MARCHING TO ARMAGEDDON

MARCHING TO ARMAGEDDON

Canadians and the Great War 1914-1919

Desmond Morton and J.L. Granatstein

LESTER
&ORPEN
DENNYS
PUBLISHERS

FIRST EDITION

Canadian Cataloguing in Publication Data

Morton, Desmond, 1937-
   Marching to Armageddon

Includes index.
ISBN 0-88619-209-9 (bound)
ISBN 0-88619-211-0 (pbk.)

1. World War, 1914-1918 – Canada. 2. Canada –
History – 1914-1918.* I. Granatstein, J. L., 1939-
II. Title.

D547.C2M67 1989   940.3'71   C88-094588-5

Design by Don Fernley
Picture research by Susan Renouf
Maps by Jonathan Gladstone, j.b. geographics

Typeset in 11 pt. Aster by Alpha Graphics Limited
Printed and bound in Canada by Metropole Litho Inc.

Lester & Orpen Dennys Limited
78 Sullivan Street
Toronto, Canada M5T 1C1

CONTENTS

ACKNOWLEDGEMENTS

Any book is a team project and this is no exception. Our first debt is owed to the scores of veterans of the Canadian Expeditionary Force and the British forces who shared their letters, diaries, and photographs with us and who enriched our understanding of their war by their memories. These are men and women who made us proud and happy to be fellow Canadians.

Many have helped with their expertise. Dr. Margaret McCallum, one of Canada's most promising young historians, shared in the research. We were helped by many of our colleagues, including Professor Craig Brown, Professor Michael Bliss, and Professor Thomas Socknat of the University of Toronto. Miss Barbara Wilson of the Public Archives of Canada spared us and our readers countless errors, as did our editor, Beverley Endersby. Those that remain are proof only of our sin of "invincible ignorance". Malcolm Lester and Gena Gorrell gave us added evidence that Lester & Orpen Dennys deserves its reputation as Canada's best publisher.

The publisher would have waited in vain for a manuscript had the University of Toronto not allowed the principal author a three-month leave from his duties as principal of the Erindale Campus in Mississauga and if two wonderful people, Clara Stewart and Kathie Hill, had not sacrificed time and energy on repeated versions of the text. Finally, this book, like all its predecessors, is the product of family forbearance. It is dedicated to our respective and long-suffering wives, Jan and Elaine.

D.M. and J.G.
October 1988

INTRODUCTION

In 1914, with bands playing, flags waving, and crowds cheering, Canadians marched off to Armageddon. "Some may not return," the Minister of Militia told the departing troops, "and pray God they may be few." One in ten of those who joined Canada's wartime army died in its ranks. As many more returned so maimed in body or mind that they could never wholly resume their lives. At Ypres, Passchendaele, the Somme, Vimy, and in the bloody battles that ended the war, Canadians shared in a conflict as terrible as any in human history.

For Canada, the years of the Great War are a great divide. In the aftermath, Canadians tried to return to their old ways but found they could not do so. The war cost them their innocence. Never again could they share a strong and all but universal faith in divine providence, the perfectability of man, or the righteous wisdom of Britain or her allies.

Contemporaries preached that the war would be a "fiery furnace" from which Canada would emerge purified. In wartime, Canadians had put an end to the liquor traffic, brought women to equal partnership in democracy, conscripted wealth as well as manpower. However, cynics would point to bootleggers, "flappers", and profiteers.

The Great War demonstrated the limits of voluntarism, and the inefficiency of market capitalism, and in so doing, forced Canadians to measure the strengths and limits of the modern state. Canadians learned how far the state could manage, and sometimes mismanage, the market, and the memory of that lesson would not fade. Canadians also saw the struggle of capital and labour reach a new ferocity, and that memory would not fade either.

Even though Canadians fought as allies of the British, for Canada the Great War was a war of independence. By 1918, the self-governing colony that had trusted its fate to British statecraft was not only committed to speaking with its own voice in the world, it had won on the battlefield the right to be heard. Yet, the war would mute that voice. It would force Canadians to look into the abyss in their own confederation. The war did not forge a nationality for Canada, as it did for Australia. Instead, it revealed to a generation of leaders how delicate and painstaking their task must be.

Canadians marched to Armageddon in 1914. Those who returned were transformed by the experience.

I
OVER BY CHRISTMAS

A HOT AUGUST WEEKEND

The murder of an Austrian archduke and his wife in a small Bosnian city was hardly big news anywhere in Canada in 1914. Balkan crises and wars had been brutal perennials for a generation. Canadians with a taste for foreign news followed, instead, the trial of Mme Caillaux, wife of a former French premier, who had shot the editor of *Le Figaro* to stop his slanders. A jury set her free. Across the channel, the "Curragh Mutiny" had seen senior British army officers defy a constitutional government and win. If Herbert Asquith, Britain's Liberal prime minister, wanted to force the Protestant North into a self-governing Ireland, he could fight the Ulster Volunteers himself. An army officered largely by Irish Protestants would do little to help him.

That summer, Canadians had enough concerns of their own. On the prairies, a second year of drought turned wheat fields to parched desert. The two new transcontinental railways, the Grand Trunk Pacific and the Canadian Northern, plunged deeper into debt, while the thousands of men who had built them drifted into the army of unemployed. Those ranks swelled; Canada that summer was adjusting to the worst depression since the 1890s. Ontario employers complained that they were working at half-capacity. Still, outdated immigration propaganda drew shiploads of young Britons to win their fortunes in "The Last Best West". Others were not as welcome. Some were not welcome at all. In Vancouver harbour that July, Canada's only available cruiser, HMCS *Rainbow,* cleared for action against a defiant immigrant ship, the *Komagata Maru;* when the two hundred Sikhs abandoned their resistance British Columbians had won another battle against Asian immigration.

There was no way, in Canada, in 1914, to count the unemployed or to poll public opinion, but most barber-shop pundits could predict the fate of Sir Robert Borden's Conservative government. Three years of failure, misman-

2

agement, and bad times would bring back the Liberals and their trusted old leader, Sir Wilfrid Laurier. Liberals were sure of it. Conservatives, of course, could argue that railway bankruptcy was a legacy of Laurier's folly, that Liberal senators could be blamed for blocking Borden's gift of $35 million to pay for three badly needed British battleships, and that, in June, Ontario's Tories had won a powerful new mandate — largely because their Regulation 17 would partially strip Franco-Ontarians of their French-language schools.

A country so preoccupied had little thought for the outside world. When the Toronto *Globe* wrote, on July 22, of "The Nation's Defences", it was referring to germs and the need for vaccination and chlorination. As for Europe, the great powers would surely keep the peace. "Let us hope," *La Presse* serenely observed, "that they will use their influence for a prompt settlement of differences." A cartoon in the *Vancouver Sun* had a more jocular view: "Hi mates," John Bull and Uncle Sam call to the German Kaiser and the Russian Tsar. "Come and sit on the fence with us an' we'll see if we can't settle this dispute without mussin' up your pretty uniforms."

Certainly the great powers had kept the peace in a dozen earlier disputes in the century. Even the assassination on June 28 of the heir to the Habsburg monarchy raised no insoluble problems. Two generations had passed since 1870, when Europe's power structure had been defined on one side by a triumphant Prussia and on the other by a vengeful France. Weaker than the newly proclaimed German Empire, France had bided her time, rebuilt an army, and, in 1894, forged an alliance with Russia. It was a marriage of questionable convenience. The Tsar's army was enormous, and Russia was the one continental power no one had ever defeated. But was there really a community of interest between the Third Republic and a vast, underdeveloped Russian autocracy? For all her enormous and powerful armies, Germany too felt threatened. In the ramshackle, disintegrating Austro-Hungarian Empire, she found her only dependable friend.

Alliances are often controlled by their weakest, not their strongest members. While the Archduke Franz Ferdinand was little mourned, his death at the hands of Bosnian terrorists had to be avenged or the Dual Monarchy would look feeble. Since Serbian plotters had helped hatch the assassination at Sarajevo, Serbia must be punished. That was the judgement of General Conrad von Hötzendorf, the chief of staff of the Habsburg armies, and neither his eighty-eight–year–old master, Emperor Franz Josef, nor any mere civilian opposed him. On July 23, Vienna issued its little neighbour an ultimatum so stinging that it was sure to be rejected. When the Serbs swallowed almost all of it, the tiny exception became the pretext for war. On July 28, Austrian artillery opened fire on Belgrade.

Conrad von Hötzendorf was not the only general who supplanted diplomats. Russian pride and dynastic survival dictated that Serbia had to be defended. Russia mobilized, but her generals had only a single plan, directed at Germany as much as at Austria-Hungary. Berlin commanded that the Russian mobilization cease in twelve hours. That ultimatum, too, was a pretext: Kaiser Wilhelm II and his generals had given up on peace. Indeed, it was the German generals who had the tightest grip on their country's choices. General Count Alfred von Schlieffen, chief of staff of the Kaiser's army, died in 1913, but he had left a plan that could give Germany victory in a two-front war. Not Russia but France would be the target. While a few divisions held off the slow-moving Russians, the highly developed road and rail system of Western Europe would carry more than a million Germans west across Belgium and northern France to envelop the French armies, much as Hannibal had swept up the Romans at Cannae. If the Belgians did not like their role as doormat for the German armies, they could, as the German ambassador politely explained, lump it. Belgium's King Albert I neither liked it nor lumped it: he mobilized his little army and called for help. On August 3, France and Germany went to war.

So far, the British Empire had no need to get involved and, in the view of many of Asquith's Liberal colleagues, no wish to do so. Germany had been a traditional friend — Kaiser Wilhelm was a cousin of King George V — France and Russia, the old enemies. But times had changed. The British and German monarchs detested each other. So did their countrymen. The Prussian victories in 1870 had alarmed Britain, as had Germany's remarkable industrial growth and trading rivalry. Most serious was the Kaiser's determination to challenge Britain's naval and imperial dominance with his own high-seas fleet and colonial empire. During the Boer War, 1899–1902, Britain had felt her isolation when Germany joined other European powers in righteous sympathy for the Boers. Painfully, the British had come to an understanding or "entente" with, first, the French, then the Russians. Unofficially, Colonel Henry Wilson met with Colonel Ferdinand Foch in 1907 to discuss what a British army might do if war came. The French now counted on British divisions on their northern flank. To match the Kaiser's growing array of battleships, the Royal Navy brought most of its fleet back from the Mediterranean. The French would look after Britain's interests while Britain would safeguard the English Channel coast. Of course, there were no written promises.

There was, however, a half-forgotten treaty. In 1839, Britain, France, and Prussia had all agreed to protect Belgian neutrality. Dividing the ownership of the European coastline was a vital British interest, but would it really matter to a peace-loving government with a small, troubled army? Would Britain embroil herself in a European war for the sake of what one German dismissed as "a scrap of paper"? The reluctant answer was yes. As German shells began to pound King Albert's frontier fortresses, a British ultimatum commanded the Kaiser to withdraw. At midnight, August 4, 1914, the ultimatum expired. The British Empire was at war.

In Canada, August 1 to 3 was widely observed as the Bank Holiday weekend. Only a wealthy minority, of course, escaped to cottages. Most crowded the beaches, amusement parks, or downtown streets, where excitement grew hourly. Prime Minister and Lady Borden had long since fled the aftermath of a tiresome parliamentary session for a few weeks of golfing at Port Carling. They were there as the vague Balkan crisis took shape. On July 31, Borden returned to Ottawa. That day, copies of the *Globe* reminded readers that the money-lenders would be the final arbiters of war: "If they refuse to finance it, it cannot be carried out." By Saturday, war news had finally captured Canadian newspapers. On Sunday, a few papers brought out special editions, the *Manitoba Free Press* apologizing for breaching the Sabbath and explaining that it had permission from the provincial government. On Monday, holiday crowds jammed the streets in front of newspaper offices to read the bulletins. Most Canadians waited for Britain's decision.

A few Canadians were already busy. On July 29, Britain warned its colonies to take precautions. Recent wars, notably the Russo-Japanese War, had begun with surprise attacks. Soldiers and Canada's few sailors manned the Halifax fortifications and dragged some guns to command the St. Lawrence below Quebec. The *Rainbow* headed south, mindful of German cruisers but determined to warn a couple of tiny British warships that had no wireless. At Victoria, Premier Richard McBride signed a cheque for $1,150,000 and bought two submarines from a Seattle shipyard. British Columbia's coast would not, now, be utterly defenceless. On Sunday, August 2, armed militia mounted guard on bridges, canals, tunnels, and railway stations. Crowds cheered them. Reporters visited local consulates to watch Austrian, Serbian, and French reservists arrange passage home. The Austrians, reported the Montreal *Gazette*, were "slightly undersized as to height, but sturdy specimens". In Winnipeg, Bishop Nicholas Budka reminded his Ukrainian flock of their duty to their Habsburg emperor, a message Canadian patriots would not allow him to forget.

In Ottawa, the Minister of Militia, Colonel Sam Hughes, was almost out of control. For most of his sixty-one years he had dreamed of leading Canadians to war. Immune to persuasion and ridicule, he had preached and prepared for war with Germany. Now he had to wait on London. The worst feature of the British Empire was that it was run by the English. "They're going to skunk it," he raged. An aide was ordered to haul down the Militia Department's Union Jack. The octogenarian quartermaster general, Major-General Donald Alexander Macdonald, persuaded Hughes to be patient. At 8:55 P.M., Ottawa got the news; Hughes was ecstatic.

"When Britain is at war, Canada is at war," Sir Wilfrid Laurier had explained in 1910; "there is no distinction." Nor was there consultation. No one in 1914 cared. In Quebec City, Montreal, Toronto, excited crowds filled the downtown streets. In Winnipeg, where the Knights of Pythias had gathered for an international convention, local citizens made certain that American delegates could report the patriotic fervour. The pleasure was marred when "some unknown maniac" drove his high-powered car into the crowd. In Vancouver, local militia regiments had time to organize a parade. The Associated Canadian Clubs cheered when Talbot Papineau, a Montreal lawyer and a descendant of the Patriote leader of 1837, rose to assure them "that there would be as many French Canadians as English Canadians to take up arms in defence of the Empire in this crisis". W.J. Bowser, a future B.C. premier, rejoiced that the pacifists had been driven from power in Britain: "fortunately the spirit of the people pushes such undesirables into the background when the honour of the nation is to be maintained...."

"Ready, Aye, Ready!"

Canadians, that August, were united. Immediately Laurier summoned journalists to pledge a party truce for as long as Canada was in danger. Dissidents in his caucus agreed to hold their tongues. Borden summoned Parliament for August 18 and then met for endless hours with cabinet colleagues to wrestle with a hundred unfamiliar problems. For the MPs, the prime minister struggled to rise to the rhetorical occasion, pledging Canadians "to put forward every effort and make every sacrifice necessary to ensure the integrity and maintain the honour of our Empire". As usual, it was Laurier who found the magical phrase. Recalling what he had said in 1910, he asked what Canada must do: "When the call comes, our answer goes at once, and it goes in the classical language of the British answer to the call of duty, 'Ready, aye, ready!'" Without division or significant debate, members approved an overseas contingent of 25,000 men, with Canada bearing the full cost: a war appropriation of $50 million and a Canadian Patriotic Fund to support the families of men who would fight for the Empire.

The government needed more. In the days before Parliament met, the Cabinet wasted hours trying to devise adequate emergency legislation. Exasperated, Borden handed the task to W.F. O'Connor, a Halifax lawyer. "Make absolutely sure that you omit no power that the government may need," insisted a Liberal MP, and O'Connor's draft War Measures Bill met the challenge. The Cabinet, it decreed, would have full authority to do anything it deemed necessary for "the security, defence, peace, order and welfare of Canada".

Canada, of course, was not ready for war. Indeed, no belligerent was prepared for the kind of struggle that began in 1914. Only old men could even remember the last real European war of 1870 or the American Civil War of 1861–65. A single Canadian officer had seen the Russo-Japanese War for himself. For soldiers and civilians alike, images of war were shaped by peacetime manoeuvres, colonial forays, and romantic lithographs of sword-waving heroes leading attacks. Experts and amateurs agreed that, if the generals did not end the war by Christmas, the financiers would. No national economy could stand the strain for more than a few months. European armies had patiently planned and organized to make their full strength available in the first few weeks. Building reserves of men and munitions was unnecessary and unwise.

There were dissenters. Field Marshal Lord Kitchener, summoned by Herbert Asquith to take over the British War Office on August 5, shocked his cabinet colleagues by predicting three years of war and a British army of a million men. As usual, the conqueror of dervishes and Boers gave no reasons. A generation earlier, Warsaw financier Ivan Bloch had predicted that modern weapons would lead to mass casualties, military stalemate, and ultimate exhaustion for one or both sides. Only the Tsar had listened to Bloch, and his arguments left their mark on two Hague conventions to limit such horrors of war as the use of poison gas. The generals were unimpressed; generals did not like to take military lessons from Polish-Jewish bankers.

By her own modest standards, Canada was better prepared in 1914 than for any earlier or later war. The South African War had given Canada some experienced officers and an incentive to think about war. Prosperity in the Laurier years made it easy to expand, rearm, and reform the militia. In 1907, the British had won agreement from their dominions to standardize military training, organization, and equipment. Keen militia officers had learned from able British instructors. For a few pre-war years, militarism had been in fashion in Canada, as a conservative response to urbanization, industrialization, and immigration. "The school mistress with her book and spectacles has had her day in the training of boys," boasted Professor Andrew Macphail of the *University Magazine,* "and sensible parents are longing for the drill-sergeant carrying in his hand a good cleaning rod or a leather belt.... That is the sovereign remedy for the hooliganism of the town and the loutishness of the city." In 1909, most provinces, including Quebec, agreed to institute cadet training in their schools. The Canadian Defence League, headed by a galaxy of clergy, physicians, professors, and business magnates, urged universal military training.

In such a setting, Sam Hughes was a model Minister of Militia. Borden had had misgivings about him in 1911 and had warned him that he was beset by two unceasing enemies, his tongue and his pen. Hughes, an editor and militia officer from Lindsay, was the pride of Ontario's Orange Lodge, a charming braggart with just a hint of mental imbalance. In 1899, he had bullied his way to South Africa and had come home strengthened in his faith in citizen-soldiers and his contempt for military professionals, popular prejudices widely shared in Canada. In 1902, Hughes had persuaded the Laurier government to order the Ross rifle. A marksman, Hughes knew it was a fine target rifle. Sir Charles Ross agreed to build his factory in Quebec, close to Laurier's constituents. However, the Ross was also a foot longer, a pound heavier, and a third more costly than the British Lee-Enfield, and it jammed easily and seized up when fired rapidly. The faults, shown up at the first trials, were never corrected. Hughes treated them as irrelevant or fabricated by British rivals, and the Liberals were happy to agree.

As Minister of Militia, Hughes ignored the constraints imposed on all civilian ministers. Borden, he believed to be "a most lovely fellow, gentle as a girl" — easily bullied. The militia prospered under its new minister's bullying and charm. In 1904, 25,000 volunteers had drilled; under Hughes, in 1913, 55,000 militiamen and 44,000 cadets went to camp. Militia spending rose from $7 million in 1911 to $13.5 million in 1913. Orders were issued for new guns and equipment to land in Canada as fast as British factories could deliver them. That was not very fast: in 1914, Canada had modern artillery for only two of the six divisions in its paper organization. Hughes ignored criticism, whether it was for equipping militia staff officers with Ford cars; banning liquor from training camps; or escorting a bevy of officers and their wives to the British, French, and Swiss manoeuvres in 1913. One pre-war Swiss notion, a shield-shovel with a stubby four-inch handle and loopholes for sighting and firing a rifle, he judged to be ideally suited for modern warfare. He patented it in the name of his secretary, Ena MacAdam.

Fashions change. By 1913, the depression had taken the starch out of Canadian militarism. "Drill Hall Sam" had become an embarrassment. His constant warnings that war with Germany was imminent cost votes in German-Canadian ridings. Even Conservatives began to wonder if Hughes might be crazy. But, on August 4, he suddenly looked very sane.

Hughes, though not a man of system, had better subordinates than he deserved. An able British officer, Major-General Willoughby Gwatkin, served as Chief of the General Staff. Thanks to him, a mobilization plan for a force of 25,000 to fight "in a civilized country in a temperate climate" was on file. By mid 1914, an interdepartmental committee had finally completed a "War Book", detailing all the precautions, from censorship to guarding cable stations, that the country must take on the outbreak of hostilities. Across Canada, the militia was more a social and political organization than a military force, keener on bands, dress uniforms, and mess dinners than on dusty manoeuvres, but scores of officers, professional and amateur, had done all they could to prepare themselves for war, often at the cost of income, careers, and ridicule. Their turn had come.

In one respect, the Borden government left Canada less ready for war than it had been in 1911. Conservative candidates had won votes by promising to scrap Laurier's "tin-pot" navy. Quebec voters, at least, had never grasped Borden's alternative: a $35-million gift to Britain to buy three of the huge Dreadnought battleships. When they did, a Liberal Senate sank the Naval Aid Bill. As for the navy, Borden let it wither to a few hundred men. Ironically, on August 5, the navy was Canada's front line. HMCS *Rainbow*, lacking crew and ammunition, narrowly missed the German cruisers that would have sunk her off San Francisco. Naval reservists were hurriedly mustered to man McBride's submarines. When the Germans sank Sir Christopher Cradock's squadron off the Chilean coast on November 1, four of his midshipmen became Canada's first war dead.

"THE WORLD REGARDS YOU AS A MARVEL"

If the war was to be over by Christmas, Canadians would have to hurry to share in the glory. In 1899, it took Ottawa two weeks to recruit and despatch a regiment of 1,000 men. In 1914, Britain had accepted the Canadian offer of an infantry division with supplementary units, a force of 25,000. It was what Gwatkin had anticipated in his plan, which, on July 31, Hughes cancelled. The minister would run the mobilization his way, free of interference from despised professionals. On August 6, hundreds of telegrams notified militia colonels to recruit volunteers aged eighteen to forty-five, physically fit, able to shoot, and, if married, armed with their wives' permission. Later, Hughes explained that his mobilization was "like the fiery cross passing through the Highlands of Scotland or the mountains of Ireland ... in a short time we had the boys on the way for the first contingent, whereas it would have taken several weeks to have got the word round through ordinary channels." This was nonsense; it took weeks to sort out the confusion. For maximum effect, the minister insisted that "his boys" would assemble at Valcartier, a sandy plain twenty miles north of Quebec City, designated earlier that year as a future militia camp. At once special trains went into service, ferrying workers, equipment, and building materials to the site. Units of the tiny permanent force arrived to help. Within days, the beginnings of roads, a water system, and a 1,500-target rifle range appeared. By the end of August, so did volunteers.

Recruiting was as easy as Hughes had expected, though not for his reasons. British immigrants flocked to enlist. So did the unemployed. Ontario, hard-hit by the depression, produced almost a third of the recruits; the western provinces almost half. Two-thirds of the volunteers were British-born. Few came from the Maritimes, and just over a thousand were French-speaking. Most came from the cities: Toronto, Montreal, and Winnipeg each sent enough men for two battalions, Vancouver sent one and a half, and Edmonton's 101st Regiment arrived at full strength. By September 4, there were 32,000 men and 8,000 horses in camp, far more than expected. Across the St. Lawrence, at Lévis, was a separate unit, the Princess Patricia's Canadian Light Infantry. Raised at the expense of Hamilton Gault, a Montreal millionaire, the unit was filled with British Army reservists, diverted from their regiments. The officers were Canadian, among them Lieutenant Talbot Papineau.

Even cynics were impressed by Valcartier, with its acres of tents, its showers, and its large rifle range. What he wanted, Hughes insisted, were men who could "pink the enemy every time". Hughes was everywhere, on horseback and in uniform. Ostensibly, Colonel Victor Williams, the militia's adjutant-general, a permanent-force officer, was in command, but the minister was in charge, greeting cronies, bellowing abuse, boasting of his achievements to admiring journalists.

"Pipe up, you little bastard, or get out of the service," Hughes bellowed at a captain. Another, whom he addressed as major, was promoted on the spot. Having created chaos, he alone would create order, forming ad hoc battalions and shifting them when fresh troops arrived. Four Ontario battalions formed the 1st (Provisional) Infantry Brigade under Colonel M.S. Mercer, a Toronto lawyer. Four Western battalions were grouped in the 2nd Brigade. Hughes's son Garnet recommended an old friend for the command: Arthur Currie was a Victoria real-estate dealer, a Liberal, and a former militia gunner who had commanded the 50th Highlanders. The third brigadier, Colonel Richard Turner, was a Quebec City merchant and a Tory. Slight and bespectacled, Turner gave no hint in his appearance of the heroism that had earned him a Victoria Cross in South Africa. To command the artillery, Hughes chose another South African veteran, Colonel E.W.B. Morrison — "Dinky" to his friends — the editor-in-chief of the Ottawa *Citizen*.

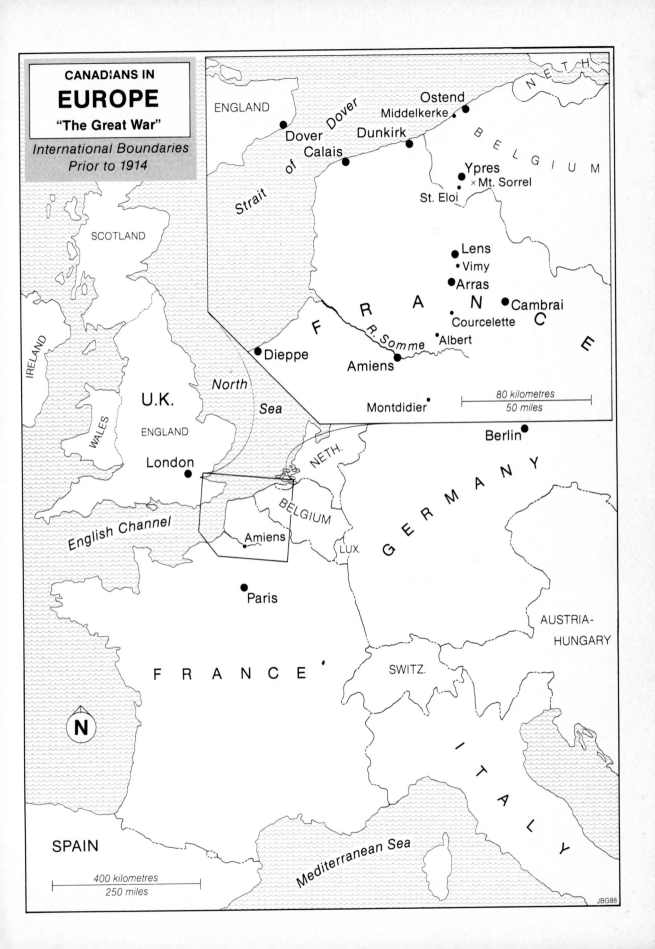

Uniforms, equipment, and weapons had to be found. The Ross Rifle Company factory in nearby Quebec worked overtime. So did textile mills and clothing factories because no one had thought to stockpile the new khaki serge uniforms that the Empire's armies had gradually adopted since 1900. Farm wagons, their paint still damp and the green timber already warping, were delivered as divisional transport. A bewildering variety of motor vehicles arrived as well: Hughes and the auto manufacturers agreed that the Contingent would be a showcase for Canadian products. In the South African War, soldiers had suffered miseries from Canadian-made Oliver pattern leather equipment but thousands of new sets arrived in Valcartier. Hughes believed in it. MacAdam shield-shovels also appeared, but most of the Colt machine guns, ordered from American factories, were delayed. Even Hughes admitted that the British water-cooled Vickers was better but the American gun would have to do.

Except for the governor general, the Duke of Connaught — an old soldier — and a few other veterans, visitors to Valcartier found it all marvellous. Never had Canadians seen so many soldiers or such purposeful confusion. With so many responsibilities, surely Canada's War Minister could be forgiven occasional rudeness to an Anglican bishop or a Humane Society official. Soldiers, after all, were supposed to be abrupt men of action. Only one cloud hung over Hughes's joy: how could he choose the units to go overseas? When Sir Robert Borden solved his problem, saying that all could go, Hughes wept with gratitude.

Embarkation was a nightmare. Ignoring the few professionals he had available, Hughes put William H. Price, the contractor who had built Valcartier, in charge of the docks. Extra ships were chartered to carry the additional men. Some arrived loaded down with private cargo and with 132,275 bags of flour — Canada's special wartime gift to Britain. Battalions were marched aboard only to be marched off again when they did not fit. Units ignored orders and schedules and crowded to the docks to avoid waiting. When the last of 30 ships had cleared Quebec harbour, 863 horses; 4,512 tons of baggage, vehicles, and ammunition; and a few soldiers remained. Price hired an extra ship.

At the Gaspé basin, the armada stopped to form convoy. The transports in their long lines looked to spectators like a vast battle fleet. On October 3, Hughes passed through the convoy on a final visit, delivering bundles of his farewell message. "Soldiers," it proclaimed, "The World regards you as a marvel." Crumpled copies soon dotted the dark surface of the St. Lawrence.

IVAN BLOCH'S NIGHTMARE

By the time the First Contingent reached England on October 14, the Polish banker had proved to be a better prophet of war than most of Europe's generals. The law of uncertainty still governed human affairs. The war would not be over by Christmas.

More than any other power, Germany had gambled on quick success. By the end of August, that gamble was paying off. The Belgian forts, expected to resist for months, were pulverized in a few days, thanks to huge guns borrowed from the Austrians. A campaign of terrorism discouraged even the slightest civilian resistance. At Dinant, almost seven hundred people, including a three-month-old baby, were shot. At Louvain, the university was sacked and burned. German soldiers, enraged that anyone dared oppose their desperate mission, added scores of smaller private atrocities. The purpose was clear: terror was the fastest, cheapest way to neutralize resistance. Dusty columns of infantry poured through Belgium and into France at an exhausting thirty miles a day. King Albert's army was shoved back to Antwerp.

Von Schlieffen's plan had discounted French resistance, an expectation the French fulfilled. Their strategy, Plan XVII, seemed designed to help the Germans. France almost ignored its northern frontier; huge armies were mobilized opposite the lost provinces of Alsace and Lorraine, poised to hurl themselves at the Germans. That was what von Schlieffen had hoped for when he had ordered the defenders to pull back, drawing the French deeper into a trap and making it easy for the huge German attack force to surround them. For years, French officers had concentrated only on the attack. French courage, willpower, *élan*, would overcome anything. In the Battle of the Frontiers, an almost metaphysical faith in the *attaque à outrance* would be tested. Instead, the French army proved only that it could die. Led by officers in immaculate white gloves, masses of infantry in old-fashioned blue coats and red trousers raced forward to be massacred by German artillery and machine guns. In the rugged terrain of Alsace, the wonderful French 75-millimetre guns were useless. High velocity and rapid loading meant nothing if a hill stood in the way of the shell. In a few days, 140,000 of France's best soldiers were killed or wounded and one officer in ten was dead. With no training or equipment for defence, the survivors reeled back from the frontier, a beaten army.

The British, unlike the French and Germans, had no plan. On August 5, Asquith met with Kitchener; Winston Churchill, the First Lord of the Admiralty; and Britain's generals and admirals to make one. Could Britain's little army be sent to Belgium? Perhaps it might be landed on the German coast?

Should it go to Amiens to build up its strength from reservists and Territori-als, the British counterpart to the militia? Sir Henry Wilson, now a general, gave a chilling answer. His conversations years ago with Ferdinand Foch left Britain no choice: the French expected the British on their left flank. On August 23, five divisions of British regulars, 100,000 superbly trained troops, moved up to the Mons canal, just inside Belgium, in the path of sixty-one advancing German divisions. For a day, the British held their ground. That afternoon, pilots from the new Royal Flying Corps reported that the Germans were lapping around the British flanks. Sir John French, the aged and mer-curial British commander, ordered a headlong retreat. A few days later, too exhausted to move, Sir Horace Smith Dorrien's II Corps gave further battle, beating back the Germans. Otherwise the British were out of the fight.

German victory seemed certain. Or did it? Belgium had collapsed but not before its railways had been sabotaged. German troops could march but could they be fed? Von Moltke's army was a horse-powered juggernaut; his cavalry divisions and artillery batteries were immobilized for lack of horseshoe nails. Troops were hungry. The French army had fallen back in defeat, away from its trap. To the east, Russia's "steamroller" had rumbled into Germany territory sooner than expected. Prussian *Junkers* demanded protection for their rural estates. Surely the victorious armies in the West could spare a few army corps. By the time help arrived, the crisis was over. A brilliant staff officer, Colonel Hoffmann, noted that the Russian armies had been split by the Masurian Lakes. Intercepted wireless messages told him the Russian plans. Railways concentrated the German defenders against one of the invading armies and, by August 30, the Russian general had shot himself, and 90,000 of his men were prisoners. By then, the battle in France had turned.

On August 29, the French general next to the British redirected his army and administered a stinging set-back to the weary, advancing Germans. If Sir John French had followed up, the Allies might have had a stunning victory. But, in his view, the British were too tired. The Germans, too, were growing cau-tious. With several of their divisions sent to Prussia, the Germans decided to shorten their swing, passing east of Paris. For weeks, with ox-like imperturb-ability, General Joffre, the French commander-in-chief, had watched events unfold, quietly gathering his reserves north and east of the German flank. The new air arm changed history. Pilots spotted German columns pushing east of the French capital, not beyond it as von Schlieffen had intended. Suddenly, it was the Germans who were in the bag. From Paris, General Galliéni sent his garrison in taxis and buses to spring the trap. To the south, the French retreat ended as Joffre attacked a hungry, exhausted invader. Even the British rejoined the battle, moving cautiously from the Marne to the hills overlooking the Aisne. There, faced by a German army corps too weary to move, their advance stopped. Much the same thing happened along the line, and both sides dug in. The chance for rapid victory had passed.

By October 10, the German guns had smashed Antwerp's defences. The Belgians and a few British marines fled along the coast to the Yser. There, just inside his country's border, King Albert ordered his army to fight. Pursuing Germans found the sluice gates opened and the land flooded. The Germans then sent troops to outflank the Belgians through the railway town of Ypres. On October 21, they ran into Sir Douglas Haig's I British Corps, bent on the same mission of out-flanking the enemy. For twenty days, the best of the British and German armies battled each other on the low ridges that surrounded Ypres. On November 11, the fighting died away, and both sides dug in. The Germans, remembering whole battalions of university students sacrificed in the struggle, called it the *Kindermord von Ypern*, the "child-murder of Ypres". The British knew only that 58,000 men, the best of their peacetime regular army, had been lost. Entire battalions had been virtually annihilated. The Ypres salient might be a useless excrescence in a line of trenches that now extended five hundred miles from the Channel to the Swiss frontier. Officially, the blood-soaked ground would be justified as a remnant of the Belgium for which Britain had joined the war. To British generals, whose sons and friends had died in the rain and mud, Ypres also was sacred soil. Canadians would come to know and curse those memories. They, too, would die at Ypres, among the millions who would perish in a war only Ivan Bloch had truly foreseen.

Departing soldiers and "the girls they left behind them." Until 1915 wives had to give written permission for their husbands to depart — but the mood of the times favoured sacrifice for king and country, and the Patriotic Fund promised to compensate for a soldier's meagre pay.

Above Artillerymen, in a motley collection of uniforms, practise on an 18-pounder field gun. In patriotic passion, Colonel Sam Hughes shipped all the modern guns in Canada to Britain, leaving none for later contingents or for training.

Right Hughes watches "his boys" off the Gaspé coast in 1914. As a minister Hughes had an imperfect grasp of the separation of civil and military powers. He also had supreme confidence in his own judgement.

First Contingent men at Valcartier wait for kit inspection. Waiting, as soldiers soon discovered, was the army's prime occupation. Drill, route marches, physical training, and "bayonet-fighting" were other ways to fill time.

A shipload of Vancouver Island volunteers leaves Victoria for the mainland. Remote from European battlefields, but hard-hit by a depression and "British to the core", B.C. provided far more than its share of men for the First Contingent.

A practice trench in Winnipeg would have looked ridiculous to any veteran of
France or Flanders, but Canadians were trained by officers and soldiers whose
only knowledge of war came from manuals, newspapers, and perhaps memories
of service in South Africa.

Motor vehicles for the First Contingent parade the mechanized modernity of Canada's army. Nine different manufacturers provided 140 cars and trucks for the Contingent. Hughes boasted that they would show Canada's industrial potential, but because of a lack of parts or poor design most never got farther than England.

Toronto's Mayor Tommy Church bids farewell to Italian reservists after Italy joins the Allied side in 1915. Thousands of immigrants returned to their European homelands to fulfil reserve commitments — including a good many who slipped out via the neutral U.S. to fight for Germany or the Austro-Hungarian Empire.

II
DOING YOUR BIT

GIVING 'TIL IT HURT

A German triumph or a diplomatic compromise might have ended the war in 1914. Neither was possible. The generals had failed; compromise was unthinkable. By Christmas, France had 900,000 dead and maimed soldiers to avenge. Germans remained convinced that war had been forced on them, with the British, perversely, as the chief culprits. When the British learned of the atrocities in Belgium, some of them touched up by clever journalists, they knew that there could be no peace with the barbarian Hun. The Belgian horrors, sometimes corroborated by American reporters, were also a useful lever to shift neutral opinion, particularly in the United States.

In August, it had been enough that England was in danger; by early 1915, the war was a moral crusade. Canadians were a church-going people; among Protestants, crusading was a congenial act. If mankind was hard to perfect, society could certainly be improved, and the task might even be easier overseas than close at hand. In his day, Sir Wilfrid Laurier had warned Canadians against "the vortex of European militarism". Now, J.W. Dafoe of the *Manitoba Free Press* insisted that Canadians were in the war to defeat Prussian militarism. C.W. Gordon, the Presbyterian cleric who wrote popular novels under the name of Ralph Connor, put in verse what countless clergymen were to thunder from their pulpits:

> O Canada, What answer make to calling voice and beating drum
> To sword gleam and to pleading prayer of God
> For right? What answer makes my soul?
> Mother, to thee! God, to thy help! Quick, my sword.

A moral crusade transcended mere politics and government. Canadians, on the whole, expected little from their political rulers, and that little would be badly done. For a hospital, a college, or a waterworks, people looked to civic and business leaders. Apart from the alleged wastrels of the permanent force, even the Canadian militia was essentially a network of regimental clubs financed by wealthy families like the Gooderhams, the Pellatts, and the Olands. It was natural that Hamilton Gault should finance a regiment. A Yukon millionaire, Joe Boyle, raised his own machine-gun battery. So did Sir John Eaton, heir to the Toronto merchandising empire. Jack Ross, another scion of wealth, transferred half a million dollars to the Patriotic Fund, lent his yacht to the navy, and went off to war in command of HMCS *Grilse*.

A government with little idea of what to do about the war and, fearful of doing too much, found voluntarism a blessing. The Canadian Patriotic Fund (CPF) was a marvellous start. In the War of 1812, its forebear had financed pensions and a campaign medal; in 1914, under Sir Herbert Ames, a Montreal MP and businessman, the CPF was content to support soldiers' families. Admittedly, the government could have increased a private's pay from $1.10 a day but, as Borden explained, "It would be most undesirable to discourage private enterprise." In three months, the CPF collected $6 million. With the slogan "Give 'til it hurts", Toronto gathered $312,551; Montreal promptly raised $750,000. Led by the example of the Canadian Pacific Railway, employees of large companies were persuaded to donate a day's pay. The CPF continued to grow. By 1916, the national fund supported 55,000 families; in 1919 Ames reported a total income of $47 million. The fund did more than raise and spend money; organizers congratulated themselves on teaching thrift to soldiers' wives, discouraging foolish purchases, and depriving immoral mothers of their children. No state agency, Ames boasted, could have done as much or as economically, and none would have been able to discriminate against the undeserving.

Soldiers' families were not alone in sharing in wartime generosity. Christie Brown and Co., the biscuit-maker, offered full salaries to employees who enlisted. Ottawa, most provinces, and many employers followed suit. None realized how long the war would last. In 1915, it appeared that the war would end sooner if Canadian soldiers had more machine guns. With some Toronto judges as inspiration, service clubs, businesses, and school children launched an informal Machine Gun Fund. By the time Sam Hughes put a stop to it — on the grounds that factories were over-booked with government orders — fund collections had reached $731,000. An attempt to divert part of the money to launch a Disablement Fund to care for wounded soldiers was scotched by Sir Herbert Ames: the Patriotic Fund wanted no major competition as the biggest claimant on public generosity. Realism was intruding.

Other war charities were busy enough. Canadians were besieged by tag

days for causes ranging from Belgian or Serbian relief to hospitals for
wounded horses. The YMCA needed money to provide soldiers with stationery
and sports equipment. The Red Cross collected $21,271,000 in cash and sup-
plies. The Canadian Field Comforts Commission needed money to ease the lot
of soldiers in the trenches. Late in 1915 Colonel William Hamilton Merritt, a
passionate convert to the new dimension in war, launched a Canadian Aviation Fund to help would-be aviators finance flying lessons and to buy aircraft
for the British flying services. In Montreal, a Khaki League opened hospitals
for returning invalids. In Winnipeg, the same task was assumed by the Imperial Order Daughters of the Empire. The Boy Scouts volunteered to run messages. In Toronto, for a time, school children were required to salute soldiers;
elsewhere, they collected scrap metal; and everywhere they were alert in
looking for behaviour that would betray a German spy or saboteur.

Churches took a lead in patriotic causes. Before the war, reform-minded
clergy had often declared themselves to be pacifists: since militarism was now
the enemy, it took only a slight twist of convictions to preach war. "If ever a
war in all history was seeking first the kingdom of God," S.D. Chown reassured Methodists, "this is, so far as we are engaged in it." "War is never
wrong," declared the *Presbyterian Record*, "when it is a war against wrong."
Preachers found a unifying theme in the image of the fiery furnace, in which
society would be purged of its impurities. While theological reformers and
conservatives differed over the list of evils, all promoted the cause. "If a man
cannot conscientiously declare himself a patriot," warned W.B. Creighton of
the *Christian Guardian*, "he has no business in any Church that prides itself
upon its patriotism."

Thanks to Michael Fallon, the Catholic bishop of London and a fervent supporter of Regulation 17, most Irish Catholics refused to be distracted by the
Easter Rising of 1916 in Dublin or its bloody aftermath. More than one in ten
of those who joined the Canadian Expeditionary Force was an English-speaking Catholic, a figure comparable to that for Presbyterians. The thousands of
English immigrants helped swell the Anglican ratio to almost one in five.
Methodists lagged at one in twelve.

Like Creighton and Chown, pre-war feminists had denounced war. Votes for
women, they insisted, would be votes for peace. Like the clergy, most women
changed their minds when war came. The British suffrage leader Sylvia
Pankhurst travelled across Canada, giving them reasons. "If this struggle is
lost," she warned, "civilization that is based on right and justice will disap-
pear...." War offered Canadian women some new roles. Almost three thousand were commissioned as nursing sisters; others went overseas to manage
field comforts. Tens of thousands, after 1915, worked in an expanding muni-

tions industry, sometimes in trades traditionally performed by men. A few
went too far for conventional opinion. The Toronto women who bought uniforms, drilled, and learned to fire rifles were soon ridiculed into oblivion.

For most Canadian women, voluntarism largely confirmed traditional
roles. Men collected the money for the Patriotic Fund; women distributed the
charity and delivered the lectures on thrift and domestic economy. Women
worked for the Red Cross, rolling bandages, knitting socks, packing food par-
cels, and serving meals. When the Militia Department wanted convalescent
homes for invalid soldiers, women answered the call. When the businessmen
who formed the Military Hospitals Commission in 1915 realized that discipline, not "a motherly touch", brought faster recovery, the women were
thanked and the homes were closed. Certainly there were women who issued
white feathers to men in civilian clothing or publicly denounced "slackers"
and "shirkers", but such tactics were notorious, not effective, and male officials did their best to discourage them. In recruiting, women's real role was
to persuade wives and mothers to release their men for war. Even when
women took jobs as "conductorettes" on streetcars or as members of
Ontario's Women's Emergency Corps, special uniforms and rates of pay
maintained an "appropriate" distinction between the sexes.

The war would be won, a popular slogan insisted, if all Canadians "did their
bit". Men, women, and children would, of course, do their best "bit" if they
performed in their own spheres.

Not Quite Unanimous

A national crusade is more natural if a nation is united. In 1914, French and
English, Liberal and Conservative, Catholic and Protestant were united on the
issue of Canada's role in the war. Dissenters were silent or inaudible, and foreigners, as the *Manitoba Free Press* noted on August 5, "made themselves
scarce".

The war created acute tensions. After the British and French, Germans
contributed Canada's third-largest ethnic element, with roots as deep as the
1780s. Immigration in the Laurier years had brought tens of thousands more
from Germany and even more from the Habsburg Empire. Berlin, in western
Ontario, prided itself on being a German city, complete with a statue of the
Kaiser. Most Ukrainians, despite Bishop Budka's advice, remembered that
they had fled Habsburg rule. In the circumstances, the government urged tolerance for all newcomers. "Having invited them to become citizens of this
country," Sir Robert Borden explained, "we owe to them in the trying circumstances in which they are placed the duty of fairness and consideration."

Weeks passed before "enemy aliens" were ordered to register and it was October before internment of Germans and Austrians of military age began — long after the few Canadians in Germany had been confined. When a Montreal judge decreed that a German had no rights in a Canadian court, he was swiftly overruled.

Public opinion was not satisfied. The pre-war naval debate had conditioned many Canadians to believe that Germans were dangerous. The troops posted at public buildings and along the Welland Canal fed expectations of sabotage, probably in alliance with that traditional Irish-American bogey, the Fenians. In one of the more bizarre episodes of the war, rumours of an air raid from Ogdensburg in February 1915 blacked out Ottawa's government buildings. In fact, boys in the United States had released balloons to commemorate the centennial of the end of the War of 1812! In British Columbia, where thousands of militiamen were mobilized at the outset of war, local businesses found hysteria was an ally in keeping a profitable arrangement going. Troops meant public spending in a province hard hit by depression. Racial prejudice and unemployment fed hostility to Ukrainians. At Nanaimo and in the Crowsnest Pass, miners struck until "foreigners" were interned. At the Lakehead, municipal officials demanded that Ottawa lock up and feed hundreds of unemployed "enemy aliens" who otherwise required local charity. By the end of 1914, the government found itself guarding six thousand men in a dozen internment camps. Magistrates, acting on information gleaned from gossip or neighbourhood malice, daily added to the number. Under the War Measures Act, internees had no recourse to appeal. In May 1915, mobs reacted to the torpedoing of the *Lusitania* by pillaging German businesses in Victoria, Winnipeg, and Montreal. More "enemy aliens" were locked up. By the summer, more than eight thousand were confined. Economy, labour shortages, and common sense led to the release of most of the so-called Austrians so that, by the end of 1916, only a couple of thousand internees, most of them German, remained at Amherst, Nova Scotia; Kapuskasing, Ontario; and Morrissey, British Columbia.

Public passions were not satisfied. At Berlin, Ontario, on February 15, 1916, a crowd led by unruly soldiers threw the Kaiser's statue in a local lake. Resentful citizens fished it out. In May, the threat of a boycott of the city's industries forced Berlin to change its name to Kitchener, even though the margin was only eighty-one votes. In 1917, when a newly elected council proposed to restore the old name, riots and a boycott changed its mind. Across Canada, persecution spread. German-born officials and civil servants were fired and university professors and teachers were driven from their jobs. Patriotic Winnipeggers agreed that hamburgers would henceforth be known as "nips". Orchestras stopped playing the works of Wagner and Beethoven. In 1918, the government banned all publishing in "enemy" languages and then relented, provided that English translations were run alongside the foreign text.

On the scale set by European horrors, such persecution was minor but it left ugly memories and uglier precedents. Apart from a few trivial incidents, there was no sabotage and pathetically little espionage in Canada. When the Parliament Buildings burned on February 3, 1916, only the most ardent patriots blamed enemy agents.

Amid the patriotic consensus in English-speaking Canada were a few voices of dissent. Not all pacifists had changed their minds. In Toronto, Alice Chown argued with her prominent uncle that Methodists had been duped by militarism. Laura Hughes, the Minister of Militia's niece, came home from the International Congress of Women at the Hague in 1915 and joined Chown in forming the Canadian Women's Peace Party. In Winnipeg, Fred Dixon condemned the war from his seat in the Manitoba legislature, with moral backing from a dwindling handful of journalists and friends. In time, he was overshadowed by the Reverend James Shaver Woodsworth, a Methodist minister and expert on urban social problems. In contrast to Chown or Creighton, Woodsworth had been converted to pacifism by the war. He was appalled by its pointless cruelty and shocked when clergy turned their pulpits into recruiting platforms. In 1917, Woodsworth's convictions cost him his job and forced him, middle-aged and underweight, to find work loading ships on the Vancouver docks. Less famous was the case of Harry Erland Lee, a Toronto teacher whose attempt to explain both sides of the war led school trustees to rule that he was "unfit to discuss the war before loyal British children". Driven to enlist, Lee became the first Toronto teacher to be killed in the war.

Opponents of the war could hear a discreet supporting chorus of Canadian labour leaders. More had been expected in 1911 when, in sympathy with European socialist and union organizations, the Trades and Labor Congress (TLC) pledged itself to a general strike against war. As happened in Europe, labour's anti-militarism was washed away on the tide of patriotic euphoria. In 1914, so many trade unionists enlisted that some union locals collapsed. J.C. Watters, the TLC president, and his supporters retreated to a position of cautious but persistent criticism of a national war effort that offered neither consultation with labour leaders nor protection for working people. When war fever and wartime wages were forgotten, union officials hoped, members might again follow their chosen leaders.

Neither unions nor pacifists had much impact on French-Canadian opinion. Foreigners of any description found as cold a shoulder in Quebec as anywhere in Canada. In 1914, cheering crowds, political speeches, and earnest twinning of the Union Jack and the French *tricolore* suggested that Henri Bourassa, leader of the *nationalistes*, might be right about his *Union sacrée*. "There are no longer French Canadians and English Canadians," rejoiced *La Patrie*. "Only one race now exists, united by the closest bonds in a common cause." Lorenzo Prince of *La Presse* called for a French-Canadian regiment to join France's heroic army.

It was not to be and the government should have been the first to know it. In 1911, Conservative funds had helped elect *nationaliste* MPs, on the specious grounds that Laurier was subservient to Britain and that his navy would lead to conscription for British wars. Settled into their minor portfolios, Borden's French-Canadian ministers might change their views but their supporters would not. Nor did the France of the Third Republic, secular and corrupt, command more than a superficial affection in Quebec. To a Canadien, France was as foreign a country as England was to a Rhode Islander. As for moral crusading, it was not a Quebec style.

Besides, Quebec had an issue closer to home: Ontario's Regulation 17. "The enemies of the French language, of French civilization in Canada, are not the Boches...," thundered Bourassa, "but the English-Canadian anglicisers, the Orange intriguers, or Irish priests." If Borden wanted national unity for the wartime struggle, let him persuade Ontario to restore the educational rights of Franco-Ontarians. Borden insisted that he could do nothing: education was a provincial matter. Indeed, by 1916, Manitoba had followed Ontario's oppressive lead. Wartime patriotism was making it easier for English Canadians to insist on a homogeneous, English-speaking, British Canada. In Quebec, Bourassa's following grew correspondingly.

It was not yet dominant. Crowds cheered in October 1914 when Laurier invoked the memory of Adam Dollard des Ormeaux, the saviour of Montreal from the Iroquois, to raise recruits for the war. In 1916 a Conservative minister, Arthur Sévigny won his rural seat in a hard-fought by-election. There was more talk than money when Bourassa appealed for aid for *les blessés de l'Ontario*. If Quebec's Cardinal Bégin did little to conceal his suspicions of the Borden government and the war effort, Montreal's Archbishop Bruchési was openly sympathetic to the Conservatives. At root, most French Canadians felt little engagement with the issues of the war or of Ontario schools. Few enlisted in the Canadian Expeditionary Force; few sent money to the numerous Franco-Ontarian appeals. Bourassa spoke most eloquently for Québécois when he insisted that the first duty of all Canadians was to themselves. Canada should profit from the war, like its American neighbours, by sending food, shells, and other supplies, and keeping strict account of the bills. To send more and more men to the war was "to reduce the number and influence of...real Canadians, whether of British or French extraction, and to increase the power of the foreign element, especially of German and Slavs".

In March 1916, Talbot Papineau, now a captain, tried to counter Bourassa's growing leadership of French Canada by pleading for a common devotion to Canada. "At this moment as I write, French and English Canadians are fighting and dying side by side. Is their sacrifice to go for nothing, or will it not cement a foundation for a true Canadian nation?..." It was a message without meaning for Quebec. Bourassa dismissed it as a fake, from someone "utterly unqualified" to speak for French Canada.

It was a view that extended beyond Quebec. French Canadians were not the only people whose links to a mother country were attenuated by centuries. Middle-class crusading patriots did not speak for all Canadians. The war was a long way off. "Doing your bit" could mean profiting from soaring food prices, collecting wartime wages, or bidding on a profitable munitions contract as well as buying a tag for Belgian relief. It need not mean risking life or limb in Flanders. Canadian-born recruits had been scarce at Valcartier; they took time to convince.

JOINING UP

When the Canadian Contingent reached England in mid-October, the famous recruiting posters — Lord Kitchener, grim and finger-pointing, with the words "Your King and Country need you" — were rain-soaked and fading. By January 1915, Kitchener had collected 1.2 million volunteers for his New Army. Sam Hughes believed that Canadians would do just as well. At New York, as he boarded a liner for England, he boasted to reporters, "We could send enough men to add the finishing touches to Germany without assistance either from England or France." A Second Contingent, twelve more battalions, was authorized on October 9. In November, after militia cavalry complained of being overlooked, the government approved thirteen new regiments of Canadian Mounted Rifles. In January, Hughes announced a Third Contingent: "I could raise three more contingents in three weeks," he added. Promoted to major-general — out of British gratitude for not trying to command the Canadians in France — Hughes covered seven thousand miles that month, making recruiting speeches. "We are coming, General Kitchener, 500,000 strong!" he shouted. Audiences roared. Hughes was sublimely happy.

Hughes had a simple view of recruiting: he wanted the largest army imaginable. A thousand recruits meant a battalion; half that made a cavalry regiment. In early 1916, he promised audiences an army of twenty-one divisions, five of them from Toronto alone. The draining away of manpower through sickness, desertion, unsuitability, and battlefield casualties did not interest him. How Canadian divisions in battle were to keep their ranks full when every recruit joined a new battalion was not his concern. Perhaps, as one of Hughes's biographers suggests, his mind "could not handle these sorts of details". They were left to the weary General Gwatkin, armed with British figures showing that each division in the field needed between 15,000 and 20,000 new men each year. At that rate, Gwatkin advised, Canada could support two, perhaps three, divisions: "who shall say how long this war will last," he warned.

Hughes paid no heed. Neither did Borden. Canadian men would "do their bit". At Halifax, in December 1914, the prime minister insisted: "There has not been, there will not be, compulsion or conscription." By the end of 1914, the Canadian Expeditionary Force (CEF) had enlisted 56,584 men. In June 1915, the government set the authorized strength at 150,000. In November, after a discouraging visit to England and France, Borden raised the total to 250,000. An even grander gesture was needed. In his New Year's message for 1916, "in token of Canada's unflinchable resolve to crown the justice of our cause with victory and with an abiding peace," Borden announced that the CEF would rise to 500,000 men.

For a country of eight million people, it was a bold promise. For once, there was criticism from the government's side. Lord Shaughnessy, president of the CPR, warned that so large a commitment might endanger Canada's productive strength. "Piffle," said Hughes. In 1915, monthly enlistments rose from 9,363 in January to 22,581 in December. Of seventy-one battalions authorized by the autumn of 1915, all but two raised their full complement and thirty-four sent extra reinforcement drafts overseas. Not only were young Canadians eager to enlist, the government's recruiting methods proved the cheapness of voluntarism. Without asking for a penny from Ottawa, militia units paid the costs of raising new battalions from their own regimental funds. With expenses ranging from advertising to band instruments, reported the *Toronto Daily Star,* the price of recruiting a battalion averaged $13,384. To back up the effort, women's organizations, recruiting associations, and a Speakers' Patriotic League held meetings, raised money, and spotted likely prospects. Hundreds of young men, eager to join the exciting new war in the air, learned that both the Royal Flying Corps and the Royal Naval Air Service demanded prior qualifications. When J.A.D. McCurdy, Canada's aviation pioneer, opened a school for pilots in 1915 at Lakeview in present-day Mississauga, he charged $400 for 400 minutes of flying. Hundreds lined up for a chance. Hundreds more went to the United States for pilot training. By 1917, 750 young Canadians had left Canada to join the British flying services; others joined overseas.

It went without saying that voluntary recruiting and enlistment guaranteed a CEF that would make Canadians proud. Colonels could choose who joined their battalions. Germans, of course, were banned after the rumour that a former RNWMP sergeant had been found dead in a German uniform. Native Indians were welcome despite official fears that they might not enjoy "the privileges of civilized warfare"; Asiatics were not welcome, though a handful of Japanese Canadians fled B.C. prejudice to enlist in Alberta battalions. Despite occasional support from Hughes, blacks found it impossible to enlist. In 1916, "coloureds" were finally allowed to join a labour company that went to France to chop trees. Some battalions had a harder time finding men. A company of Russians and other assorted naturalized "foreigners" filled out the ranks of the 41st French-Canadian Battalion.

Despite Borden's pledges and Hughes's optimism, there soon were warning signs. As early as January 1915, results from the hinterland led the Toronto *Globe* to ask: "Is rural Ontario losing its imperial spirit?" Recruiting lagged in the Maritimes and, more notoriously, in Quebec. In July, the Militia Department cut its standards for height and chest measurement. In August married men no longer needed a wife's permission to join up; men who had enlisted lost the right to buy their way out for $15. By the autumn, even wealthy militia regiments had exhausted their funds. Increasingly the recruiting leagues turned their fire on a government that was doing nothing to help. Patriotic rallies heard demands for conscription or at least national registration so that "slackers" and "shirkers" could be identified and prodded to "do their bit".

Hughes briskly turned the tables on his critics. If the militia was failing, civilian organizations could do far better. Colonels did not have to be soldiers; what he wanted were "strong men who have successful business or professional training". Between the autumn of 1915 and the summer of 1916, 150 new battalions were authorized. Recruiting entered its most frenzied phase. In Toronto, by early 1916, eight battalions competed for men; in Winnipeg there were six; in Edmonton, three. Colonel Vaux Chadwick's 123rd Battalion led the way in "shaming" tactics, urging women to refuse their favours to lily-livered men who would not fight for their country; Colonel Kingsmill's 124th Battalion, in contrast, invited "pals" to enlist. Both Toronto units got their quota. Three battalions invited Irish recruits; a score offered the attraction of Highland kilts and bagpipes. A Winnipeg battalion got its quota by promising strict temperance; a similar Toronto battalion collapsed when its colonel suffered a nervous breakdown. Two western battalions sought Scandinavians; three Ontario units insisted upon having "Men of the North"; and five looked south of the border — to the dismay of the British Foreign Office — to recruit an "American Legion" (about a thousand joined, though half of them deserted; among those who stayed, four earned the Victoria Cross). Two battalions accepted "Bantams" — men below the minimum height of 5'2"; two others appealed for "Sportsmen". Five companies enlisted university students; they were used to fill the depleted ranks of Princess Patricia's Canadian Light Infantry.

No one had ever claimed that Hughes's recruiting system was efficient. Gwatkin had pleaded in vain for recruiting depots, with proper medical inspection, training, and discipline to fill the ranks of existing units. The minister dismissed such notions as military red tape. Under the pressure of time, sympathy, or a demanding colonel, doctors passed thousands of men as fit who promptly became medical and pension burdens. Elderly patriots who broke under the strain, tubercular cases, and sufferers from insanity added nothing but trouble to the CEF. One man, Wilfrid Lavalée, joined six times and got to England twice though he was variously described as "vagrant", "violent", "alcoholic", and "a dangerous moron" in his numerous discharge papers. He and others like him helped explain why, after 400,000 enlistments, close to one-quarter had "wasted away" without seeing action. The 210th Battalion, "Frontiersmen" raised around Moose Jaw, Saskatchewan, enlisted 1,020 men, paraded 782 for inspection, and embarked only 505 of them for England: 59 had deserted and 152 had been discharged. The high-spirited 118th Battalion, responsible for most of the anti-German riots at Berlin-Kitchener, managed to take only 231 soldiers to war.

On April 14, 1916, leaders of the recruiting leagues brought their frustrations back to Ottawa. Something a lot like coercion was wanted. When a meeting with the prime minister proved futile, they created a Canadian National Service League, with John Godfrey, a Liberal lawyer from Toronto, as chairman. Encouraged by Sir George Foster, Minister of Trade and Commerce, Godfrey identified Quebec as the stumbling block to successful recruiting, voluntary or compulsory. Godfrey also had an answer: a "Bonne Entente" movement to iron out the differences between the French and English. "The Freudian philosophy can be employed with races," he explained, "...the best method of getting rid of interracial differences is by the process of psychoanalysis."

Godfrey was by no means wrong in his observations. While recruiting in the Maritimes also proved disappointing, Quebec's poor results were too obvious to be missed. A more sensitive minister than Hughes might have addressed

On the Edge of the Wood, Alfred Munnings. Famous in peacetime as a painter of racehorses, Munnings was one of the British artists Max Aitken (Lord Beaverbrook) recruited for the Canadian War Records Office (CWRO). The soldier is a horseholder from the Canadian Cavalry Brigade. (NWM 8587)

The Canadian Mounted Veterinary Corps at Work with the Field Artillery, 1916, R. Caton Woodville. As an illustrator, Woodville had portrayed British battles on land and sea to generations of readers of the *Illustrated London News.* Only the stiffly appropriate poses of the men here suggest to a perceptive observer that reality may have been a little reorganized. (NWM 75100)

9.2-inch Howitzers, a Night Shoot, Thurston Topham. The British artist was struck by the light and shadows created by the Canadian howitzers — squat, heavy guns that could pulverize trench lines and dug-outs but usually focused on enemy artillery. (NWM 8884)

Moonrise over Mametz Wood, Thurston Topham. This has been described by veterans as an eerily accurate impression of the Somme battlefield in 1916. Patrols, understandably, preferred moonless nights. (NWM 8893)

Seven A.M., April 22nd, 1915, Arthur Nantel. Nantel's battalion, the 14th, watched people and livestock flee the German bombardment of Ypres on that date. Nantel was among those Canadians who survived the battle to spend the rest of the war in a German prison camp. (NWM 8629)

Trench Fight, H.J. Mowat. The heroic tradition of war art survived, even among men who had seen fighting. Mowat, a Canadian who served with the British Army, must have known that soldiers almost never advanced in dense waves or crossed bayonets with an enemy. Only rarely did they see the enemy they killed. (NWM 8562)

Forging the Nine-Inch Shell, Frederick Waistell Jopling. Perhaps this violent scene suggested to the home-front audience the shell's ultimate detonation. To support the war effort, artists were encouraged to record the otherwise dreary face of industry. (NWM 8330)

the problem. If recruiting depended on strong militia regiments, French Canada had very few of them. The few French-speaking senior officers were mostly long past their prime. As for fervent wartime patriotism, it hardly existed outside English-speaking Montreal. In the First Contingent, a single French-speaking company represented Quebec's majority. In October 1914, a delegation of fifty-eight leading Quebeckers persuaded the government to include a French-Canadian battalion in the Second Contingent, but it took wearying months to find the men. When the 22nd French-Canadian Battalion left in May, it took most of French Canada's military spirit with it.

By 1916, eleven battalions were hunting for French-speaking recruits in Quebec; a few more sought Acadians and Métis in the Maritimes and the West. Figures are unreliable since enlistment forms did not indicate a soldier's language, but Militia Department statistics for June 1917 reported 14,100 French-speaking members of the CEF; fewer than half had been recruited by Quebec battalions. More than half the province's infantry recruits were English-speaking. With distinguished exceptions, as the historian of the 22nd Battalion discovered, the quality of French-speaking recruits was dismaying. Olivar Asselin, a wayward disciple of Bourassa, found fellow idealists for the 163rd Battalion, the "Poil-aux-Pattes", and the 189th Battalion found tough, hard-fighting farmers and fishermen from the Gaspé. Other recruits had too evidently been attracted by the promise of regular meals and a warm overcoat, or by the 206th Battalion slogan, "le dernier régiment à partir; le premier à profiter de la victoire".

Justifications for French Canada's dismal performance flowed easily. Hughes's Orange bigotry, refusal to form a French-Canadian brigade, failure to give commands to Major-General Lessard (aged fifty-five) or the stone-deaf Colonel Pelletier, and the choice of a Methodist clergyman to inspire recruiting in Montreal were all charges reiterated by Liberals. Later observers noted that, like Maritimers, Canadiens married young and stayed on the farm, two of many arguments against enlistment. The plain fact was that French Canadians felt little identity with the war, and very few in French Canada attempted to change their minds. Laurier gave speeches of remarkable eloquence, once in 1914 and once again in 1916. When Borden's ministers spoke, they were reminded of their *nationaliste* speeches of 1911. In 1916, the Militia Department finally recognized that Quebec was not a province like the others, appointed a patriotic pharmaceutical manufacturer, Arthur Mignault — not a Methodist! — as chief recruiting officer, and gave him staff and a budget. The effort utterly failed. The luckless Mignault only added his recriminations to those that flooded into the government's mail.

Outside Quebec, Borden's 1916 appeal and the recruiting leagues had some effect. January 1916, with 28,185 recruits, was the best month ever, until March, with 33,960. Then the totals fell — 10,059 in June, 5,717 in September, 4,930 in December. Almost no one had volunteered for the infantry. Kilts, white feathers, displays of German atrocities, speeches by war heroes — nothing made any difference. Instead of 500,000 men, the CEF ended 1916 with 299,937 men and women in its ranks. Most who joined after mid-1916 enlisted in the Canadian Forestry Corps or the fast-growing Corps of Canadian Railway Troops, not the infantry battalions.

Bonne-Ententism led to a couple of talkative meetings with prominent Quebeckers, but no change of policy or attitude. Appointment of Montreal financier Sir Thomas Tait as Director General of National Service led only to his indignant resignation when his choice of staff was criticized. In the fall, R.B. Bennett, a millionaire lawyer and Calgary MP, reluctantly agreed to chair the National Service Board. Its role was to conduct a national registration through the distribution of cards, although their completion and return was not compulsory. Voluntarism died hard. Only in June 1917 were the cards fully counted: four out of five had filled them out; perhaps 286,976 could be available for service. A little more hard work by the recruiting leagues showed that *available* did not mean willing to enlist. Those Canadians who would "do their bit" in the war had done it. Voluntarism was over.

ORGANIZING SIDE-SHOWS

By 1915, the war in France and Belgium had settled into a stalemate. The Western Front stretched along a five-hundred–mile belt of trenches and barbed wire. The Eastern Front, vast, more sparsely fortified, and mobile, offered no greater hope of easy victory. The victors of Tannenberg had advanced cautiously into Poland but their Austrian allies had suffered only defeats. Habsburg forces had dissolved before the advancing Russians, leaving 350,000, either dead or captured, and falling back to the Carpathians. Even the Serbs had found the strength to hurl the Austrians from their soil. Everywhere the generals and politicians faced the new year with promises of early victory and secret quandaries about how to achieve it.

The French and Belgians saw few options. King Albert had to cling to the little strip of Belgium that remained, preserve his army, and hope that it would be strong enough to justify renewed Belgian independence if the Allies ever won. The French, too, were almost wholly preoccupied with regaining the ugliest, coldest, wettest, and most valuable part of their country. General Joffre's strategy, faithful adherence to Plan XVII had cost France most of its iron, its coal, and a great many of the factories that could produce the munitions of war. He and his generals promised that it could all be won back. The French faith in the offensive was unbroken. If the French allowed themselves any distraction, it was to coax, bribe, and bully Italy into the war. One of their paid agents was an ex-socialist agitator named Benito Mussolini. On May 23, 1915, the French had their way; Italy declared war on Austria-Hungary.

The Russian Tsar and his generals had no plans at all. At the end of 1914, Grand Duke Nicholas, the commander-in-chief, let his allies know that Russia could do no more. Victory and defeat alike had exhausted Russia's reserves of ammunition, artillery, and even rifles. Without weapons, the Russian steamroller could not move. In October 1914, after years of German influence, Turkey entered the war against the Entente. Not only did the Russians face a new enemy, but their only warm-water ports were cut off from the Mediterranean. Getting supplies from Arctic ports or from Vladivostok was a near-hopeless expedient, though a few Canadians were sent to help build railways. Without massive Allied help, the enormous potential power of Russia would be lost.

Perhaps because they had thought harder about war than other people, German leaders were even more desperate. They found themselves in the two-front war their strategists had always predicted they would lose. Britain's maritime blockade, proclaimed at the outset of war, reminded Germans that their faith that the war would end quickly had kept them from stockpiling scarce materials. German divisions would also be needed to prop up her hopeless Habsburg ally. Germany's magnificent fleet sat impotent in harbour. An early brush with the Royal Navy off Heligoland had cost three cruisers. "The Emperor," reported Admiral von Tirpitz, "did not want losses of this sort."

Germany's battleships were not quite useless. As the American naval theorist Alfred Mahan had taught both German and British admirals, a "fleet in being" was a powerful threat. In case the Germans ever came out, Britain was forced to keep her Grand Fleet, twenty-seven Dreadnoughts strong, ready and waiting at dreary Scottish naval bases. The British also discovered another danger. On September 22, 1914, in a couple of hours, a single German submarine torpedoed three elderly British cruisers. The Grand Fleet headed to sea in panic; its wartime bases had yet to be protected against the U-boat menace. Germany could open a new front: on February 4, 1915, neutrals and belligerents alike were notified that their ships might be sunk on sight: Germany was blockading Britain. The British were appalled. There was virtually no effective countermeasure against submarines; they could not even be detected unless they surfaced. There was, however, one weapon: public opinion. Sinking ships without allowing the crews to find safety was shockingly contrary to the rules of war. On May 7, 1915, the Germans were taught a lesson when a U-boat sank the British liner *Lusitania*, sister-ship of the *Titanic*. Many American passengers were aboard; 128 of them were among the 1,195 who drowned. British propaganda, shrewdly managed, amplified American indignation. In August, the Germans ended their unrestricted blockade.

For the most part, the Kaiser's far-flung empire and naval bases proved useless. The German China squadron, hurrying home, had demolished Admiral Cradock's obsolete cruisers off Chile only to be utterly destroyed off the Falklands on December 7 by a more powerful British squadron. By 1915, almost all of Germany's commerce-raiding cruisers had been destroyed, one of them by an Australian cruiser. In South Africa, Louis Botha and Jan Smuts forgot the bitterness of the Boer War, crushed a revolt of fellow Afrikaners who did not, and rewarded themselves by acquiring German South West Africa. Other German colonies fell as easily, from Tsingtao, captured by the Japanese, to Togoland. The sole exception was German East Africa, where General Paul von Lettow-Vorbeck smashed a British landing force at Tanga on December 5 and then led his tiny army inland to out-run and out-fight vastly superior British and South African forces for the rest of the war. Von Lettow-Vorbeck's 3,500 white and 12,000 black troops kept 372,950 of the enemy engaged until November 1918. It was Germany's most economical and successful side-show.

The Germans' second most economical side-show opened January 19, 1915, with the first Zeppelin raid on England. The Kaiser had forbidden attacks on residential areas and "above all on the royal palaces" but, at 11,000 feet, bombing was indiscriminate. Forty airship raids killed 537 people and injured 1,358. That was trivial by the standard of other losses but more than enough to persuade editors and politicians to denounce government negligence while Anglican bishops demanded condign vengeance. When the Royal Flying Corps's few planes utterly failed to drive off the invaders, fliers on leave were mobbed. In 1917, when the Zeppelin threat had been beaten by improved fighters, the Germans sent twin-engined Gothas at 15,000 feet. Again civilian casualties mounted, frightened crowds packed London's Underground stations, and factory production on the night shift fell 73 per cent. As the Germans had hoped, the Royal Flying Corps (RFC) was forced to bring its best pilots from France and to build up an air-defence organization that absorbed 200 first-line aircraft and 15,115 men. Thousands of young Canadians were trained for the new air war, particularly in 1917 and 1918, after a few Canadians had proved their courage and skill as pilots and aerial fighters. German bombing and British reaction forced a doubling of the RFC and, ultimately, the creation of a single flying service, the Royal Air Force, as the means of organizing retaliation on Berlin. A Canadian, Colonel W.R. Mulock, commanded the force designed to begin attacking the German capital in December 1918.

In London, most British generals were as scornful of "side-shows" as their French counterparts. Wars could be won, they insisted, only by destroying an enemy's army. Some politicians were equally insistent that there must be a more ingenious way. The solution pointed to Turkey. The British were outraged that an old, if despised, ally had lined up with the enemy. Yet the Ottoman Empire, with its corrupt leaders and hopeless army, surely offered a chance of easy victories unavailable in France. The point was made when the Turks launched an army of 90,000 into the Russian Caucasus; only 18,000 frozen, beaten survivors straggled back. A smaller Turkish army attacked at Suez. A weak British garrison, backed by the newly arrived Australian and New Zealand Army Corps (ANZAC), drove them off. Dreams of conquering Palestine and Syria blossomed in British minds. A force from India landed at the Persian Gulf and captured Basra. Soon the British edged north, up the Tigris towards Mesopotamia and Baghdad.

No one could claim that winning Palestine and Mesopotamia would defeat Germany but they were irresistible prizes to a country that had always used war to add to its empire. Once launched, the British campaigns could not be limited. Nor could they be easily won. The Turkish army was ill-equipped and horribly administered but its troops were brave, German-led, and provided with artillery, machine guns, and shovels — the implements of the Western Front war. British generals assigned to the Turkish campaigns were old, stubborn, and often second-rate. Their armies were savaged by sickness, heat, maladministration, and a sense of futility. The British finally took Baghdad in 1918 but not before 889,702 British and Indian troops had gone to the Persian Gulf and only after a British division was forced to surrender at Kut-el-Amara in April 1916 and marched into a horrible captivity, which few survived. The Palestine campaign won Jerusalem at Christmas 1917, but not until a series of humiliating defeats had first drawn 1,192,511 men from Britain, India, and the Antipodes.

Only one thrust at Turkey promised a war-winning dividend. By forcing the Dardanelles, the straits that separated European and Asiatic Turkey, Russia's allies could open a way to the Black Sea. Russian wheat could then pay for Allied munitions and the Russian military steamroller could move again. Forcing the Straits was no new idea; the Royal Navy had repeatedly planned such an operation before the war and it had regularly concluded that the job *could* be done — but only if troops were landed to neutralize the Turkish guns. At the Admiralty, an ambitious Winston Churchill was bent on building his reputation. There were no troops: Lord Kitchener refused to provide them. Churchill demanded action anyway. A fleet of obsolete British and French battleships twice silenced the Turkish forts, only to withdraw for rest. The Turks rebuilt the forts, mined the Straits, and, on March 18, sank four old Allied battleships and damaged others. It was all they could do. The rest of the fleet could have sailed on to Constantinople. Instead, it turned back. The Allied admirals had had enough: they would not proceed without an army.

Another month passed. A German general, Otto Liman von Sanders, took command of the defences. On April 25, a small army of ANZACs and British regulars poured ashore at the tip of the Gallipoli peninsula; they met barbed wire, machine guns, artillery, and valiant resistance from Turkish troops, commanded in part by Kemal Pasha, the future creator of modern Turkey. The survivors clung to a couple of narrow beach-heads. Through the heat of the summer, sickness and snipers took a terrible toll. Both sides attacked with huge losses and no more success than assaults on the Western Front. On August 6, the British landed more divisions, at Suvla Bay. Inexperienced troops and hopelessly unenterprising generals turned a near-victory into another stalemate. In December, in the only brilliant operation of the campaign, the British and ANZACs slipped away from Gallipoli and Suvla without leaving a man. They had lost 213,890 casualties, a majority of them through sickness, a few from frostbite. For Australians, the suffering, losses, and futility of ANZAC Beach and Gallipoli became a unifying national memory.

The fiasco had other consequences. Bulgaria watched the disaster, waited for its 1915 harvest, and, on September 6, joined Germany and Austria. Vengeance was a motive: in 1913, Serbia had robbed her of Macedonia. In October, as German and Austrian divisions drove south into Serbia, the Bulgarians struck from the east. Serbian resistance collapsed. Half the Serbian army and tens of thousands of refugees perished in a winter retreat across the mountains to Albania and the Adriatic. The starving, frost-bitten survivors were taken to Corfu to recuperate.

There was almost nothing more the Allies could do for land-locked Serbia. The French dictated the response: a landing at Salonika with 150,000 troops to force neutral Greece into the war, and to drive north against Belgrade and Bucharest. The drive failed at the Vardar: the despised Bulgarians turned out to be tough soldiers, with machine guns too, if not very many of them. The usual stalemate followed. The British suggested withdrawal; the French insisted on staying: by 1917 more than half a million British, French, Serbian, and Russian troops were camped at Salonika, facing a Bulgarian army that had no intention of moving. Like Gallipoli, the Salonika front was hot in sum-

Internees and guards at Yoho National Park, B.C., in 1916. While some internees might have aided the enemy, many were just recent immigrants who had jobs that other workers wanted, or whose unemployment made them a burden on municipal relief.

The sinking of the *Lusitania* was pretext enough for gangs of rowdies to smash German-owned property like the bar of the Kaiserhof Hotel in Victoria.

While some women broke stereotypes to fill a variety of wartime jobs, most channelled their support into traditional female tasks. Knitting produced a phenomenal output of socks, scarves, wristlets, and other goods. Men overseas cherished them for their quality — and for the unexpected personal notes they sometimes found enclosed.

Toronto women "do their bit" for the Victory Loan campaign in 1917 by dancing a hornpipe on University Avenue. The sight was doubtless a reminder to older spectators of how war upsets normal standards of behaviour.

A militant minority of women joined quasi-military organizations, drilled, and learned how to shoot. Ridicule from both sexes soon drove such groups out of existence; in any case, there was plenty of more conventional patriotic work for them.

The 163rd Battalion was one of the few successful recruiting efforts in Quebec after 1914. While Henri DesRosiers, a veteran of Ypres, was in command, the real attraction was Henri Bourassa's errant lieutenant, Olivar Asselin. While Asselin insisted that he was doing his duty for France, his memoirs show him responding to his yearning for adventure. The "Poil-aux-Pattes" — literally the "hairy paws" — appealed to the best and brightest in French Canada.

Native Indian parents and their newly enlisted son. Though military authorities worried that Germans "might refuse to extend to them the privileges of civilized warfare", native Canadians were eagerly sought as volunteers and many enlisted. Wartime service and sacrifice seemed to many native groups a solid argument for better treatment from the Canadian majority.

III
LEARNING WAR

Liverpool was the normal destination for Canadians crossing the Atlantic but the Admiralty's new fear of submarines sent the Canadian convoy to the little West Country port of Plymouth. At dawn on October 15, welcoming crowds saw the first mist-shrouded ships enter Plymouth Sound. The welcome turned chilly. After days on board ship, officers and men broke ranks to try the potent English beer. Captain J.F.C. Fuller, an officer sent by the War Office to help with disembarkation, was told that Canadians were not "coolies" and would not unload their own ships. He managed it in nine days with a thousand British "New Army" recruits. A nightly "Drunkards' Express" delivered Canadian stragglers to their new camp on Salisbury Plain. Their equipment was piled along a country road near Plymouth for units to sort and collect. With six months' training, Fuller told his mother, Canadians would make fine soldiers "if all their officers were shot".

The Canadians had less than four months to become an infantry division. At Salisbury, conditions were ideal — for a week. Of 123 days the Contingent spent in England, it rained for 89. Gales flattened tents, rain turned to sleet and snow, and the thin topsoil turned to mud. Soldiers learned the dilemma of whether to sleep in a sodden uniform or to put it on again in the morning. Some officers joined their wives in nearby hotels or fled to London. The men stayed put or went absent without leave. Under the driving rain, with a handful of British instructors, battalions practised route marching, bayonet fighting, and, when the few ranges were available, shooting. Much of their equipment was gratefully abandoned. Canadian boots dissolved in the mud, Bain wagons collapsed under a full load of ammunition, and MacAdam shovels — impossible to carry and by no means bulletproof — were left to rust. For all its defects, the Ross remained: with fourteen Territorial and eighteen

"New Army" divisions to equip, the British had no better rifles to spare, even if Hughes had allowed them.

By January, the best twelve battalions of the First Contingent had been selected and their organization was set, for the third and final time, at four companies each. Days of drill and polishing climaxed on February 4, 1915, in a review for King George v. A week later, the Canadian Division had left for France.

Raising a second contingent took longer. Most of the experienced officers and almost all of Canada's tiny stock of modern weapons had gone in October. The British pleaded a lack of accommodation. It was spring before the infantry battalions left Canada and August before the last artillery batteries reached England. Sensitive to Canadian outrage at the conditions on Salisbury Plain, the War Office evicted a British division from huts at Shorncliffe Camp near Dover and installed the Canadians. As scores of new battalions were authorized in Canada that summer, more and more units were despatched overseas. Canadian camps spread to Witley, Bramshott, Seaford, Hastings, and other towns of southern England. Scores and ultimately hundreds of surplus officers, left over from contingents and broken-up battalions, manoeuvred themselves into staff positions.

Men in the ranks rarely had that kind of influence. Whatever his high patriotic motives, once a man mumbled his oath of allegiance and signed his attestation papers, he had lost most of the rights he had ever enjoyed as a civilian. Under military law he could suffer "death or lesser penalty" for a score of acts, from cowardice in the face of the enemy to sleeping while a sentry. Lesser penalties ranged from extra drill to "Field Punishment No. 1" — being lashed to a wagon wheel for an hour each morning and evening for such offences as "absence without leave", forgetting to shave, or "dumb insolence". A soldier forfeited privacy, dignity, and autonomy. Obey orders was the general principle; ask questions later — or never — was the army's rule. Drill, with sergeants bellowing personal abuse, attempted to turn a soldier into an obedient automaton. In 1914, Hughes had insisted that "his boys" could choose whether to be inoculated for typhoid fever. That kind of choice faded fast. By 1916, medical officers regularly instructed men to drop their pants so that their genitals could be inspected for symptoms of gonorrhoea. In camp, soldiers were jammed ten or fifteen to a tent twenty feet in diameter; in barracks, they were crowded into ill-heated frame huts, occasionally two to a bed.

Canadians modelled their army on what they had learned from childhood was Britain's greatest military institution, the infantry battalion. Pre-war militia units had painstakingly imitated the uniforms, customs, and traditions of British regiments; under their drab khaki uniformity, CEF battalions did the same. Militia Headquarters issued a standard maple-leaf badge but battalions designed and purchased their own. Kilts and bonnets for would-be Scottish battalions, black buttons for the Winnipeg and Nova Scotia "Rifles", even the white goats some units boasted as mascots were borrowed from British regimental traditions in hopes of instant *esprit de corps.*

Canadian volunteers inherited less traditional features of Queen Victoria's armies. Peacetime soldiers had been recruited from the bottom of society, from men who were presumably unfit for better work. Even in the army's idiom, "soldiering" meant shirking. Endless supervision and brutal punishments were necessary because peacetime soldiers could be counted on to dodge work, malinger their way to hospital, and do the least possible. In army language, any chore was a "fatigue". Even in wartime, a soldier's pay, clothing, and food ranked him among society's poor. At $1.10 a day, a Canadian private was better off than any Allied soldier but he earned half the rate paid a Canadian unskilled labourer in 1915. In camp, his meals consisted of a few monotonous staples: porridge and tea for breakfast; stew and a pudding for dinner; bread, cheese or jam, and tea for supper. Over longjohns or a cotton vest and underpants, a soldier wore a coarse grey-flannel shirt, khaki serge jacket and trousers, heavy boots, and puttees — long strips of wool that an infantryman wound up from his ankles to his knees (a cavalryman or gunner wound them down his legs).

Officers, in contrast to "men", were gentlemen, a breed apart. They were commissioned, not enlisted. They wore tailored uniforms, with a collar and tie, and a leather Sam Browne belt carefully polished by a soldier-servant or "batman". Soldiers saluted officers, called them "sir", and spoke to them only when spoken to. Striking an officer was a capital offence. Officers — and sergeants, too — lived and ate separately. Table manners and an ability to abide by "mess etiquette" were among the expectations imposed on a would-be officer. The sergeants' mess aped the officers'.

Over time, the CEF evolved its own style. It was a slow process. Until October 1916, Canadian soldiers were part of the British army, disciplined by the Army Act. Officers were issued British as well as Canadian commissions. The affinity was more than legal. Every senior officer in the CEF and a quarter of the men in the ranks had belonged to the pre-war militia, with its British-style uniforms and procedures. Almost 20,000 had served in the British regular army. Next to the colonel, the most important figure in many new CEF battalions was an elderly British veteran who acted as regimental sergeant-major. He and the sergeants, chosen from those with any prior military experience, indoctrinated raw Canadians in their new way of life. British soldiers were the backbone of many CEF units, passing on the customs and language of Indian cantonments a decade earlier. A "chit" was any army form, a "dekko" was a look-see, a "wallah" was anyone of importance.

In Canada, soldiers discovered that "kicking" and complaining would win public sympathy against harsh conditions or over-zealous officers. At Camp Borden in June 1916, anger at the heat, blowing sand, and shortage of water produced a noisy demonstration against Sam Hughes that no hurriedly imposed censorship could suppress. Once in England, there was no audience for such protests. Soldiers also found that they had spent months and even years in Canada without adequate training. Officers appointed because they could attract volunteers usually had no time, knowledge, or inclination to be instructors or disciplinarians. In England, British instructors usually rated newly arrived Canadians as two-week recruits. Drill, route marches, and shooting began again. Once in England, battalions raised on the pledge that friends would fight shoulder to shoulder with friends were ruthlessly dissolved. By 1916, the army in France needed only privates and lieutenants.

In Canada or in England, soldiers learned that they were part of a complex organization. In the infantry, a soldier knew his section best: ten to fifteen men under a corporal or lance corporal. A lieutenant commanded a platoon of four sections, with a sergeant as *alter ego* and second-in-command. Four platoons formed a company, under a major or captain. A battalion of four companies, with a lieutenant-colonel in command, was a soldier's "unit", the "family" to which he returned from hospital or a course. That was why breaking up any battalion was traumatic. Soldiers soon formed new loyalties to the 8th "Little Black Devils" from Winnipeg; the 29th Battalion, "Tobin's Tigers" from Vancouver; or the elite 42nd, one of three CEF battalions raised by Montreal's Royal Highlanders. A division — 18,000 to 20,000 men — was commanded by a major-general and included three infantry brigades of four battalions, each commanded by a brigadier-general. Two or more divisions formed an army corps under a lieutenant-general. An army controlled several corps. Staff officers, with red tabs on their collars and a red band around their caps, were a hated and despised by-product of the army's higher organization.

A battalion was the limit of most soldiers' horizon, but a growing range of supporting arms, services, and specialist organizations developed during the war, from cyclist battalions to a veterinary corps. Just behind the infantry were batteries of field artillery with 18-pounder guns. Much farther back was heavier artillery — 4.5-inch howitzers and 60-pounder guns, with shells able to collapse dug-outs or shatter concrete. Trench mortars, throwing a few bombs and rushing away to leave retaliation to fall on the infantry, were both effective and deeply disliked. In time, machine-gunners became a specialist corps, with their heavy Vickers guns. By 1918, each infantry platoon had its own temperamental Lewis gun. Men specialized as snipers, machine-gunners, rifle grenadiers, and "bombers". Sick and wounded depended for evacuation and treatment on the Army Medical Corps, while the unloved but essential Army Service Corps delivered food, ammunition, and fuel — usually at a safe distance from the fighting.

The British, and some Canadians who should have known better, imagined that Canadians (and Australians) adjusted well to soldiering because of their customary robust, outdoor life. In fact, barely a quarter of the CEF came from farming, mining, or frontier occupations. Almost as many were from clerical, sales, or professional backgrounds and more than a third were recruited from urban manufacturing, construction, and labouring jobs. What such men brought to the army was the rigid discipline of pre-1914 industrial society. Teachers, parents, foremen, and employers had exacted conformity and obedience. The army reinforced what society had begun in the home, school, factory, or office. Civilians also enjoyed fewer creature comforts in 1915; it was no sudden hardship to be cold, wet, or hungry. If there was a British accent to the CEF it was also, conveniently, the accent of most of the men in the ranks of the Canadian Corps until 1916.

That did not guarantee that "soldiering" came easily. Canadians resented the "coolie" burden of large pack, haversack, greatcoat, spare boots, water-bottle, rifle, bayonet, 150 rounds of ammunition of "full marching order", when transport could easily halve the eighty-pound burden. Grudgingly and seldom did Canadian soldiers accept the special privileges of junior officers when they knew that a commission in the CEF usually rewarded social or political "pull" or a few extra years of education. Until 1916, commissions were awarded to men who could persuade a militia colonel in Canada to make them officers. Even officers promoted from the ranks were suspect, perhaps all the more so because they had abandoned their comrades for a life of relative privilege. Like army food and the weather, officers were accepted by soldiers as part of a temporary and unnatural existence, but some day there might be a reckoning. Robert Correll, a quiet, friendly soldier with two more months to live in the summer of 1916, explained to his sister: "I guess you will notice that a number of officers have been killed or wounded. It seems a hard thing to say but from what we can learn the ones that used the men dirty over here sometimes get 'accidentally' shot during a charge...."

TRENCH WARFARE

A legend that Hughes stopped the break-up of the Contingent by bearding Lord Kitchener at the War Office is colourful fantasy. The British had intended, from August 1914, to use the Canadians as a division. To ensure that Sam Hughes would not take command, they offered a choice of their available generals. Hughes settled for Sir Edwin Alderson, a conscientious fifty-five–year–old veteran who had commanded Canadians during the South African War.

By no means all those who had landed at Plymouth went to France with the 1st Canadian Division. Newfoundland's contingent, raised in a dominion with no better peacetime army than the popular Church Lads' Brigade, reached England without rifles, equipment, or even military caps. To safeguard their separate identity, the Newfoundlanders left the CEF in December 1914, went north to Scotland, joined the British 29th Division at Gallipoli in September 1915, and returned with it to France in 1916. The Princess Patricia's Canadian Light Infantry (PPCLI), with its trained British reservists, went to France on December 20, 1914, as part of the 27th Division. Canada's two permanent-force cavalry regiments and a brigade of Royal Canadian Horse Artillery formed most of the Canadian Cavalry Brigade. To Hughes's indignation, the War Office gave the command to Colonel J.E.B. Seely, a British amateur soldier, adventurer, and politician who had been Kitchener's predecessor at the War Office until the "Curragh Mutiny". Never again, Hughes insisted, would Canadians be denied a voice in choosing their commanders.

Normally, British troops crossed the Channel from Dover or Folkestone to Le Havre. Fear of losing a shipload of Canadians to a U-boat persuaded the Admiralty to order a longer, rougher journey from Avonmouth to St. Nazaire, on February 16. Officers climbed into battered coaches; other ranks squeezed into tiny French cattle cars with the familiar markings: "Hommes — 40 Chevaux — 8". Two days' journey across France took them to Hazebrouck on the Belgian border, headquarters of General Sir Horace Smith-Dorrien and his new Second British Army. By the end of the month, twinned with British units, most of the battalions had experienced trench warfare in a quiet sector near Armentières.

The worst of a bad winter was almost over by the time the Canadians arrived, but the British trenches along the Flanders plain were as wet, muddy, and dreary as any on the Western Front. Water lay only a couple of feet below the surface. An army that believed its own legends was convinced that it was un-British to retreat to dryer and more defensible ground, even if it could be found. The French and Belgians, whose ground it was, agreed. British defenders did their best in appalling conditions, made worse because no one had foreseen the vast quantities of tools, lumber, barbed wire, and duck-boards, to say nothing of flares, grenades, and artillery ammunition, that trench warfare consumed. A virtual truce at Christmas 1914 helped the British even more than the Germans to improve their defences, but generals, far from the line, punished fraternizers and preached the "offensive spirit". The PPCLI, in the line by December 1914, had won early distinction by launching one of the first trench raids of the war in February 1915.

Canadians learned that front-line defences ideally consisted of three lines of trenches behind a barbed-wire entanglement. A fire trench faced the enemy; a second or "support" trench lay behind it; and a reserve trench was a third line of defence. The French put few men in the front line and counted on destroying attackers with a storm of shells from their famous 75s, followed by a counter-attack. The British insisted on doggedly holding every inch. Brigades manned their sectors with two battalions in the trenches, a third in reserve, and a fourth back under the control of the Division.

Trench routine turned day into night. At dawn and dusk, the likeliest times for an attack, every soldier stood to, fully armed, for an hour. At night, work began: repairing barbed-wire entanglements; shoring up trenches after artillery fire or erosion; fetching and carrying up food, water, ammunition, and building materials. A few men, faces blackened and armed with clubs, knives, and grenades, set out to patrol no man's land, perhaps to seize a prisoner or collect identification from a dead enemy. Periodically, flares lit the sky, machine guns emptied belts of ammunition into the darkness, and artillery would join in until quiet returned.

After the dawn stand-to, most of the troops could rest. Officers could authorize an issue of SRD ("service rum, diluted") after a cold or particularly unpleasant night. Rations, brought up in a sandbag, with tea and sugar tied into separate corners, were distributed—a can of bully beef or Maconochie stew between two or three men, a can of jam or butter between five, a few hard-tack biscuits for each man. It was a diet, historian Denis Winter has noted, that left men hungry, flatulent, and afflicted with boils. British generals did not believe in comfort in the trenches: after all, troops should remember that they would be moving on in the spring or summer offensive. Dug-outs were reserved for headquarters and officers' quarters. Soldiers built a shelf or burrowed a "funk-hole" in the trench wall, rolled themselves in a greatcoat and a waterproof sheet, and tried to sleep.

Common sense and military values came into frequent conflict. To the dismay of sergeant-majors and the stuffier officers, soldiers took the stiffening from their caps and hacked off the long skirts of their greatcoats so that mud would not cling to them. Though men in kilted battalions suffered from the cold and from cuts inflicted on the back of their knees from mud-encrusted cloth, pride denied them trousers. In 1916, long after the French and Germans, the British provided their men with steel helmets. The goatskin jerkins and leggings and the washbasin-shaped helmets made soldiers resemble medieval pikemen.

Day and night, soldiers lived in the miasma of rotting corpses and latrines, turned acrid by the odour of chloride of lime. Rats prowled the trenches and gorged on human flesh. Within a few days of reaching France, officers and men alike were infested with lice. Such was the misery that men woke up bleeding from scratches gouged to relieve the itching. In the foul conditions, infection often followed. Only in 1918 was trench fever — "pyrexia of unknown origin", or PUO — traced to body lice. Standing for hours and even days in freezing water produced trench foot, akin to frostbite. Rubbing feet with whale oil and changing socks regularly seemed to curb the swelling. That took systematic discipline: officers of units that reported too many cases of trench foot were warned and then fired.

Armentières was a quiet part of the trench line, where both sides had learned to live and let live. It was a style, British historian Tony Ashworth claims, Australian, Canadian, and Scottish divisions rarely adopted. Letters and memoirs suggest little of the front-line comradeship that purportedly united trench soldiers of both sides against all staff officers, generals, and gunners. Canadians certainly saw the staff as enemies, but they hated Germans too. War was too cruel to love one's opponents.

Even a few days in the front line cost a battalion a dozen or more killed and wounded. On both sides, snipers hid themselves and waited for the unwary. The Germans, who stayed in the same sector for months, were better at their job. Machine guns were no threat to men under cover, but night patrols and wiring parties were easily caught in the open by flares. The worst threat was from mortars and artillery: more than half of all Canadian casualties were the victims of shelling. Until 1917, infantry were the main victims of artillery duels. Under shelling, soldiers could join in a deadly game, dodging from traverse to traverse to escape a slow-moving mortar bomb. More often, men developed a carapace of fatalism; they were safe until that inescapable shell or bullet "with their name on it" arrived. Under a heavy barrage, with the earth shaking and the sky hidden by smoke and dust, there was no fatalism or even courage. It was then that brave men cried, fouled themselves, waited for a sordid death. Charles Yale Harrison, an American in the CEF, recalled a German *minenwerfer* barrage:

I am terrified. I hug the earth, digging my fingers into every crevice, every hole.

A blinding flash and an explosive howl a few feet in front of the trench.

My bowels liquefy.

Acrid smoke bites the throat, parches the mouth. I am beyond mere fright. I am frozen with an insane fear that keeps me cowering in the bottom of the trench. I lie flat on my belly, waiting....

Suddenly it stops.

No single weapon transformed war as much as aircraft. Few foresaw what airplanes — barely eleven years old when the war began — would do, although all the belligerents had them. A single plane had changed the outcome of the Battle of the Marne in 1914. As trench war developed, aircraft and balloons became the only means of seeing beyond the enemy's front line. From the sky, observers spotted artillery targets and guided fire. Air photos became instant maps and the best source of information for army staff officers. Aircraft forced armies to move and work at night and to hide under camouflage. Anti-aircraft guns became a new form of artillery. By the end of the war, they had shot down more planes than the specialized fighter aircraft that caught the public's eye.

The Germans had a technological lead, as in much else, in aircraft engines and frames. By adapting a primitive device on a captured French plane, Anthony Fokker devised an interrupter gear that allowed machine-gun bullets to get past propeller blades. By adapting this to his *Eindekkers*, Fokker created the first real fighter plane. Pilots could merely point their craft at the slow-moving two-seater observation planes, fire, and score a kill. In self-defence, pilots learned the violent evasive manoeuvres their instructors had forbidden because, until 1916, no pilot knew for certain how to pull out of a spin. Fighters became instruments in a struggle for supremacy in the sky. For the winner, the reward was uninterrupted aerial observation and the kind of help Canadians needed on the Somme and at Vimy Ridge to locate German guns and troop movements.

In 1915, Lord Kitchener had invited the dominions to set up their own squadrons. The Australians did so, but a Canadian government that had rejected its own navy wanted no air force. Air-minded Canadians flocked to join the Royal Flying Corps and the Royal Naval Air Service. Though the British tried to reserve their pilot ranks for "officers and gentlemen", Canadians, with their ambiguous class status, met fewer obstacles. Britain's reward was some of its most skilled pilots. Of twenty-seven top Empire "aces" who downed thirty or more aircraft, eleven were Canadians. The best was Lieutenant-Colonel W.A. "Billy" Bishop, who ranked third among all the aces of the war, with seventy-two victories. Lieutenant-Commander Raymond Collishaw of the RNAS was fifth with sixty. Without the Canadians, historian Denis Winter concedes, the British record of victories would have been thin.

Despite legend, few Canadians escaped the trench war into the flying services. In 1916, a shortage of good, experienced infantry officers led the CEF to ban transfers. Instead, ordinary soldiers and their officers faced the alternation of terror and boredom as long as the war — or their lives — continued.

The "front" was only part of their lives. Within battalions, companies rotated from the fire trench to support and reserve. Even in 1915, a division had only four of its twelve battalions in the trenches at one time. Once relieved, almost always at night, troops filed their weary way back through a maze of communications trenches to form up and march to billets, perhaps in a battered farmstead, in rain-sodden tents, or even in prefabricated huts. "Rest" was a relative term. The infantry was the army's labour force, compelled to dig trenches, repair roads, bury the dead, or load supplies, usually under the supervision of men from other corps, such as the Engineers, whose work it might have been. Generals chose rest periods to inspect troops: that meant that soldiers spent time practising drill, polishing buttons, and burnishing steel. Out of the line, soldiers were paraded to baths and waited, naked and shivering, for a minute of tepid and sometimes scalding water. Shirts and underwear were handed in to be laundered, disinfected, and returned — usually with the lice and their larvae intact. Not until 1918 did a Canadian, Colonel J.A. Amyot, devise adequate sterilization equipment for the British army.

At each relief, a few men earned a brief escape. Ordinary soldiers could expect a week's furlough to England once a year; officers went three or four times as often. Perhaps no grievance in the ranks was more bitter. Courses were another escape. Brigade and divisional schools taught sniping, signalling, patrolling, or the new-fangled Stokes trench-mortar. A few weeks of spit and polish was a small price for learning new weapons, tactics, or techniques and to escape the trenches.

Soldiers dreamed of a more enduring escape, a "Blighty", borrowed, like so much army language, from Hindustani, for "a country across the sea". With rare, Victoria-Cross–winning exceptions, wounded men dropped out of the battle. If they could, they made their own way back; if they were lucky, comrades or stretcher-bearers would help. Army doctors, faced with mass casualties, practised a ruthless sorting of those they could help and those who must be left to die — discreetly concealed by its French name, *triage*. A lucky man with a "Blighty" could be in an English hospital by nightfall. The less fortunate might convalesce just behind the lines. The luckless died in slow misery, beyond the help of medicine or friends. Stomach wounds and fractured thighbones were agonizing and usually fatal.

Courage, whatever the original stock, is a wasting asset, exhausted by too many hours of anxious stand-tos, earth-crunching bombardments, and night patrols. Over time, the letters and diaries of Canadians in the trenches reflect the strain and deepening despair. Some men sought death. Some fled it. Some deserted; a few wounded themselves; so many thousands were diagnosed for "shell shock" that the Medical Corps banned the words and boasted of cures by massive electro-shock. In the end, discipline and military law held soldiers to their appalling duty. In all the wars of the Victorian era, only three British soldiers had been shot for military offences; in France and Flanders, the British Expeditionary Force executed 304 men, 265 for desertion or cowardice. The CEF followed suit: by the end of the war, 25 Canadians had been shot, 2 for murder and the rest for failing the test of courage in battle.

"SAVING THE SITUATION"

The Canadians entered the line near Neuve Chapelle in March. Though a handful of Territorial battalions had reinforced the over-strained British regulars, the Canadians had preceded all but the regular army divisions raised in England since August 1914. Now they were on the fringes of their first battle. For weeks Sir Douglas Haig's First Army had rehearsed, studied the unfamiliar new air photos, collected ammunition, and waited. On March 10, British and Indian troops attacked at Neuve Chapelle behind a short artillery barrage. The British took much of the German front line on schedule and waited for the second phase. Hours passed. A merciless rain of German shells cut telephone lines and smashed into waiting troops, as reinforcements rushed into place. When their attack resumed, the British were slaughtered. Further attacks on March 11 and 12 met the same fate. When the fighting ceased, Haig's army had lost 12,892 men, 100 of them Canadians, caught in incidental shelling. Perhaps the French and the Germans had an improved opinion of the BEF but it was a costly lesson in "enterprise and initiative" in the attack.

In early April, the Canadians marched back to Smith-Dorrien's Second Army. By April 17, they had replaced a French division in the Ypres salient, with the British 28th Division on the right and a French Algerian division on the left. The Algerians and a division of French Territorials linked up with King Albert's Belgian army. It was a quiet sector with historic memories of famous regiments and the brutal fighting six months earlier. Ypres — "Wipers" to the troops — had survived almost intact and it was easily visible from the low ridges the Canadians occupied. The immediate concerns were prosaic ones: the French trenches were "filthy" and "in a deplorable state" and the Canadians must bring them up to British standards. However, the weather was getting warmer, the skies were clear, and the enemy was quiet.

Duke Albrecht, of the German Fourth Army opposite, had no grand plans but he had been given a chore. In 1909, the Germans had signed the Hague Convention against asphyxiating gases, but war was war. Germany's chemical industry produced vast quantities of chlorine, a deadly gas that was heavier than air and would certainly invade enemy trenches and dug-outs. Albrecht had been given six thousand cylinders of the gas and orders to try it out. There was one problem: as flyers were already discovering, the prevailing winds blew from the west into the German lines. From January to April, the Germans waited. Finally, they lugged the cylinders to the north side of the Ypres salient, facing the French. If the cylinders worked — and sensible people doubted it — the Germans could collapse the salient and win a reassuring little victory. If they didn't....

On April 11, the Germans were ready. Belgian spies sent word. German prisoners reported the cylinders. Joffre's headquarters was contemptuous: "All this gas business need not be taken seriously." The British headquarters was no more concerned.

Thursday, April 22, was a beautiful day with a gentle westward breeze. Two brigades, Brigadier-General A.W. Currie's 2nd on the right, R.E.W. Turner's 3rd on the left, held the Canadian line. M.S. Mercer's 1st Brigade was far to the rear, training for a possible future attack. For a week, German shells had battered Ypres. The Cloth Hall was soon in flames; fleeing civilians and their possessions crowded the few roads out of the town. At 3:00 P.M., Turner's headquarters got orders to collect a hundred mouth organs from the Division. An hour later, the German guns began pounding the French lines. In minutes, the shelling spread to Turner's trenches. At 5:00 P.M., observers saw two greenish-yellow clouds rise from the German lines, merge, and roll forward like a dawn mist. Minutes later, stricken Algerians, choking and crying from the gas, poured from their trenches. A few fell into trenches held by the 13th Battalion, Royal Highlanders from Montreal. Most poured back towards Ypres. French guns burst into action, slowed, and stopped as the cloud of chlorine reached them. Behind the cloud German troops, protected only with face-masks purchased days before in Brussels, picked their cautious way over Pilckem Ridge, past Langemarck, and towards Kitchener's Wood where British gunners abandoned their heavy guns. Little but their own caution remained to keep the Germans from Ypres.

Brigadier-General Turner grasped the situation. His flank was open. Neither he nor anyone else could realize that fully four miles of defences lay unmanned because of the gas cloud. Reserve companies were ordered into St. Julien, a village on the Canadian flank. As dusk fell, Sir Edwin Alderson ordered an attack to retake Kitchener's Wood and the British guns. The surviving Algerians, he was told, would help. In the darkness, the 10th Battalion, from Alberta, and the 16th Canadian Scottish, from B.C. and Ontario, formed a dense mass. At 11:30 P.M. they moved forward. Half-way, five hundred yards from the wood, flares suddenly lit the sky and machine guns spat fire. The survivors rushed the woods but the Germans kept fighting. The French never came. By dawn, only one-third of the 1,500 Canadians had crawled back to form a thin line of defence. The rest were dead or captured.

The Canadian attack had at least stalled the German advance. All night and the next day, British and Canadian battalions rushed up to plug the gap. Alderson found himself struggling to control a score of units. By now, Ypres was a burning ruin. German artillery pinpointed roads forward to the battle, where they crossed the Yser Canal and the reserve trench lines, to kill the reinforcements. On April 23, more battalions were poured in piecemeal in an attempt to drive the Germans back. All they could do was stabilize the line. At St. Julien, Lance Corporal Fred Fisher of the 13th Battalion lugged his heavy Colt machine gun forward to fight off German attackers. His heroism earned him the first 'Canadian' VC of the war. He died on the 24th. Sergeant-Major Fred Hall of the 8th Battalion was killed trying to haul wounded men to safety. He also earned a VC.

On Saturday, April 24, the Germans turned on the two Canadian brigades that still held out in the salient. At 4:00 A.M., shells blasted the shallow ditches where the Canadians waited. A few minutes later, gas was released. The 8th Battalion, Winnipeg's "Little Black Devils", and the 5th Western Cavalry had been issued cotton bandoliers to cover their mouths. Dry or soaked in urine the cloth made no difference. Scores of men lay coughing and gasping, faces black from asphyxiation. Survivors opened fire on the mass of advancing Germans. As their over-heated Ross rifles seized, cursing soldiers slammed open the bolts with their boots or shovels. Colt machine guns, heavy, awkward weapons, jammed or ran out of their special ammunition.

Captain Edward Bellew of the 7th Battalion fought his gun until the Germans overran his position. Out of ammunition, he smashed the mechanism and was taken prisoner. His VC was announced only after he returned to Vancouver in 1919. On the right, most of Currie's brigade clung to their trenches. On the left, remnants of the 3rd Brigade fell back. Germans on their flank blasted them with enfilade fire and closed in on St. Julien. In the wild confusion of his headquarters, Turner and his brigade major, Garnet Hughes, misinterpreted Alderson's order to hold the village as a directive to withdraw to a stronger line. By 3:00 P.M., St. Julien's defenders, left to their fate, had been overwhelmed. On the right, with his men clinging to the apex of a shrinking

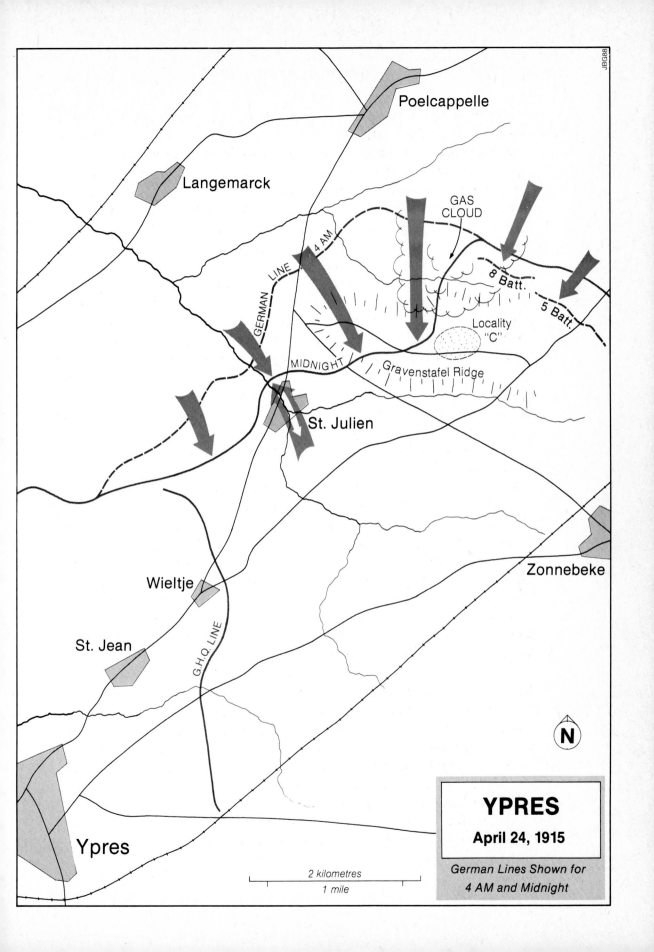

Poelcappelle

Langemarck

GAS
CLOUD

4 AM

GERMAN LINE

8 Batt.

5 Batt.

Locality
"C"

MIDNIGHT

Gravenstafel Ridge

St. Julien

Zonnebeke

Wieltje

G.H.Q. LINE

St. Jean

N

YPRES

Ypres

YPRES

April 24, 1915

German Lines Shown for
4 AM and Midnight

2 kilometres

1 mile

JBG88

triangle, Currie told his two colonels, Lipsett and Tuxford, to pull back to the reserve line and then walked back through the shell fire to get help. The British commander of the 27th Division, Major-General T.D'O. Snow, treated Currie to contempt and outrage, appalled that a brigadier would leave his headquarters on such an errand. If the Canadian had got his men into trouble, said Snow, he could get them out again. Currie walked back with a handful of Canadian stragglers to find that his two colonels had ignored the order to retreat. Their men would have been slaughtered if they had moved.

The battle continued in utter disorder. On Sunday, British and Canadian battalions kept struggling to regain the lost ground. A British brigade of regulars lost half its men in a valiant, unsupported bid to retake St. Julien. Virtually isolated and assailed by two German brigades, Currie finally pulled his men back to join the remnants of the 3rd Brigade on Gravenstafel Ridge. By April 27, Alderson's Canadians had withdrawn to count their losses. In the salient, the battle continued with growing ferocity. On May 8, as part of the 27th Division, the PPCLI valiantly held the shoulder of a German drive on Frezenberg Ridge. Of 550 Patricias who began the day, only 150 remained that night. Somehow they had held their ground.

Second Ypres was no triumph. In a savage defensive battle, the Canadians had fallen back two miles and lost 208 officers and 5,828 men. The inexperience of a raw division had shown; so had its courage. Survivors would argue about Turner's remoteness from the battle and the British official historian would condemn Currie's decision to go back for help. One battalion commander, Lieutenant-Colonel J.A. Currie, MP, was removed for drunkenness and cowardice in the battle (and, once back in Canada, promoted). Men sent into battle with a bad rifle had every reason to be bitter and demoralized. However, in a brutal baptism of fire, the Canadians had not broken. They had done all they could be asked to do and more. Four Canadians won Victoria Crosses for their courage in the fight or in risking their lives for wounded comrades. One of them, Captain Francis Scrimger, a medical officer, had risked his life rescuing wounded men as Germans shelled his dressing station. Another doctor, Lieutenant-Colonel John McCrae, would win immortality for a poem he scribbled in the wake of the battle, as he remembered how the wrecked bodies of men he had known had been dragged into his field hospital.

> In Flanders fields the poppies blow
> Between the crosses, row on row,
> That mark our place; and in the sky
> The larks, still bravely singing, fly
> Scarce heard amid the guns below.

We are the Dead. Short days ago
We lived, felt dawn, saw sunset glow,
Loved, and were loved, and now we lie
   In Flanders fields.

Take up our quarrel with the foe:
To you from failing hands we throw
The torch; be yours to hold it high.
If ye break faith with us who die
We shall not sleep, though poppies grow
   In Flanders fields.

Canadians would come to curse the Ypres salient and the battered ruins it now surrounded. Thousands more would fight and die for muddy fields that their generals should cheerfully have abandoned. But in April 1915, Canadians wanted to be proud of their sacrifice at St. Julien and Kitchener's Wood and of the terse words in the British official communiqué: "The Canadians had many casualties but their gallantry and determination undoubtedly saved the situation."

A Dreadful Equilibrium

The second battle of Ypres ended, like the first, in a bloody stalemate. For a few square miles of ground and the odium of adding poison gas to the battle-field horrors, the Germans had lost 35,000 casualties; to preserve a largely symbolic salient, the British had sacrificed 59,275, of whom only a few dozen actually died from the gas. In its outcome, the battle reflected the war in 1915.

For the Germans, Ypres had never been more than an incident. Having missed victory in the west in 1914, it was time for the generals to turn eastward. With France's falling pre-war birthrate, French military manpower would only shrink in number. Russia's immense manpower could only be disarmed. Germany's strategy, insisted the Kaiser's new chief of staff, General Erich von Falkenhayn, must be to destroy the Russian army without invading Russia. More Austrian setbacks in early 1915 confirmed that the Habsburg armies would now be little help, but a new German army, thrust into the midst of their line, might find a complacent as well as ill-equipped Russian opposition. So it proved. On May 4, 1915, some 700 German and Austrian guns opened fire. Russian defences collapsed. By the end of the month Field Marshal August von Mackensen's Eleventh Army had collected 153,000 prisoners.

It was just a beginning. In Poland, Warsaw fell to von Hindenburg's armies on August 5, 1915. By the end of the month, Brest-Litovsk was in flames. Then, to the dismay of subordinates and allies, von Falkenhayn reined in his armies and suggested a separate peace. The Russians had lost two million soldiers, half of them as prisoners; three thousand guns; and uncounted rifles. Men could be found; the weapons never would be. At Petrograd, the Tsar ignored the peace offer and clung to his European allies. Henceforth, he announced, he would command his armies in the field. As much as the politicians in France and England, the Russian autocrat realized that only victory would satisfy his people.

Von Falkenhayn had won a victory, not the war. Thanks to Nicholas II, Russia would fight on. In the south, Serbia was conquered, and the road to Constantinople again lay open through Bulgaria but only to drain off more German men, money, and equipment. The Italian front gave the Germans more comfort. Having declared war in return for secret Allied promises, Italy had launched her armies towards Trieste. Her fourth battle for the Isonzo River ended like the first three and the next seven, with cruel losses and no gains. At the end of 1915, a quarter-million Italians were dead or wounded.

In the West, it was France that insisted on early victory; the British were content to wait until their armies were ready in 1916. Joffre's faith in the offensive was unmarred by experience, and his target stared from the map. The German trench line formed a huge bulge into France; it would be pinched out of existence from its two flanks, the Artois and the Champagne districts. The British, feeble fighters if their 1914 performance was any evidence, could best help by occupying more miles of trenches and by making diversionary attacks.

It was what the Germans had expected. Unlike that of their enemies, their pre-war planning had included defence. They knew they would need picks, shovels, and millions of miles of barbed wire. They had huge trench-mortars and heavy artillery too, while the British depended on obsolete naval guns so inaccurate that the troops christened them "Strictly Neutral". When Joffre launched his first attack in the Champagne, the Germans were ready and waiting. The resulting disaster cost France 200,000 men. Neuve Chapelle in March won the British a little grudging respect, but Ypres in April was a distraction. In May, General Ferdinand Foch launched his Artois offensive with fifteen divisions. A couple of them almost captured Vimy Ridge. Canadians found the dead bodies two years later. They were among 100,000 French casualties.

The British helped out with their own attack at Festubert. The Canadian division, hurriedly filled with men who had been left behind in February, sent the 2nd and 3rd brigades into assaults across open ground on May 23 and 24.

German machine guns opened fire, troops stumbled into uncut wire, and the price was 2,468 Canadian dead and wounded. A month later, at Givenchy-lez-la-Bassée on June 15, it was the turn of Mercer's 1st Brigade to attack. A British mine exploded prematurely and the 2nd Battalion, which tried to attack across uncut barbed wire, lost 366 men in a few minutes.

Through the summer, Joffre demanded renewed offensives. Russia's plight and the growing disaster in the Balkans were added arguments. By the time the French moved, von Falkenhayn had brought four divisions back from the east. On September 25, Haig's First Army attacked at Loos. The lessons of Neuve Chapelle were absorbed. A far heavier bombardment and careful rehearsals allowed some of the British, at enormous cost, to struggle through to the German second line despite huge losses. Others were trapped when their poison gas blew back on them. Haig appealed for reserves. Reluctantly, Sir John French sent him two New Army divisions. Hungry and weary after struggling along jammed roads, the raw British troops were still in mass formation when German shells tore into their ranks. Losses were appalling. Whole battalions broke and fled. The Guards Division plugged the hole but the British had few gains. Sir Douglas Haig had his revenge. His friends at court spread word of Sir John French's incompetence. By Christmas, Haig had taken his place.

The new British commander did not entirely fit the stereotype of a mindless ex-cavalry officer. Except in French, which he spoke well, Haig was painfully inarticulate, acutely unimaginative, and conventional; he shared a military contempt for politicians and their art but he was no fool. At fifty-four he was young enough to learn both politics and war. Neither was Haig a genius: the pre-war British army would not have accepted him if he had been. Haig's chief eccentricity was a profound Christian faith and a calm conviction of divine mission. He was proof against a general's worst enemy, despair. Haig knew that he would succeed and, if one means failed, he would find another.

Both Joffre and von Falkenhayn had failed to break the stalemate in 1915; perhaps Haig would succeed in 1916.

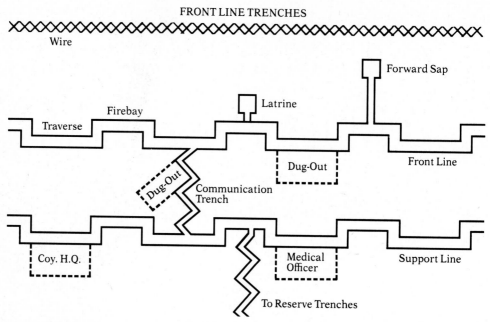

Above A diagram of a trench system, showing the first two lines. Naturally, nothing on the ground was this systematic. But photographed from a kite balloon, *facing*, trench systems give almost diagrammatic clarity to the appearance of a quiet sector.

THE CANADIAN CORPS 1917

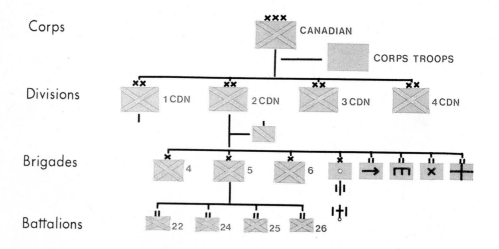

The organization of the Canadian Corps in 1917. By 1918 a brigade of engineers had been added to each division, and machine-gunners were grouped in a battalion for each division as well.

The people of Plymouth, England, awoke to find ships carrying the Canadian Contingent entering harbour. Their welcome lost a little of its enthusiasm after the newcomers encountered the strong local beer.

Sir Sam Hughes's first official visit to Camp Borden on July 11, 1916 included a march-past through heat and swirling sand. Thirty-five men collapsed and one man died of heat exhaustion. The minister was booed and, when the news broke through censorship, the legend that the "boys" loved Hughes was shattered.

Men of the 15th Battalion line up for kit inspection on Salisbury Plain. Such was the Scottish mystique in Canada that four of the battalions in the First Contingent wore kilts. The khaki aprons were supposed to provide a little discreet camouflage and to keep the kilts clean when men were forced to crawl.

A Curtiss Jenny takes off from the flying school aerodome at Long Branch, outside
Toronto. Canadians who wanted to fly for the army had to qualify at their own
expense. The Curtiss school charged $400 for as many minutes of flying time.

Colonel William (Billy) Avery Bishop was Canada's leading air ace in a realm
where Canadians excelled. The top dozen aces in the war shot down 757 aircraft;
the four Canadians among them, Bishop, Raymond Collishaw, Donald MacLaren,
and William Barker, accounted for 247.

While officers slept in dug-outs, men in the ranks made themselves comfortable on narrow steps carved out of the trench wall. The mark of a veteran soldier was the ability to sleep anywhere.

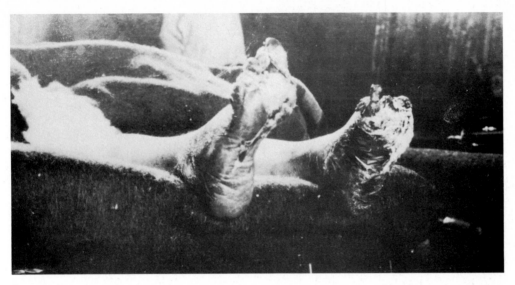

An acute case of trench foot. Days of standing in freezing mud and water produced a condition akin to frostbite. The best cure was prevention, with regular foot inspection and changes of socks. Defeating trench foot gave medical authorities a prestige they then used to tackle a series of other military hygiene problems.

A couple of soldiers try one method of aiming a Lewis gun at passing enemy aircraft. The round magazine was awkward to handle and was too easily damaged. For all their tendency to jam, Lewis guns were also the principal weapon used in the air.

Soldiers called this chore "chatting": hunting "chats", "seam squirrels", or just plain lice in the seams of their clothing. A Canadian doctor, Colonel John Amyot, devised a steam disinfector which, by 1918, at least guaranteed that the blood-sucking parasites did not survive army laundries.

Canadians from the 15th Battalion — Toronto's 48th Highlanders — in the trenches during the winter of 1915. A year later, the survivors would be wearing the washbasin-shaped "trench helmets" that became the trademark of Great War soldiers.

First aid in the trenches. A wounded soldier grimaces as a comrade applies a dressing. The septic Flanders mud could make even minor wounds fatal. Gas gangrene was a terrible way to die.

Two soldiers badly burned by a German flame-thrower are evacuated by
ambulance. Many horror weapons were more effective in hurting morale than in
causing death.

USE FOR PACIFISTS ON WESTERN FRONT

Put Them in Cages and Let Them Sniff for New Deadly German Gas.

HAS "ODOR LIKE GARLIC"

Letter From Canadian Officer Describing Enemy War Weapon.

Special to The Mail and Empire.

Ottawa, Aug. 26.—A vivid description of the new German gas and its deadly effects is given by a Canadian artillery

A modest contribution to wartime nastiness from the pages of the Toronto *Mail and Empire*. A public starved of war news by bland "official communiqués" eagerly devoured letters from the front, and absorbed the anger common enough among those on active service.

ordered by the War Office for New Army recruits, became a byword in Britain for bad fit and quality. Canadian greatcoats were rejected as too thin and shoddy for British use. Rumours that cardboard had been used in the boots issued to the CEF offered the Liberals such a scandal that they abandoned party neutrality. In April 1915, Borden dismissed two of his back-benchers for gross profiteering. In May, he created the War Purchasing Commission to remove from Hughes and his department a function the minister and his cronies had obviously abused.

In the sorry mess of Canadian war procurement, Hughes deserved credit for one glowing accomplishment. At Valcartier in September he had summoned a few industrialists and, on the basis of a pencilled note, constituted them a Shell Committee, with authority to carry out any contract the War Office cared to place. Within weeks, the British had ordered 200,000 shells; by May 1915, the Shell Committee had distributed $170 million in contracts to 250 firms, large and small, across Canada.

Canada, of course, had no real munitions industry. In 1914 a single government factory at Quebec produced enough shells and rifle ammunition for the annual militia camps. A shell, the cast-steel projectile that delivered high explosive or shrapnel to the enemy, was not complicated but it had to be machined to a fine tolerance, and any flaw in the casting could lead to a premature explosion, demolishing gun and gunner. In all of Canada there were half a dozen experts and only ten sets of gauges. The War Office, to add to its problems, had its own version of an inch, 0.010 smaller than anyone else's. Workers had to be trained, machinery purchased, and costs estimated on the basis of a war that might be over in months.

It was a typical Hughes venture. Politicians demanded and got favours for constituents, from a job as inspector to a contract for a firm that needed business. Sir Alexander Bertram, the Shell Committee chairman and a major contractor, tried to run the business from his Montreal office. Hughes ordered a transfer to Ottawa; there Bertram's son struggled with the mounds of paperwork while waiting contractors perched on ammunition boxes. To spread the work, shells shuttled back and forth across Canada so that small firms in Lethbridge or Lindsay could add a little polish or paint. The British, after all, would pay. But were the British getting deliveries? Lloyd George discovered that, of the $170 millions' worth of shells on order, Canada had delivered $5.5 millions'. Without reorganization, the Canadians would get no more business.

Hughes was defiant. D.A. Thomas, a Welsh colliery-owner sent to investigate, reported on the Shell Committee's costly chaos and left without results. Four months passed without orders. That was enough. Over Hughes's objections, the Shell Committee was shoved aside and, by December 1915, Borden had approved a new Imperial Munitions Board (IMB), responsible solely to the British but run by a Canadian, Joseph Wesley Flavelle, a Toronto millionaire whose management skills as a bacon exporter were respected on both sides of the Atlantic. Flavelle picked a team of skilled managers and backed them as they cut prices, tightened quality, and resisted political pressure.

Flavelle made himself few friends and some well-earned enemies. A Toronto firm had counterfeited inspection stamps. A Montreal manufacturer tried to slip through a batch of faulty shells by painting over the pinholes. To keep peace, Flavelle granted contracts to prairie and B.C. firms, despite high prices, and then was denounced for keeping IMB business in Ontario and Quebec. When unions demanded the fair-wages clause guaranteed in other government contracts, Flavelle insisted that they were working for Britain and their members should be glad to have jobs. In June 1916, Hamilton and Toronto machinists walked out. Flavelle broke the strike and, with backing from the War Measures Act, banned reporting of the dispute. Lloyd George had opened the way for hundreds of thousands of women to work in British munitions factories. The IMB followed suit, promising equal pay, female inspectors, and separate lunchrooms. By 1917, more than 30,000 women were employed. The War Measures Act was again used to suppress any reports of discontent, bad working conditions, or sexual assaults on women munitions workers.

The Imperial Munitions Board was easily the biggest business Canada had known, with six hundred factories in 1917, a quarter of a million workers, and production worth $2 million a day. From producing shells, the IMB expanded to fuses, brass casings, and propellants. Close to a third of the shells fired by the British army in 1917 were Canadian-made. When contractors proved greedy, incompetent, or recalcitrant, Flavelle took them over or built his own factories. British Munitions loaded shells at Verdun. British Explosives bought out ill-managed companies at Renfrew and Trenton. Canadian Explosives built its own factory at Nobel near Parry Sound during the harsh winter of 1917. British Acetones took over the Gooderham and Worts distillery at Toronto. Nearby, at Ashbridge's Bay, British Forgings was Flavelle's answer to the price-fixing "buccaneers" of the Canadian steel industry. In 1918, the IMB added a shipbuilding department and, by the end of the year, launched 103 steel and wooden vessels.

Late in 1916, as the Royal Flying Corps (RFC) struggled to find pilots to replace losses from superior German aircraft, months of negotiations with Canada finally jelled. Thousands of Canadians had already joined the British flying services; it made sense in the crisis to go to the source. In weeks, the IMB bought the Curtiss operation from its Canadian promoters. Its tiny aircraft factory became the nucleus for Canadian Aeroplanes Ltd. By the war's end, the IMB had produced 2,600 Curtiss JN-4 trainers and 30 F-5 flying boats.

In British Columbia, the IMB employed 24,000 workers to hunt for the prime spruce and fir needed by British aircraft factories. Flavelle did more. IMB agents scoured the countryside around Toronto for bases and developed airfields at Camp Borden, Beamsville, Hamilton, Armour Heights, and Deseronto. The British created RFC Canada as a training organization, recruited 9,000 cadets and 7,500 mechanics, and graduated 3,372 aircrew at a cost of 129 lives. In all, 22,812 Canadians served with the British flying services in every role from trying to spot submarines to piloting heavy bombers over Germany. Of 13,160 Canadians who served as aircrew, 1,388 were killed, 1,130 were wounded or injured, and 377 became prisoners of war. Canadians were 6 per cent of British flying casualties in 1915 and 16.8 per cent in 1918. The IMB had contributed more than shells.

If the IMB was the most spectacular creation of Canada's wartime economy, it was not unique. Textile mills rolled out khaki serge for uniforms, flannel for hospital sheets, and miles of canvas for tents and tarpaulins. Paper and wood-pulp production doubled with the appetite for war news and propaganda. With wartime prosperity, an automobile became a luxury a lot more Canadians could afford: car registrations rose from 74,416 in 1914 to 342,433 in 1919. Only construction stayed in a wartime slump.

For the common cause, Canada's new industries mattered less than her old export staples. With French farms stripped of manpower and Russian wheat blocked in the Black Sea, Allied countries needed all the food Canada could produce. As usual, Ottawa looked to voluntarism. A "Patriotism and Production" campaign in 1915 urged farmers to grow all they could. With the promise of wartime prices, farmers obliged by planting a record 40 million acres. The climate obliged. By November 1915, Canadian farms had yielded 393.5 million bushels of wheat at an average of 26 bushels an acre. It had never happened before — nor would it again. In 1916 and 1917, acreages grew and yields fell. Heat, drought, a late frost in 1917, and the relentless results of soil exhaustion cut wheat production to only 189 million bushels in 1918, 11 bushes to the acre. Canada's wheat exports fell 238 per cent between 1915 and 1918.

The 1915 bumper crop kept prices close to 1914 levels but, from 1916 on, scarcity shaped the market. When Italy led Allied attempts to corner the 1916 crop, Ottawa helped dealers form the Wheat Export Company. In 1917, the government went further, closing the Winnipeg Grain Exchange and handing wheat-marketing to a new Board of Grain Supervisors. When prices rose from

$1.70 to $2.40 a bushel, farmers and politicians learned the delights of orderly marketing. Much of the new wealth was spent on automobiles. For a lot of prairie farm families, cars bought from wartime incomes ended rural isolation.

Wheat, of course, was only one crop and the prairies were only one region. Until the war, Canadian cheese and meat had fought a losing battle in British markets. With the Danes and Dutch briefly cut off by the conflict, Canadians had a fresh opportunity to compete. In the war years, Canadian fishermen doubled their landings and their exports. By 1917, Canadian pork exports tripled and beef exports grew sevenfold. Food processors packed pork and beans, bully beef, and all the cheese they could produce. Ontario was the main beneficiary. Its farmers also had their frustrations. Ideal growing seasons in 1917 and 1918 fulfilled all the hopes of "Production and Thrift" campaigns, but who would harvest the crops? The spirit of voluntarism turned women into "farmerettes" and boys into "Soldiers of the Soil". Civil servants, teachers, retail clerks, and clergy sacrificed annual holidays for harvest duty. Farmers soon discovered that city folk did not make efficient harvest labourers. Much of the crop rotted in the fields.

FINANCING THE WAR

Canada entered the war as a debtor nation. In 1913, its balance of payments was $408 million in the red. While patriotic crowds marched and cheered, the Montreal stock markets closed to forestall a panic. An order-in-council took Canada off the gold standard. To reassure the banks, Ottawa for the first time printed its own dollar bills. Fiscal prudence was not universal. Despite solemn pledges to respect strict accounting procedures, the War Appropriation Act became a licence to print money. By the war's end, the original $50 million had grown to $1,069 million, by no means all of it wisely or honestly spent. After a vigorous year in 1915 pursuing malefactors, Parliament's public-accounts committee lapsed into exhaustion. A year later, the ailing auditor general, John Fraser, also abandoned his struggle. To its dismay, the Department of Finance found itself compelled to hand over huge sums with little to say in their use.

Almost every issue of wartime finance and politics was entangled in the fate of the two transcontinental railways Laurier had helped create as rivals to the CPR. The Canadian Northern had given cheap, popular service to the prairies until its promoters, William Mackenzie and Donald Mann, persuaded the Bank of Commerce and Laurier to finance a line from Vancouver to Toronto. Charlie Hays of the Grand Trunk talked his British shareholders into similar folly before he drowned with the *Titanic*. Laurier had helped by offering to build a line through the northern Quebec and Ontario bush and a bridge across the St. Lawrence at Quebec City for the GTR's convenience, all at public expense. Perhaps symbolically, the Quebec bridge collapsed twice, in 1907 and 1916. The Liberals had basked in the glory of big spending; the Conservatives inherited the bills: two unfinished railways on the verge of collapse, and a disastrous national credit rating.

The war was the railways' salvation and their ruin. Borden's finance minister, Sir Thomas White, had long condemned the railway deals and their promoters but he understood that railway bankruptcy could wreck Canada's credit, to say nothing of that of the prairie provinces and the wealthy Torontonians who had given their money to Mackenzie and Mann. In wartime it was easy to argue that every railway was needed and, grudgingly, money was found for the Grand Trunk and the Canadian Northern. However, the war was also a patriotic excuse for the Board of Railway Commissioners to hold down freight rates. The CPR grumbled publicly but quietly rejoiced at the spectacle of despised rivals being squeezed to death by low revenues. As costs soared — the price of a freight car tripled — the Grand Trunk and the Canadian Northern gradually crumbled. By 1917, the majority of members of a royal commission recommended a solution Borden had urged since 1904: nationalization.

Whatever their fate, the railways devoured money. So did the war. In relative terms, the war took only 15 to 16 per cent of the gross domestic product — far less than the 1939–45 war — but a nation that had spent $13 million on defence in 1913 was shouldering a military budget of $311 million three years later. Even in 1915, shocked officials calculated that Canada was spending half a million dollars a day for military purposes; by 1917, the daily outlay was close to a million dollars. Raising the money from taxpayers, White concluded, was out of the question. Investors and immigrants would shun a country with high taxes. Of course, as he admitted in his 1915 budget, both rich and poor would have to make sacrifices. That meant increased tariffs, and a range of duties on bank notes, cheques, telegrams, railway tickets, and insurance premiums. In 1916, Ottawa cautiously levied its first direct tax — a business war-profit tax — designed less for revenue than to demonstrate government indignation at profiteering. Public cries for the conscription of wealth drove White against his will to an Income War Tax in 1917: 3 per cent for a family earning over $3,000 or an individual earning over $1,500. The prime minister, one of only 31,130 Canadians who paid, would have owed about $80 on his official salary. The income tax, White promised, would end with the war.

The real money would have to be borrowed. War, White and his advisers agreed, was "an extraordinary expense", to be financed like a railway, a waterworks, or a bridge. "We are justified in placing upon posterity the greater portion of the financial burden of this war," White explained, "waged as it is in the interests of human freedom and for their benefit in equal if not in greater degree than for our own." In short, the children would pay, but who would lend the money?

Not the British. By 1915, they were struggling to finance their own war effort. To the dismay of Canadian bankers, White turned to New York: it was costly but he saw no alternative. By the summer of 1916, Canada had borrowed $220 million. Sir Joseph Flavelle, White's former boss at the National Trust, shoved the minister in another direction. Canada, he pointed out, was recovering. There was money to borrow. White's officials protested that there was no precedent. In November 1915, the finance minister nervously floated a domestic war loan for $50 million at 5 per cent, tax free and fully convertible. In a week, big investors had subscribed $100 million. Smaller investors took $79 million. Flavelle got his cut: since the IMB would create still more wealth, White could advance him the surplus from the loan to finance more British munitions purchases.

The 1915 war loan set a durable pattern in Canadian public finance: Canadians would lend to their own government. In September 1916 and March 1917, the government asked for a total of $250 million and took in $460 million. For the fourth loan, in November 1917, White tapped small investors with Victory Bonds at 5½ per cent. A sea of posters in French and English helped attract 820,035 subscribers and $398 million. A fifth loan a year later raised $660 million from 1,067,879 Canadians. The sixth and final war loan, in November 1919, produced $680 million. Between them, the war and the railways quadrupled Canada's national debt; four-fifths of it was owed to Canadians.

Flavelle's deal, by helping the British to borrow, also helped fill the IMB's order books and expanded its contribution to the wartime economy. By 1917 Britain's credit was nearing exhaustion, its own munitions factories were running full out, and Canadian shells were becoming a luxury. Luck and Flavelle's ingenuity came to the rescue. On April 7, the United States entered the war. Flavelle collected his staff and headed for Washington. Americans welcomed him as a fellow spirit. As unready for war as Canada had been three years earlier, the United States needed just about anything the IMB factories could produce. If the Canadians tendered at least 7 per cent lower than U.S. contractors, they could have the business. With trained workers and most of their machinery paid for by the British, most of the IMB's companies could compete. IMB activity in 1918 slumped by about a third from the 1917 peak but American orders helped diversify its operations into shipbuilding and additional aircraft manufacturing.

For the rest of his natural days, Sir Thomas White insisted that his fiscal policies had not contributed to inflation. Economists would disagree. Until late 1919 the Canadian and U.S. dollars remained virtually at par and banks bought relatively few of White's bonds but, as an improvised central bank, the Finance department was generous with its paper. As the money supply grew from $1,108 million in 1914 to $2,091 million in 1920, Ottawa printed the notes. Borrowing on the future heated an economy that, by 1916, had more money than ways to spend it. Inflation indexes were even more imperfect in 1914–18 than now, but they told a story. The Department of Labour family budget index, set at 100 in 1913, fell to 98.7 in 1915, reached 147.2 in 1918, and climbed to a height of 184.7 in 1920. A price-level index based on 100 for the 1935–39 period was 85.4 in 1914, 166 in 1918, and 203.2 in 1920. Simply put, purchasing power in the war years was halved.

Inflation was not necessarily a disaster. Tight money, when the rest of the world was on a spending spree, would have priced Canadian food and munitions out of competition. Exports paid for the war. Britain's bill — $252,567,942.03 — for providing food, clothing, transportation, munitions, and just about everything but pay to the Canadians overseas, was more than offset by what Britain owed the IMB. Nor was inflation solely a result of fiscal policy. Bad harvests tightened food supplies and raised prices. The U.S. entry into the war and a harsh 1917 winter produced fuel shortages. Though governments did nothing to restrict the output of consumer goods, wartime affluence encouraged higher prices. Wages slowly followed inflation, with the usual noisy accompaniment of strikes and lock-outs. Then further increases could be justified to meet the added labour costs. There was no such relief for the elderly, the poor, and those on fixed incomes. They tightened their belts and suffered, often in silence.

Three-quarters of a century later, it is easier to understand the wartime inflation. Historians have argued that Canadian prices and wages, after half a century of remarkable stability, had actually started to climb in 1907. No one took strong objection until the increases soared in late 1916. Nor were the causes easily grasped. Fiscal policy, labour shortages, and crop failure were too banal or complex. The public wanted a scapegoat: greedy profiteers satisfied the need.

Canada Regenerated

Profiteers especially fitted the demonology of a moral crusade. Canada's leaders in mobilizing a voluntary war effort were predominantly English-speaking middle-class Protestants, often with rural roots. Like most people, they thought their own ideas should fit just about everyone. In the struggle against Kaiserism, all people of goodwill must surely agree on the need to purge Canadian society of greed, corruption, partyism, vice, and the liquor evil. Wartime solidarity left no room for the arrogance of capital, the violence of revolutionaries, or the selfishness of sects. Middle-class feminists who had led the struggle for the vote found a fresh argument in the war: if victory depended on moral regeneration, the most moral members of the race must extend their power beyond the family. "Women have cleaned up things since time began," declared Nellie McClung in 1916, "and if women get into politics there will be a cleaning up of pigeon-holes and forgotten corners in which the dust of years has fallen."

By no means all Canadians, not even middle-class Protestants, saw the war as a crusade. For politicians in 1914, it was business as usual. Ontario's "Doc" Reid; Manitoba's Bob Rogers, the notorious "Minister of Elections"; and George E. Foster, a passionate patronage-monger, constituted themselves a cabinet committee to ensure that the War Appropriation was spent to the Conservatives' advantage. Hughes did not want their help. As an aide, John Bassett, explained to an enquiring friend: "Contracts are sent to a great extent to those firms who have political pull...." If the friend wanted a share, he could line up with the others. Another aide, Harold Daly, helped guard the minister's door. "I was particularly good to lawyers," he recalled, "because I knew what business I was going into when I got out of the army."

The Tories needed friends in 1914. After three years of "Bad Luck" Borden, Laurier and the Liberals were convinced that voters would undo the cruel injustice of 1911. Conservatives feared that legislative fiascos and the 1913–14 depression might prove the Liberals correct. Would the war give the Tories a renewed chance? Rogers and the rest of the old guard were eager to try a snap election in November 1914. Borden finally drew back: it was too opportunistic. The spring of 1915 would be better. Meanwhile, over Laurier's objections, soldiers were given the right to vote and Harold Daly sailed on the *Lusitania* in May to manage the overseas campaign. He survived the sinking and reported from London: "I am still glad to die for the Conservative Party but I am glad I didn't drown for it." By then, Borden had changed his mind. A stack of letters and renewed pressure from colleagues persuaded him that an election would be inappropriate while Canadians digested the casualty lists from Ypres and Festubert. Laurier had drawn applause from a Toronto audience when he proclaimed: "I do not care...so long as the war lasts, to open the portals of power with that bloody key." In September, the two leaders negotiated a one-year extension of Parliament until 1917. Surely the war could not last that long.

Laurier's motives were clear. He knew what had happened to British Liberals in the patriotic "Khaki Election" of 1900; he could easily have guessed Bob Rogers's proposed slogan for the campaign: "Vote Conservative for Borden backs Britain". The Liberals had much more work to do in revealing just how corrupt and patronage-ridden Borden's patriotism really was. In 1915, they exposed boots, binoculars, and spavined old horses. For 1916, private detectives helped untangle the affairs of the Shell Committee, Sam Hughes, and his favourite honorary colonel, J. Wesley Allison. By threatening to "rawhide" his critics and by claiming that Allison had "more honour in his little finger than the Auditor-General had in his entire carcass", Hughes added colour to the language and deepening embarrassment to the government. Ministers distanced themselves from the hero of Valcartier. A particularly righteous speech by George Foster led an amused Borden to note that his veteran minister "has no more political sense than a turnip".

In fact, Foster, and Borden too, sensed that Canadians would no longer tolerate a war effort run on traditional lines. In 1914 the Patriotic Fund had given business-like management to what should have been a government function. The pattern was repeated in 1915. The War Purchasing Commission, the Military Hospitals Commission, and, pre-eminently, the Imperial Munitions Board involved businessmen and business methods. Politics, as the War Purchasing Commission files reveal, were by no means forgotten but they were buried under business-like efficiency. Through the IMB, Joseph Flavelle gained a powerful influence on policy inside the government and on attitudes of the Canadian public. At the end of 1916, after a visit to England and France taught him what defective shells meant in war, Flavelle was in no mood for Toronto contractors who pestered him about their profit margins: "Profits?" cried a suddenly animated Flavelle. "I have come straight from the seat of a nation where they are sweating blood to win this war and I stand before you stripped of many ideas. Profits! Send profits to the hell where they belong."

If the war could do that to a Methodist millionaire, it could do much. It could persuade Stephen Leacock, a deeply conservative economist, to insist that government must intervene to end "silly and idle services or...production that is for mere luxuries and comforts". It convinced Newton Rowell, Ontario's Liberal leader, that Robert Borden, a Conservative, might even be a better national leader than a man who played politics with the war effort and who pandered to Quebec prejudices in Regulation 17. Had Sir Wilfrid Laurier really followed the new gospel of "service above self"? Late in 1916, the young Ernest Lapointe had insisted on dividing Parliament on a question beyond Ottawa's powers — Ontario schools — and Laurier had not controlled him. MPs had split by language, not by party, western Liberals had abandoned Laurier, and Rowell had encouraged them. The war gave him reasons to do so again and again.

The war and the cause of regeneration fed on each other because lines were so often shared. Whatever the views of most Canadian women, their self-appointed leaders were tireless for both sacrifice and reform. In 1914, the corrupt Roblin regime in Manitoba survived the joint onslaught of Liberals and feminists; in 1915 it fell, possibly because several thousand potential supporters had left for the war but even more because its easy morals were at odds with the wartime mood. Early in 1916, the feminists got their reward: votes for Manitoba's women. Alberta and Saskatchewan followed within months; British Columbia and Ontario adopted the change in 1917. Almost automatically, the prohibition cause shared in the triumph. Saskatchewan, which had bravely banished the bar in 1915, found itself the prairie laggard a year later when it was the last to end any sale without benefit of prescription. The old counter-arguments, government meddling, personal freedom, job protection, lost their weight in the wartime mood of sacrifice and discipline. What better example of the excesses of personal freedom, cried Nellie McClung, than the Kaiser, "William Hohenzollern". Manitobans were commanded to use "ballots for bullets and shoot straight and strong in order that the demon of drink might be driven from the haunts of men". By 1917, every province but Quebec had banished booze. Thirsty souls with credit and a fixed address could summon "liquids" by mail order from Montreal.

As usual, Quebec seemed to be the exception: recalcitrant on liquor, demanding on French-Canadian rights elsewhere, uninterested in the rights of women, and indifferent to the world struggle against Kaiserism. Were the French better than the "enemy aliens" who also seemed as "unenlightened" about women, liquor, and the war? Organized labour was another reluctant warrior. The Trades and Labor Congress had waited (like the National Council of Women) until 1913 to endorse female suffrage but among its leaders only the socialist Jimmy Simpson backed prohibition and neither he nor the others showed the patriotism of "the best" British and French trade unionists by denouncing strikes. Instead they had resisted the war, resisted national registration, and would resist conscription. How did this serve the soldiers who were making the supreme sacrifice to build a purer and better Canada?

The answer, as ever in Canada, was that there was more than one perception of the new world. Those whom middle-class reformers found wanting had no common cause. Bourassa and the *nationalistes* despised the pre-1914 European immigrants as cordially as any English Canadian. No argument against the war effort seemed more compelling to their eyes than the fear of handing over Canada to "foreigners" by draining strength to serve some Imperial behest. Leaders of organized labour, predominantly British in ethnicity, saw the "foreigners" as competition for scarce jobs. Nor could they possibly cross the barriers of language and social philosophy to make common cause with the *nationalistes*. On language and culture, labour leaders were as unresurrected as the Orangemen they sometimes were.

Save for those who take character and circumstance as they find them — almost always a taciturn and placid crowd — both regenerators and their opponents could agree about the evils of profiteering. So could the government. On November 10, 1916, after public clamour, Borden announced that a cost-of-living commissioner, the useful W.F. O'Connor, would have the power to pursue and publicize offenders. The food-processing industry, intermediary between the selfless farmers and the innocent consumer, was an obvious target for investigation — and a profitable one. There were few larger or more successful firms than the William Davies Company. Its well-known president had been raised to a baronetcy in June 1917. In August, when O'Connor's report revealed that the company had earned 85 per cent on its capital in the previous year, Sir Joseph Flavelle became the most reviled man in Canada — "His Lardship", the "Baron of Bacon". "To hell with profits" indeed!

GENERALSHIP BY DEATH

From December 6 to 8, 1915, Allied generals met at Chantilly. For all its setbacks, 1915 had not been a complete disaster. Russia had survived, Italy was still fighting, France's army was strong, and, by 1916, the British would at last field the military strength of a nation of forty million. Germany, it was agreed, must be close to exhaustion. Berlin had also retreated from unlimited submarine warfare just when it was becoming dangerous to the Allies. Victory in 1916 could be achieved by co-ordinated, simultaneous attacks around the circumference of the Central Powers. That, at least, was "Papa" Joffre's view, and who could argue the principle? Practice was another matter. When would the time come? Would the Russians be able to help? Above all, where on the Western Front should the attacks be made?

The details were still far from resolved on February 21 when a German naval shell landed in the heart of Verdun. In a few minutes, 1,220 German guns, some of them the heaviest any army had ever used, had begun to devastate the old French fortress. A *Trommelfeuer* or drum-fire, designed to annihilate the French garrison, opened a year-long battle. The Germans had a strategy, too.

In 1915, General von Falkenhayn had tried to drive Russia from the war. Now it was the turn of France. "If we succeeded in opening the eyes of her people to the fact that in a military sense they have nothing more to hope for...," he argued, then "England's best sword" would be lost. Operation *Gericht* or "Doomsday" would slaughter Frenchmen for the ultimate purpose of beating Britain. The technique was simple: seize a position the French would have to recapture, have enough heavy artillery on hand to smash the counterattacks, and destroy the French army. Verdun was the place. A year earlier, Joffre had reflected on the uselessness of the Belgian fortresses and stripped Verdun of its heavy guns to give his armies more firepower against German trenches. A colonel complained; National Assembly deputies worried; Joffre was calm. Verdun, an exposed salient, should probably have been abandoned but somehow it did not seem appropriate to vacate native soil. In February 1916, Verdun became all that von Falkenhayn could wish: the most sacred soil of France, the key point in the French line, the symbolic reminder of Charles Martel's defeat of the Huns a millennium earlier.

On February 25, Fort Douaumont, key to Verdun, fell. On the same day, General Henri-Philippe Pétain took over. A cool master of defensive war, Pétain eventually used almost every French division in his struggle to hold Verdun. "Ils ne passeront pas" became France's slogan. A single road, crammed night and day with truckloads of supplies and troops, became *la Voie sacrée*. Von Falkenhayn had his strategic wishes fulfilled but the slaughter was not one-sided. Germans were drawn deeper into the battle as attack followed attack. Typically, French regiments lost a third of their strength in eight to twelve days; German regiments lost even more. A new, more terrible gas, phosgene, was introduced. It only added to the horror. Through the spring, summer, and fall, the battle ground on. In October, Pétain's subordinates, generals Robert Nivelle and Charles Mangin, persuaded him that a major counter-attack could work. French factories were now pouring out artillery shells. It was the French turn to flood down fire by the ton. "When the trench is well turned over, off we go," explained Mangin. "Any Boches who are still there are ours." On October 24, the French retook Douaumont. In November, the Germans fell back. In three days in mid-December Nivelle took 11,000 prisoners. "We know the method and we have the Chief," boasted Mangin. "Success is certain."

That was premature. Von Falkenhayn's strategy had cost the French 362,000 men but, even by their own questionable statistics, Verdun cost the Germans 336,831. On August 29, more than a month after he had ordered the hopeless attacks to stop, von Falkenhayn was gone, displaced by his enemies, von Hindenburg and von Ludendorff.

Von Falkenhayn's other failure was in Italy. He had yielded to Field Marshal Conrad von Hötzendorf. Both of them had sent some of their best troops to attack in the Trentino in the hope that Italy, too, might be driven from the war. On May 15, the offensive began with impressive gains. Italian regiments, badly armed and worse led, crumbled. But General Luigi Cadorna found reserves and shoved them into the line. A twelve-mile advance was all the Germans and Austrians were allowed, at a cost of 80,000. Italian losses were far higher — 250,000 in dead, wounded, and prisoners — but on June 16 Cadorna began to push back. The Austrians lost almost all they had won.

The Austrian retreat was wholly unexpected. So was the reason. The Russians, by the end of 1915, had been counted out of the war. Instead, they had found a general, and their despised munitions industries had worked miracles. General Alexei Brusilov took over the Carpathian front and staged a series of small methodical attacks to discover, as he explained, which part of the enemy line was stone and which part lath and plaster. On June 4, Brusilov attacked and the Austrians — the lath and plaster — collapsed. By September the Russians had 450,000 new prisoners. Romania, which had hesitated in June 1916, joined the Allies in August. Then Brusilov's victory fell apart. The Tsar's high command did nothing. The Germans, as usual, rushed to rescue their Habsburg allies. By the time Brusilov's campaign was over, the Russians had lost a million men. Next, Germany turned on Romania. The campaign was a consolation prize for von Falkenhayn. By early December, he and Field Marshal von Mackensen marched their soldiers in triumph through Bucharest.

In the West, no one on either side knew whether the Somme was a victory or a defeat. It was certainly a tragedy. Now in command of an army of a million men — forty-three divisions and nineteen more to come — Sir Douglas Haig believed that the time had come for Britain to win the war. His army was still imperfect — "a collection of divisions untrained for the Field" — but it was in better spirits than the French. Like von Falkenhayn, Haig believed that the French were near their limit. They must be helped, but the British must take the lead. By choice, Haig would have attacked in Flanders, on ground he had come to know, but co-operation with the French dictated an attack near the British-French juncture. Joffre insisted on the Somme valley, a German salient with trenches that rose on limestone ridges beyond the river. It was hard to find a tougher German sector but its capture would be a German disaster.

Verdun altered the Allied battle. Joffre had promised two armies; he could now spare only one. Haig proposed to wait until a new British secret weapon, the "tank", was available. Joffre was almost frantic: the French armies could not hold out that long. The British must proceed. General Sir Henry Rawlinson's Fourth Army was filled with raw New Army divisions, the elite of Britain who had hurried to volunteer in 1914. For two years they had suffered from the lack of equipment, training, experience, and competent officers. Now, at last, they could begin their march on Berlin. By June 1916 there were guns and shells enough for seven long days of bombardment.

By 7:30 A.M. on July 1, 1916, 1,738,000 British shells had turned the German positions above the Somme into a cratered dusty desert. The forward battalions of eleven British divisions, dazed after the week-long storm of fire, rose at blasts from officers' whistles. Men, burdened with eighty or a hundred pounds of equipment, heaved themselves out of the trenches, formed lines, and walked forward. The officers in one New Army battalion kicked footballs. They did not reach the enemy line. Nor did most attackers. For all the barrage of British shrapnel, the German wire was only partly cut. When shelling ceased, hundreds of German machine-gunners scrambled from dug-outs twenty feet underground, adjusted their sights, and opened fire. Thousands of British soldiers fell in a few dreadful minutes.

The Newfoundland Regiment, in its first real battle, had moved up in support. At 9:05 A.M., after a report that the lead brigade had won its objectives, the Newfoundlanders were sent into the attack. The reports were false. As the men bunched at the few gaps in the wire entanglements, like cattle in a pen, the German machine guns found them. In a few minutes, 684 Newfoundlanders had fallen; 310 were dead. Along the British front, 57,470 men were casualties; 19,240 were dead. The Germans lost 2,000 prisoners and 20 guns in the first day at the Somme.

The Germans had been prepared. With such obvious British preparations in front of them, it was hard not to be. British shelling sounded fiercer than it was. Of heavy shells 30 per cent were duds; one in a thousand high-explosive shells was "premature", likely to explode in the gun barrel. British batteries called themselves "suicide clubs" and kept firing. No British shells could hurt dug-outs thirty or forty feet underground; no shrapnel — a collection of small bullets in a casing — was going to cut barbed wire. On the right, where a French attack was unexpected and the front-line trenches were close, the British attack succeeded. Elsewhere, the attackers died utterly in vain. Philip Gibbs, whose "Eyewitness" reports were the official British hand-outs to the press, reported: "It is, on the balance, a good day for England and France." History, in contrast, has judged the first day on the Somme as a military tragedy of epochal dimensions.

The battle went on. On July 14, a night attack by 22,000 raw New Army troops took the German front line. German counter-attacks almost wiped out

Men of the 8th Battalion (the Little Black Devils from Winnipeg) rest behind the lines. While staff officers did their best to keep soldiers busy, the men did their best to keep out of their way. While some watch the camera, a few stick to the business at hand — a game of cards.

Bishop Michael Fallon visits troops in France. The Roman Catholic bishop, a prime mover in Regulation 17 and other assaults on Ontario's French-speaking minority, did his best to unite Irish Canadians behind the war effort. Unlike Irish Catholics in Australia, Fallon's co-religionists responded.

Perhaps Canada would have gone dry by 1917 even without a war, but the Temperance Crusade found the Kaiser a useful ally. This petition more than two miles long, delivered in March 1916 to the Ontario Legislature, predates the Guinness Book of Records.

Henri Bourassa and his daughter Anne contemplate a cold world. Once it was clear that English Canadians would make no concessions to the French-speaking minority for the sake of national unity, Bourassa devoted his considerable talent to opposing the war effort.

Women munition workers inspecting shell fuses. Most of the vast workforce mobilized by the Imperial Munitions Board was male; employing women in a heavy manufacturing industry seemed almost revolutionary. But even here, male supervisors watch over the line.

Soldiers in the trenches rarely saw their enemy. When Canadians did invade
German trenches, they were chagrined to find an enemy better housed, equipped,
and fed than they were. This photograph of joyful German sergeants was a
Canadian war trophy.

forceful word of command. Critics immediately noted that Watson, publisher of the Quebec *Chronicle*, was an old Hughes crony while Landry's father, the Conservative leader in the Senate, had made trouble for the government over Regulation 17. General H.D.B. Ketchen, a Winnipegger, could keep the 6th Brigade but the 4th must go to Lord Brooke, son of the Earl of Warwick and a fine fellow. The minister insisted on it.

Two Canadian divisions would form a Canadian Army Corps. The Australians and New Zealanders had set the precedent of a Dominion formation. In April, Hughes's loyal agent in England, Brigadier-General John Wallace Carson, had urged formation of a corps "with your good self in command". Colonel J.J. Carrick, a Quaker businessman and MP from Port Arthur whom Hughes had despatched as his representative at General Headquarters, urged the idea on Sir John French. The Corps was welcome, but the commander must be Sir Edwin Alderson. When Borden and Hughes visited England in the summer of 1915, the arrangements were completed. Alderson could have the Corps, Currie would inherit the 1st Division, and M.S. Mercer, also promoted to major-general, would command the Corps Troops, a collection of units that came to include the Canadian Cavalry Brigade, two unassigned infantry brigades, six regiments of Canadian Mounted Rifles, and supporting units. After a firm hint from the minister, Mercer's 1st Infantry Brigade was given to Garnet Hughes. For his helpfulness, Sam Hughes received a knighthood.

In June 1915, the War Office had asked Canada for a third division, in addition to the monthly quota of five thousand reinforcements needed to complete the Canadian ranks. In Ottawa, Major-General Willoughby Gwatkin, the long-suffering chief of the general staff, warned that Canada might not be able to find enough men. Hughes overruled him and reassured an anxious prime minister: General Alderson had explained to him that the third division in an army corps was almost always in reserve and immune from casualties. At Christmas, Mercer's command became the nucleus of the 3rd Canadian Division. The six Mounted Rifle regiments were reorganized as four infantry battalions, the PPCLI came back from their British division, and the Royal Canadian Regiment of the permanent force ended its exile on Bermuda. The other battalions were chosen from the growing number in England. Since the division had no artillery, Mercer was temporarily lent the British gunners of an Indian army division that had returned to a warmer climate. The cavalry brigade went off to the British cavalry corps to await the great breakthrough.

Sir Sam had no intention of leaving the British or even his own officers to manage promotions or organization overseas. In England, Hughes preserved control by preserving confusion. At Shorncliffe, Brigadier-General J.C. MacDougall, a timid permanent-force officer, commanded the Canadian

Training Division but Major-General Steele, given command of the Shorn-cliffe District by the British as a consolation prize, insisted that he had authority over MacDougall. The two men appealed to the minister's friend and agent, General Carson, who, for his part, assured the War Office that he was responsible for Canadian affairs in England. As a further complication, when Lord Brooke had to give up his brigade, Hughes gave him command of a big new Canadian camp at Bramshott, independent of both Steele and MacDougall. The net effect was that every decision, serious or silly, had to be referred to the minister.

Since Canadians in France were under full British control, exercising influence there was more difficult. Carrick quit in August, leaving his business partner, Major J.F. Manly-Sims, in charge. The real successor was Sir Max Aitken, a New Brunswick–born son of the manse who made himself a millionaire during the Laurier boom by managing corporate mergers. In 1910, Aitken had moved to England, bought the *Daily Express*, and entered Parliament as a Conservative. Sir Max was a busy man but his stock-in-trade was information. Canada could help. The British barred reporters from the front and issued cheerfully misleading communiqués through an "Eyewitness". Hughes promptly appointed Aitken as "Canadian Eyewitness", added him to the list of honorary colonels, and thus provided the publisher-politician with the rank and status to go and come as he pleased between London, GHQ, and the front. In September, Hughes added the title of "General Representative for Canada at the front".

The minister could hardly have been better served. Aitken was an ingenious publicist, eager to glorify Canadian military exploits and ready to lavish his wealth on preserving Canadian war records. His organization in London sponsored writers, photographers, and some of Britain's most talented painters. The Canadian War Memorials Fund employed artists as diverse as Paul Nash, Augustus John, and Wyndham Lewis as well as such Canadians as David Milne and A.Y. Jackson to depict Canada's war effort. Without Aitken's patronage, this book and others like it would have been difficult to illustrate. Though a Tory, Aitken had little respect for Britain's ruling class and his contempt for its military branch developed into a vendetta. Long before the prejudice became conventional, Sir Max had concluded that the British army was led by donkeys and that Canadians could manage as well with native-born generals who had been publishers, farmers, and stockbrokers. Aside from his personal favourites, such as Lord Brooke, Hughes entirely agreed.

The dramatic expansion of the Canadian Contingent in France from a single division to an army corps with three divisions was a challenge for Aitken and Hughes. Alderson took most of his staff with him to the new corps headquarters. Dozens of Canadian colonels and majors, left behind in England, eyed the new vacancies and besieged their superiors and the minister. Officers sent home as drunks or failures insisted that they had learned their lesson or, more often, that they were victims of snobbish British prejudice. Hughes needed little prompting from Aitken to take their side: "it is the general opinion that scores of our officers can teach the British Officers for many moons to come.... There is altogether too much staff college paternalism and espionage abroad...."

It is hard to find evidence for the charge. Apart from Brooke, whom Hughes insisted on again appointing to the 4th Division, every division and brigade in the Canadian Corps had a Canadian commander with one exception: Brigadier-General L.J. Lipsett, a British instructor in Canada at the outbreak of the war, had commanded the 8th Battalion at Ypres. His men later remembered him as the most approachable and popular general in the Corps. The British sent some of their best staff officers to the Canadians. Charles Harington, Alderson's Brigadier-General, General Staff, went on to become the legendary chief of staff of Sir Herbert Plumer's Second Army, the one formation BEF divisions longed to join because of the excellence of its staff work. Harington's successors and the British officer who served as the Corps's deputy-adjutant and quartermaster general, Brigadier-General George Farmar, were of comparable stature. So were the British staff officers who played similar key roles under Canadian divisional commanders. Since the Canadians became as well known for meticulous staff work as for courage and ingenuity, "staff-college paternalism" deserves some of the credit.

Perhaps the problem was Alderson. Hughes never forgave him for abandoning the Canadian-made equipment on Salisbury Plain. He also blamed Alderson for Canadian losses at Ypres and Festubert. He remembered that Alderson had balked at giving his son Garnet a brigade. When Canadians were accused of indiscipline, Hughes complained that Alderson was too gentle to manage real men; when Alderson scolded the Nova Scotians of the 25th Battalion for panic during a German raid, he was too harsh. Alderson's greatest crime was allowing the 1st Division's Ross rifle to be replaced by British Lee-Enfields in the summer of 1915. When Hughes learned that Alderson had invited his officers to comment on the rifle, the minister was livid. The resulting replies were a loyalty test. Garnet Hughes, Turner, and Watson supported the Canadian-made rifle; Currie, Mercer, and a majority condemned it. "[It] is nothing short of murder," wrote an anonymous colonel, "to send our men against the enemy with such a weapon." After Ypres, a third of the 1st Division had rearmed themselves with Lee-Enfields. In the summer of 1915, armourers did what they could to improve the Ross. Turner threatened harsh punishment for any member of his division found with a Lee-Enfield. Mercer had to explain why the PPCLI still carried the British rifle. As for Alderson, Hughes sent him a blistering letter accusing him of undermining confidence in the Ross and failing to provide the right ammunition. Copies were distributed to every colonel. Men in the ranks could decide for themselves whether Hughes or Alderson best defended their interests.

BLOODING THE NEW DIVISIONS

Canadians knew about winter but only veterans of Salisbury Plain were prepared for Flanders. A driving, relentless, continual rain filled every trench and shell crater. Mud liquefied and oozed from sandbags. From their higher ground, Germans added their drainage to the shells and sniper bullets they poured on the Canadian trenches. Sleet, snow, and bitter winds were countered only by the morning tot of rum.

In the French sector armed neutrality was the rule between battles; but Haig's headquarters insisted that the British "dominate" no-man's land with snipers, patrols, and constant raids. The Germans responded, usually with more skill, almost always from better ground. In November, two Canadian battalions, the 5th and 7th, practised ninety-man raiding parties for ten days. On the night of November 16–17, they crossed a little creek called the Douve and one of the parties captured prisoners and a new kind of German gas mask. Both groups escaped casualties but the less successful battalion had to try again a few nights later. Haig, newly in command, was delighted. Canadians found themselves celebrated and studied as leaders in what a less enthusiastic British officer later called "the costly and depressing fashion of raiding the other side". Costly it certainly was. From its creation on September 13 to the end of 1915, the Canadian Corps suffered 2,692 casualties, 688 of them fatal.

In the new year, the 3rd Division extended the Canadian sector until the Corps held six miles of waterlogged mud south from St. Eloi. The raids and counter-raids continued. Tunnellers from both sides drove mines and counter-mines in a claustrophobic struggle to blow up enemy trenches. The Germans went deep, the British went deeper, to sixty feet. By the end of March, the Corps had lost another 546 killed and a total of 2,760 casualties from battle, sickness, and accident.

The adjoining British corps had lost a small salient on February 14. Plumer, whose Second Army controlled the salient, ordered the corps to avenge the defeat by cutting off the German salient at St. Eloi. The British 3rd Division, weary and depleted, attacked on March 27. Mud and water leaped skyward from the bursting of six British mines. The huge explosions

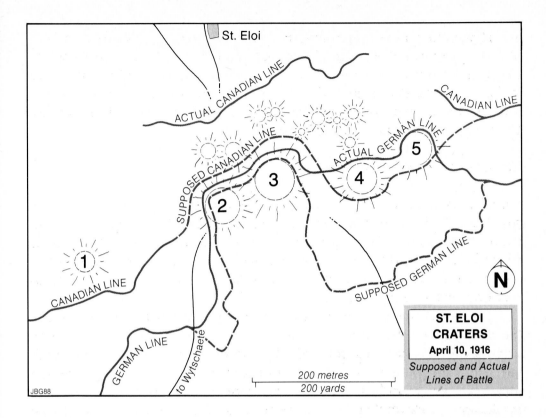

ST. ELOI
CRATERS
April 10, 1916

*Supposed and Actual
Lines of Battle*

transformed the landscape and buried the German defenders. A British brigade on the right took craters 1, 2, and 3. Machine guns held up the other
assaulting brigade. More attacks followed, and by day's end the British
claimed that craters 4 and 5 were occupied. In fact, lost in the sodden, devastated landscape, the British had actually occupied crater 6 and a seventh
from an earlier explosion. The Germans had three days to prepare before the
exhausted British discovered their error and completed the attack. Throughout the battle, German artillery saturated the tiny patch of mud and, on the
night of April 3–4, when the British moved out of the line, there was not much
left of their 3rd Division. Turner's 2nd Canadian Division took over.

The St. Eloi sector fell to the westerners of Ketchen's 6th Brigade. The battered British had left almost no trenches. The mine craters were now small
lakes, the biggest of them 180 feet across and 50 feet deep, all of them an
obstacle to supplies or reinforcements. By noon on April 4, half of the 27th
Battalion were dead or wounded by German shellfire. That night, Ketchen
sent up the 29th Battalion to relieve them as the German counter-attack
struck. It was the disaster every officer feared: trenches packed with men,
confusion of command, pitch darkness split by flares and exploding shells.
Within three hours, the Germans had taken back almost everything the Brit-

ish had captured. Ketchen's counter-attacks failed. The Albertans of the 31st Battalion regained craters 6 and 7 but, like the British a week earlier, they believed they were at craters 4 and 5. From the heights of Messines, the Germans knew better; Canadian staff officers, peering up at the muddy ridges on their skyline, did not. Geysers of spray and mud from German shells kept them from going closer. Eight days of fog and mist kept British aircraft from checking from the sky.

Turner proposed to withdraw from St. Eloi, blast the Germans as they had blasted his men, and retake the lost ground. Alderson agreed. Sir Herbert Plumer, advised that the Canadians still held key craters 4 and 5, told them to stay put. Only on April 16 did air photos finally tell Turner the truth. It was too late. On the afternoon of April 19, a crushing bombardment buried the defenders of crater 6 and then 7. "Our men were glued in the mud," wrote one of them. "The survivors were in no condition to offer fight being dazed and shell shocked. The rifles were clogged and useless, only two or three being capable of firing." The few survivors surrendered. The Germans claimed 483 casualties; Turner's division had lost 1,373. It was not a victory.

Plumer fired his chief of staff and the officers found wanting in the 3rd British Division. Turner and Ketchen, he insisted, must also go: it was inexcusable that they had not known what was happening on their front. Alderson agreed. He had not forgotten Turner's strange inactivity at Ypres a year before. Sir Douglas Haig had more political sensitivity. In his diary, he weighed "the danger of a serious feud between the Canadians and the British" against "the retention of a couple of incompetent commanders". If Turner stayed, Alderson would have to go. Aitken, when he arrived, was delighted to oblige. In Ottawa, Borden and Hughes had prepared to defend their officers: Aitken's message was a relief. On May 28, Alderson was shuffled to the wholly nominal post of inspector general of the Canadians in England. His successor was Lieutenant-General the Honourable Sir Julian Byng, a cheerfully unintellectual cavalryman known to his colleagues as "Bungo". Byng had also turned out to be, to some people's surprise, a cool and effective field commander, who had personally managed the bloodless British evacuation at Gallipoli.

When Haig concentrated his troops for the Somme offensive, the Canadians remained in the Ypres salient. The 3rd Division, more confident and at full strength, now occupied almost the only high ground the British had retained from the year before; a hill called Mount Sorrel and Observatory Ridge, which ran from Tor Top in the east a thousand yards deep into the Canadian sector. It was key ground and the Germans wanted it, not only to make the rest of the salient untenable but to hold the British troops from their coming offensive.

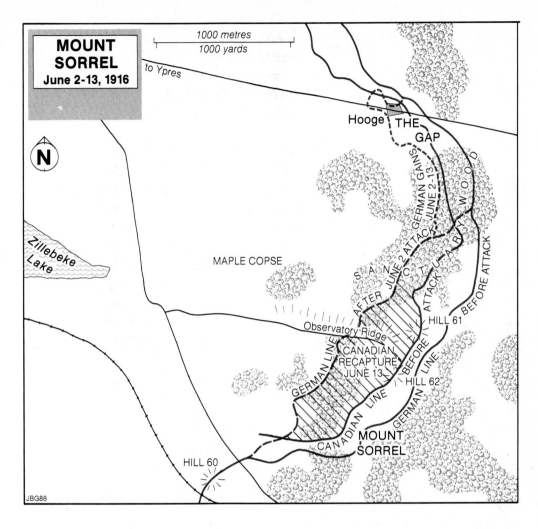

In May, British pilots spotted signs of German rehearsals behind their lines. Others saw guns and mortars in profusion. Then bad weather stopped systematic observation.

At night on June 1, German shelling stopped. Canadians were alerted but, in a few hours, when German troops had cut the Canadian wire, the shelling resumed. Next morning, Mercer and Brigadier-General Victor Williams of the 8th Brigade walked out to see the 4th Canadian Mounted Rifles position on Mount Sorrel and Tor Top. They were there when German shelling burst out with a dense fury no British troops had yet experienced. From Mount Sorrel to Sanctuary Wood, Canadian trenches and their defenders vanished. German observers saw dirt, trees, weapons, and human bodies hurled into the air. Four mines exploded under Mount Sorrel. Then, almost calmly, waves of German infantry walked forward. Dazed survivors offered little resistance. Of

702 men of the 4th Canadian Mounted Rifles, 76 survived unscathed. Two of
the four Mounted Rifles colonels were killed; a third surrendered, as did the
remnants of his headquarters, and a badly wounded General Williams. General Mercer, twice wounded, was found dead. In Sanctuary Wood, the PPCLI
lost more than 400 men as it held the flank of the German attack. Elsewhere,
scattered reserves rushed up to hold the line. With little barring them from
Ypres, the attackers unaccountably stopped after a 600-yard advance and dug
in.

   That evening Byng ordered: "all ground lost to-day will be retaken tonight".
The task was given to Brigadier-General E.S. Hoare-Nairne, commander of
the 3rd Division's British artillery and Mercer's successor. With his own
reserves and a couple of brigades from the 1st Division, Hoare-Nairne did his
best. It was a second disaster. Signals misfired. Attacking troops, packed in
trenches, were slaughtered by German guns. Artillery support, hurriedly
improvised, was feeble. Machine guns swept away attackers. At dawn, the
Germans still held their gains. On June 6, four more exploding mines slaughtered the Canadian defenders of Hooge, a little to the north. The Canadians
had lost another piece of the salient. The Germans were two miles from Ypres.
"This...goes to prove," Haig sourly noted, "that men with strange equipment
and rugged countenances and beards are not all determined fighters."

   Corps commanders who lost ground were "degummed" — fired. Byng
deserved a second chance and time. Haig refused troops: they were needed for
the Somme but he could lend some guns. This time the Germans would face
a bombardment as good as their own. Like Alderson, Byng had soon spotted
Currie as his best general: retaking Mount Sorrel would be his test. Losses
from the earlier attack forced Currie to organize his division into two com-
posite brigades. Assaulting battalions moved into the front lines, learned the
terrain, and withdrew to rest and rehearse. A gunner in his militia days, Currie insisted on knowing the artillery plan and adding a little ingenuity. Four
times, the bombardment reached a crescendo and stopped. Each time, the
Württembergers opposite scrambled to defend themselves only to be blasted
when they were in the open. On June 12, at 8:30 P.M., the guns reached a fifth
crescendo. This time the Canadian infantry advanced. They found little
resistance and two hundred prisoners. In an hour they had regained the losses
of June 4. Then, it was the Germans' turn to fight, with a hurricane of shells
and waves of counter-attacks. Both sides lost heavily, but no ground changed
hands. On June 14, the firing died away.

   In ten days, the Canadians had lost 8,000 men; the Germans 5,765, but it was
the Canadians who felt victorious. They had also learned some useful prin-
ciples for future victory: patient preparation, limited objectives, planned

artillery support. The shaken 3rd Division soon recovered under the human touch of Major-General Louis Lipsett. Best of all, Mount Sorrel confirmed a lesson of St. Eloi: Canadians could not be expected to fight Germans with the Ross. On June 21, the War Office authorized an exchange of rifles and from Ottawa, in Hughes's absence, the government cabled its consent. Among the troops, it was a vindication of Alderson: for years the myth persisted that opposing the Ross had cost him his job.

THE BLOODY SOMME

If Haig had had his way, the British offensive in 1916 would have started in Flanders and Canadians might have been involved. It was General Joffre who insisted on fighting among the hard limestone ridges and the overgrown villages that rose from the valley of the Somme. Perhaps he had spared Canadians from the horror of July 1 and the dreary, grinding battles that followed through the summer but their turn came soon enough when Haig prepared for the vast, co-ordinated Allied assault on the Central Powers, timed for September 15.

The Somme had become Haig's *Gericht*: von Falkenhayn's insistence on contesting every inch with remorseless counter-attacks matched the British tactical faith that three and four lines of infantry could swamp any defence. For the September offensive, GHQ had two innovations: enough shells for the artillery to fire "rolling barrages", leading the infantry on to their objectives so that Germans would have no time to man their machine guns; and "tanks", tracked, armoured monsters that could flatten any machine gun that did emerge. This time, Haig believed, the exhausted Germans might finally crack and his three divisions of cavalry could pour through.

The Canadians came south in late August, fifty miles along dusty roads. They would replace the Australians and New Zealanders who had struggled, with futile valour, to take the Pozières ridge, the long limestone slope that commanded the British lines. On August 31, Currie's division took over the Australian line and on September 2, his 13th Battalion shared in a last Australian attempt on Mouquet Farm. That was a distraction. Sir Hubert Gough, once the leader of the "Curragh Mutiny", now commanded the Corps in the Reserve Army. His orders were to seize Courcelette and the ridge beyond. The Canadians must do it. On the right, Turner's 2nd Division would capture Courcelette; Lipsett's 3rd, on the left, would finish with Mouquet Farm and take the long German trench, Fabeck Graben.

At 6:20 A.M. on September 15, British and Canadian guns, parked wheel to wheel, opened fire. Turner's men reached their first objectives in half an hour.

Only five of the seven tanks assigned to the Canadians started; four were blasted by German shells and a sole survivor struggled to its objective at the maximum speed of a mile an hour. Five frightened infantrymen, assigned to clear wounded from its path, found none. Though an excited British "Eye-witness" boasted that tanks had given the British a sweeping victory and that cheering British troops followed one down the main street of Flers, German generals dismissed the new devices as a toy. Haig, more far-sighted or optimistic, ordered a thousand more from the Ministry of Munitions. Canadians, on the whole, tended to the German view, though one soldier remembered that a sole tank, named *Crème de Menthe*, had allowed his company to get moving when machine guns had pinned it down.

At dusk on the 15th, Byng ordered the next attack. On the left, battalions of Lipsett's 3rd Division fought a savage battle at Mouquet Farm and along the German trench line. On the right, the 22nd and 25th battalions struggled through Courcelette and into the fields beyond only to be cut off when German defenders emerged from cellars and tunnels in the sheltered village. The New Brunswickers of the 26th Battalion, followed through Courcelette, were caught in a desperate house-to-house battle. Almost isolated, the French Canadians and Nova Scotians fought off eleven counter-attacks in two days. "Si l'enfer est aussi abominable que ce que j'ai vu," Colonel Thomas Tremblay of the 22nd Battalion recorded in his journal, "je ne souhaiterais pas à mon pire ennemi d'y aller" (If hell is as bad as what I saw, I would not want my worst enemy to go there). At Mouquet Farm, Captain George Pearkes recalled, more prosaically, that he went around stopping up German tunnels with bombs from a trench-mortar. Only when he had completed the job would a British battalion agree to take over. Private John Kerr of the 49th Battalion, wounded and losing blood, led a squad of grenade-throwing Canadians deep into German trenches and brought back sixty-two prisoners. He lived to collect his Victoria Cross.

Days of pouring rain soon dragged the fighting to a stop. Always there were more German positions farther up the slope, with fortified redoubts that commanded every approach. On the 25th, the Fourth Army, adjoining, drove its weary men forward, to Morval, Lesboeufs, and, on the 26th, Gueudecourt. That day, at Gough's insistence, the Canadians advanced as well. Now it was the 1st Division's turn to lead. Its battalions found that the Germans, to escape the shelling, waited with their machine guns in front of their trenches, crouching in craters and ditches. The Canadians fought their way through two German lines but beyond the ridge, at Regina Trench, the few weary survivors turned back. Brigadier-General G.S. Tuxford found only seventy-five men left in the 14th Battalion but he sent them back for another try at 2:00 A.M.

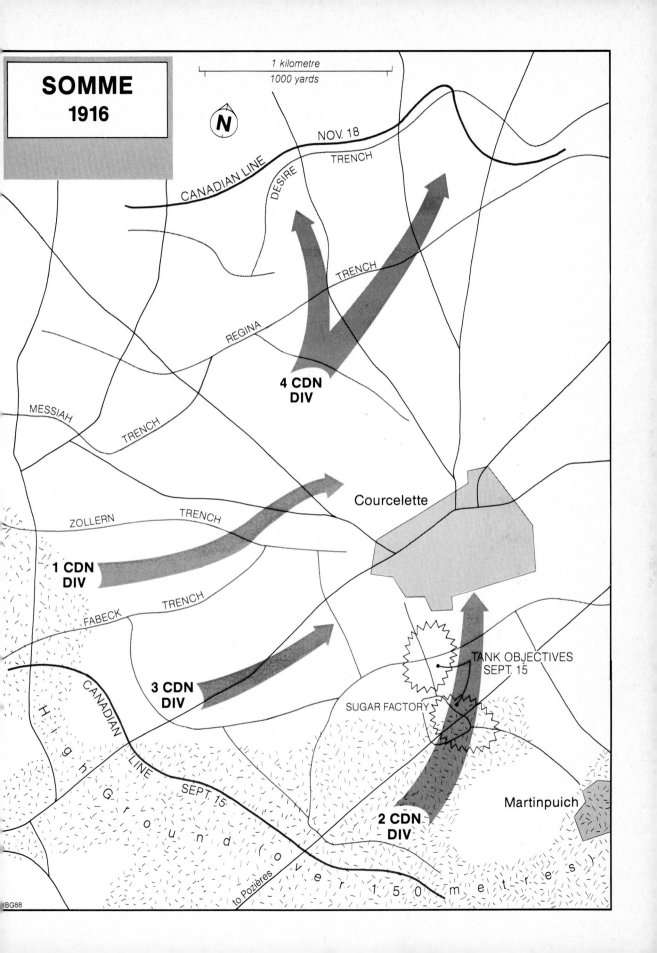

SOMME
1916

1 kilometre
1000 yards

N

CANADIAN LINE

NOV. 18

DESIRE

TRENCH

TRENCH

REGINA

4 CDN DIV

MESSIAH

TRENCH

Courcelette

ZOLLERN   TRENCH

1 CDN DIV

FABECK   TRENCH

TANK OBJECTIVES SEPT. 15

3 CDN DIV

SUGAR FACTORY

High Ground (over 150 metres)

CANADIAN LINE   SEPT. 15

2 CDN DIV

Martinpuich

to Pozières

BG88

German flares and machine guns caught them. Turner, on the right, tried piecemeal attacks and then belatedly co-ordinated them, but each assault ended in failure.

To higher commanders, Regina Trench had become the symbol of a victory they desperately wanted. It was also a desperately difficult objective, tucked behind the ridge line, fronted by tons of concertina wire which the Germans rolled out each night to fill gaps. Byng's orders were blunt: Turner's division, slightly rested but not rebuilt, would stay in the line until it had taken Regina Trench. Lipsett's division would help. October 1, 3:15 P.M., was zero hour.

It was hopeless. Driving rain turned the cratered ground to clinging, grey mud. Faulty British shells fell among the struggling infantry. Among the Canadian Mounted Rifles of the 8th Brigade, whole companies were slaughtered against uncut wire. A company that broke through was annihilated; another was driven back. In this sector, Turner depended on the depleted 5th Brigade. The 22nd Battalion struggled for half a mile through shells and machine-gun fire to find the wire uncut. "From this moment," its war diary recorded, "the attack failed." The 25th Battalion got thirty of its two hundred men to Regina Trench, and the 24th Battalion, the Victoria Rifles from Montreal, did better but the Germans drove in the Canadian flanks. The 2nd Division could manage no more than to collect its seven hundred losses.

Byng turned to Currie's 1st Division again. A week of foul weather gave both sides a little miserable time to prepare. Currie chose to attack at dawn with eight battalions in line. It made no difference. The line of German Marines, who now held the trench, was impregnable behind their wire. The 3rd Battalion, the "Toronto's", somehow got through. So did a hundred men of the 16th after an eighteen-year-old piper, James Richardson, strode up and down before the wire. His body was found later. On the 3rd Division front, some of the Royal Canadian Regiment cut their way through the wire but the Germans killed the attackers or drove them out. The cost of the day was 1,364 casualties for no gain. The post-mortems were bitter. Heavy artillery had failed to batter the German defences; shrapnel would not cut wire; the few men who broke into enemy trenches ran out of the grenades they needed to fight their way from traverse to traverse and there was no way to get them more. Replacements fresh from England, complained Currie, were virtually untrained and there were too few of them.

The reason, of course, was the chaotic Canadian organization in England, with its competing commanders and its distant, erratic overlord. Of 19,500 Canadians at Shorncliffe, more than a quarter had been diverted into odd jobs as orderlies, mess waiters, or bandsmen. Potential reinforcements were channelled into a 4th Canadian Division and then a 5th. Hughes came to England at the end of July to guarantee the command of the 4th for his old friend Dave Watson. Brigades were reserved for his brother, W. St. Pierre Hughes, of the 21st Battalion and for Lord Brooke. A hard-bitten prohibitionist newspaper owner from Vancouver, Victor Odlum of the 7th Battalion, got the third. "Big drive expected," Hughes cabled Canada, "and great desire Canadians should be first in Berlin." He planned four more divisions; Borden should send 80,000 more men.

In mid-August, Watson took the 4th Division to France. A few weeks at Ypres trained his battalions in trench fighting and a week at St. Omer allowed them to exchange their Ross rifles for Lee-Enfields. Then the division moved south to the Somme. By October 17, an exhausted and depleted Canadian Corps had moved north from the Somme to the Arras-Lens sector and the raw 4th Division took over its line. It was a horrible introduction to war. The coldest winter in memory had begun early, with sharp winds and icy rain. The trenches on the Pozières ridge were mere ditches, already knee-deep in water. Soldiers who burrowed into the walls to escape the rain risked burial in waterlogged mud.

It was long past time to stop the battle but Haig was not satisfied. The Germans, he insisted, were exhausted too. The Allies, in trouble everywhere, desperately needed a victory. He would like to announce it when the generals met again at Chantilly in November. Sir Hubert Gough wanted to oblige. On October 21, Brigadier-General Victor Odlum's 11th Brigade rushed part of Regina Trench behind a figurative wall of fire. In three hours, Montrealers and British Columbians had blocked a sector of the trench and thrown back German counter-attacks. The cost was 200 casualties and the rewards were 160 prisoners. It seemed so easy that, on the 25th, Watson sent the 44th Battalion in a similar attack. It was a slaughter. Later, the brigadier, St. Pierre Hughes, claimed that he had warned Watson that the artillery had chosen that day to switch position. As a result the barrage was feeble. German machine guns and artillery caught the Manitoba battalion in the open and killed or wounded 200.

For two weeks, steady, remorseless rain pelted the battlefield. The rest of Regina Trench still had to be captured. Gunners demanded two clear days for bombardment. On November 9 and 10, they finally got them. At midnight on the 10th, four of Watson's battalions attacked, starting from 150 yards in front of their trenches, away from the German counter-barrage. By dawn, they controlled the whole of Regina Trench, now a shallow ditch, twenty feet wide, littered with debris and corpses. Gough wanted still more from the Canadians. A week later, amid the first driving snow of the winter, with mud freezing underfoot, Odlum's 11th Brigade attacked Desire Trench beyond Regina. Perhaps Haig had a point: 625 Germans surrendered and one counter-attacking group threw down its rifles and gave up. The 11th, however, was isolated. Attacks by the 10th Brigade and a British brigade failed. Finally the Canadians withdrew from their farthest advance. For them the battle of the Somme was over.

Haig and historians would argue about its value. The few who knew what the Somme had cost Britain in the quality of its young men as much as in the appalling numbers felt numb and then furious with frustration. Yet Haig had insisted that the war could not be won until the German army was defeated and was there another way? Against an Allied claim of 623,907 dead and wounded the Germans recorded 465,525 casualties, but their statistics ignored a quarter of the wounded who recovered near the front. Von Ludendorff understood exactly what the fighting had done to his enemy when he pleaded in November for a return to unrestricted submarine warfare: "we must save the men from a second Somme battle". The Germans had sent 93 divisions into the battle, half of them twice. Most emerged with their cadres destroyed; 1,500 or 2,000 casualties in a regiment of 3,000. The old German army was gone, much as the British regulars had perished at Ypres and Neuve Chapelle.

The Canadians, too, had suffered at the Somme. The 2nd Division would proudly remember Courcelette and the 4th Division Regina Trench but, for all of the divisions, the Somme was a memory of mass butchery ordered by generals who were all-powerful and never seen. The Somme cost Canadians 24,029 men. They knew there was little to show for it but painful lessons. Like other soldiers on the Western Front that year, Canadians digested cruel experience. Infantry needed fresh, flexible tactics. Artillery had to protect attacking troops from the merciless German guns. Above all, communications had to pierce the fog of war so that generals and colonels could help front-line soldiers. Overdue but necessary, a ferment of ideas would transform the tactics and technology of fighting.

A WINTER OF DESPAIR

A war that generals had expected to win in four months had lasted twenty-eight months by the end of 1916. Now its misery was aggravated by the harshest winter since 1881. There was starvation in German and Austrian cities. Britain, the banker to the world, had mortgaged its last credit. Lord Lansdowne, Conservative leader in the House of Lords and once a governor general of Canada, pleaded privately that only peace could preserve the fabric of civilization. On November 21, 1916, the ancient Habsburg emperor died.

His heir, a nephew of the victim of Sarajevo, contacted a brother-in-law in the Belgian army to see if peace could be arranged. In Berlin, the chancellor, Theobald von Bethmann-Hollweg, again proposed a separate peace with Russia. German generals scuttled such proposals by proclaiming an independent Poland. On December 12, Bethmann announced still broader peace overtures. The terms he wisely kept secret; Germany would keep her conquests, spread her empire, and collect huge reparations from her enemies. Nothing less was now acceptable to the generals, and perhaps to the suffering German people.

The Germans at least considered terms; the Allies still thought only of total victory. In Washington, President Woodrow Wilson had tried to be a peace-maker and now he tried again. Narrowly re-elected by Americans as "the man who kept us out of war", Wilson invited warring nations to consider "peace without victory". The Allies responded awkwardly, conscious of secret promises to each other, anxious to build an image of moral superiority that might draw Americans into the war. They wanted a return to the 1914 frontiers, reparations for Belgium, France, Serbia, and other victims and, in an unexpected flourish, "national self-determination" for the subject peoples of the Habsburgs and "the bloody tyranny" of Turkey. Americans were mildly pleased but Allied terms bound Turkey and Austria all the more tightly to their German ally.

The truth was that to most people in Germany, France, and Britain, peace talk still represented defeatism and a form of treason. British seamen refused to allow delegates to a peace congress at Stockholm to board their ships. In Paris, Joseph Caillaux, the ex-premier whose wife had been acquitted of murder in 1914, urged a compromise peace with Germany. So did Louis Malvy, an interior minister who slipped money to a defeatist newspaper, *Le Bonnet rouge*. Patriots scorned them.

In every warring country, civilian ministers had helped to glorify generals as the architects of victory. The public, far removed from the battlefield, now believed in them as military geniuses. Even the soldiers at the front, yearning for peace and well aware of failures of generalship, could not contemplate defeat. Bethmann had welcomed the enormous prestige of von Hindenburg and von Ludendorff as assets in his own search for negotiated peace only to find von Ludendorff empowered by his reputation, and von Hindenburg's, to pursue grander and more disastrous strategies. There must be victory in the East, von Ludendorff insisted, not peace. In the West, though, he cancelled von Falkenhayn's policy of holding every inch. Behind the German line, 50,000 Russian prisoners laboured on a shorter, painstakingly fortified new defence line, the *Siegfried-Stellung*. Once completed, the "Hindenburg Line", as even

Germans called it, would secure the West and release fifteen divisions for other, more decisive battles. Most of all, von Ludendorff demanded that Germany take up the weapon she had abandoned in 1915: unrestricted submarine warfare. Strategy meant winning, not worrying about neutrals. German admirals now had a good reason to agree.

On May 31, 1916, the German High Seas Fleet had finally clashed with the British Grand Fleet in the foggy waters of the North Sea off Jutland. Three times the German battleships had slipped through a British trap; once the British admiral, Sir John Jellicoe, had turned away from the enemy for fear of mines or torpedoes. That was not how Nelson had fought nor did it seem a British victory to lose three capital ships to two German battleships. Jutland was another of the blows 1916 brought to Britain. The truth about Jutland was caught by an American headline: "The German Fleet assaulted its jailer but it is still in jail". Within a couple of weeks, Jellicoe was back at sea. The fatal weakness of his battle cruisers was soon repaired. Apart from a single scurry from harbour in the summer of 1916, the German High Seas Fleet now stayed in port. A few of its marines had faced Canadians at Regina Trench; most seamen waited in mutinous idleness, a fatal diversion of resources that von Ludendorff insisted must be put to real use. German admirals agreed. Who cared if sinking every ship approaching Britain brought the Americans into the war? England would starve in six months. France would collapse without her ally and, by the time Americans had an army, it would have no place to land.

One man could match von Ludendorff in ruthlessness of purpose. Alone among British politicians, Lloyd George had built a popular following. He had preached a "knock-out blow" to cheering crowds and always he had seen that blow padded by amateurism, indecision, and the refusal to mobilize national and Allied strength. Andrew Bonar Law, the Canadian-born leader of the Conservatives, shared Lloyd George's frustration: Max Aitken, another Canadian Tory, was the go-between. The decent, drunken Herbert Asquith, in his own eyes "the indispensable man", was dispensed with when 102 Liberals joined with Conservatives to make Lloyd George prime minister on December 7.

At once, Britain's wartime management changed. A tiny War Cabinet — Lloyd George, three Conservatives, and a Labour member — took charge of the war effort, most without carrying ministerial burdens. A supporting staff — Lloyd George's "Garden Suburb" — was created to carry out a prime minister's will. Merchant shipping, food production, and manpower were controlled. Only the army seemed too much to control: like Bethmann, Lloyd George realized that wartime generals had vast popular followings. Conservatives protected Haig; the King made him a field marshal. Instead of being "a butcher's boy driving cattle to the slaughter" for Haig, Lloyd George tried to persuade the Italians to lead the attack. General Cadorna, the Italian chief of staff, prudently declined. Suddenly, Lloyd George found a better agent.

The French, also, had a new leader. Joffre's miscalculation over Verdun and the terrible casualties that followed were too much even for his reputation. His reward was a marshal's baton and retirement. Verdun had produced a handsome, articulate national hero who had thrown German armies back with seemingly trifling casualties. General Robert Nivelle surely had prestige enough to allow Aristide Briand's socialist government at least to explore peace. But no; Nivelle, an artillery officer, was a man with a plan. A tornado of artillery fire, an irresistible mass of manoeuvre, and a certain breakthrough, he promised: "Laon in twenty-four hours and then the pursuit." Other generals argued that the plan was hopeless and that the French army would not be strong enough — or were they merely jealous? Lloyd George was dubious too until he met the new French commander-in-chief. Thanks to his mother, Nivelle was more articulate in English than Douglas Haig. Even better, Nivelle wanted the French to do most of the fighting. Haig and his generals learned at Calais on February 26 that the War Cabinet had put them under Nivelle's command. In united fury, they forced the prime minister to back down: the subordination would only be during Nivelle's attack. They never trusted Lloyd George again.

There was other news from that bitter winter. In Petrograd in early March, rioters smashed into bread shops. Cossacks refused to ride them down. The Tsar returned to his capital only to be turned around by defiant railwaymen. On March 15, his generals persuaded him to abdicate. Committees or Soviets of workers and soldiers took power but the government passed to middle-class liberal politicians. Once the new Provisional Government agreed to carry on the war, there was enormous relief. In the Allied countries and in the United States, Tsarist autocracy had been the ugliest blemish on the Allied cause. Doubtless too, it was also to blame for Russian defeats. Democracy would surely refuel the Russian steamroller but even optimists knew it would take months, if not years. Von Ludendorff quietly arranged for a trouble-maker named Lenin to travel home to Russia from Switzerland in a sealed railway car. Another Russian revolutionary named Leon Trotsky was released from a Canadian internment camp at Amherst, Nova Scotia, after pressure from Canadians sympathetic to Russia's new liberalism. Surely the new, democratic Russia needed men who had fought tyranny.

On January 31, 1917, Bethmann lost a bitter argument with von Ludendorff. Germany proclaimed unrestricted submarine warfare. Two days later, as he had promised, Woodrow Wilson severed diplomatic relations. He would go no further. U-boats ignored his restraint: more American ships were sunk. Alfred Zimmermann, a Bethmann subordinate, wired the German embassy in Mexico City to promise German aid if the Mexicans attacked the United States. British intelligence intercepted the message, diverted it neatly into American hands, and waited for the results. Wilson and the U.S. Congress obliged. On April 7, the United States went to war.

It was a triumph for the Allies but, like Russia's March revolution, American participation did not promise quick results. The American fleet of modern battleships made no difference to the U-boat war. The United States had no real army. To create one meant drafting, training, and equipping millions of young Americans, but only France and Britain could provide them with artillery, tanks, aircraft, and even rifles. American credit could sustain British and French finances but the American economy had all that it could do to support its own mobilization. The Yanks were coming — but not yet.

And they might not come at all if von Ludendorff was right. In March, U-boats sank 600,000 tons of British and neutral shipping. In April, the total reached 870,000 tons. No shipbuilding program could match such staggering losses. One out of four ships that left British ports never got back. In six months, the Germans had sent 3.75 million tons of shipping — and 3,833 seamen — to the bottom. The Admiralty had no answer. Since U-boats no longer surfaced to rescue crews, they were usually invisible and undetectable except when they had to charge their batteries. Admiral Jellicoe, now the First Sea Lord, dismissed convoys as impossible. Shipping companies agreed. Beginning in January 1917, Lloyd George imposed rationing. Even the rich, a visiting Canadian politician complained, could not get all they wanted to eat.

All that the French and British could hope was that General Nivelle was right.

Soldiers attend mass in a ruined French church; most have their gas masks to hand. The CEF provided Protestant and Catholic chaplains and enforced attendance at church parades, but most soldiers professed a cautious fatalism. Some senior officers tried to improve morality by enforcing a ban on swearing; others set a roaring example.

Canadian infantry attacking near Sanctuary Wood. This looks suspiciously like a rehearsal; the men are too neatly spaced for the real thing.

The front near Ypres in the summer of 1916, with a shell exploding. This shows the desolate flatness of the landscape after a year and a half of fighting. A year later, this would be the setting for Sir Douglas Haig's Passchendaele offensive.

Trenches in the Ypres Salient in the summer of 1916. Canadian positions at Sanctuary Wood were in much the same condition after the German attack had been repulsed.

The Somme battlefield in early October. Dead bodies are rare in wartime photographs and these, from the appearance of their boots, are probably Germans. The scene reflects the grim devastation in what, two years earlier, had been a green and pleasant landscape.

The Somme battlefield in front of Courcelette. As shells explode in the distance, corpses lie uncollected; the living are out of sight. After the Somme experience, the Canadians and British realized that better tactics simply had to be found.

Winter came early in 1916, and brought the coldest weather in generations. By the time the 4th Canadian Division had its last attacks in November, the ground was frozen and snow had settled in.

Canadian troops return from the trenches in November 1916. A sergeant leads the remnant of a platoon. Artillery drivers escort loaded limbers up to the gun lines. The deep mud underfoot adds to the exhaustion of weary men.

David Lloyd George and Winston Churchill. Both men sought to bring an energy and imagination to the empire's war effort that neither Asquith's Liberal government nor Britain's generals and admirals seemed capable of generating by 1916.

Sir Sam Hughes takes the salute, his son, Garnet, whispers information, and an impassive Major-General Arthur Currie watches as the 3rd Battalion, with accompanying dog, gives as smart an "eyes right" as it can manage. Military buffs will note the left-handed salute — correct drill at the time.

Sir George and Lady Perley confer with Major-General Richard Turner. As Overseas Minister, Perley was happy to leave military matters to soldiers. So was Lady Perley, once the obnoxious Colonel Bruce had been sent away.

Lieutenant-General Sir Julian Byng — "Bungo" to his friends — was no genius, but he was a sensible, experienced soldier who taught Canadians that training and careful staff work saved lives. He was also no martinet, returning salutes, so one officer recorded, as well as he could without taking his hands out of his pockets.

VI
A NATIONAL CRUSADE

A CANADIAN ARMY

Canada's acting high commissioner in London understood the status of the CEF in 1914: "as soon as the Canadian troops arrive here they will be entirely under the authority of the War Office and become part of the Imperial army in every sense of the word." That was understandable from George Perley, an imperialist, an Ottawa millionaire, and a Tory minister without portfolio who had accepted a summer in London as an ideal reward for his unpaid chores. An official reason to keep the vulgar Sam Hughes away from "his boys" was an added bonus, but Perley was perfectly correct. The CEF was as much part of the British army as any Scots guardsman or Lancashire fusilier. Canada provided the men and the money but Britain, as Hughes himself admitted, gave the orders.

In 1914, that seemed appropriate. Sir Robert Borden, and most Canadians like him, revered Britain and its institutions. The war was a test of loyalty they proudly passed. In 1915 it was different. The casualty lists from Ypres gave Canada a direct stake in a war the British seemed to be bungling. Borden went to London in 1915 to help: he found himself treated as an intruder. The dull, seemingly phlegmatic Canadian had a temper. Unless he got information, he warned Bonar Law, "I shall not advise my countrymen to put further effort into the winning of the War." That did it. Lloyd George was summoned from a country weekend and poured out almost more than Borden wanted to hear: "During my recent visit to England," Borden wrote later, "a very prominent Cabinet Minister in speaking of the officers of another Department said that he could not call them traitors but he asserted that they could not have acted any differently if they had been traitors." The department, of course, was the War Office.

Once back in Ottawa, information and even gossip were unavailable. Bor-

134

den could learn about the war only from his morning paper. Again he demanded to be informed. Well aware that the Canadian capital was a sieve for secrets, the British demurred. Bonar Law repeated what he had said in London: "if no scheme [to keep Ottawa informed] is practicable, then it is very undesirable that the question should be raised". Fury at that response fuelled Borden's New Year's pledge of half a million Canadians for the CEF. That would show the British what earnestness meant. His anger poured into a letter to Perley, to be shown to British cabinet ministers: "It can hardly be expected that we shall put 400,000 to 500,000 men in the field and willingly accept the position of having no more voice and receiving no more consideration than if we were toy automata.... Is this war being waged by the United Kingdom alone, or is it a war being waged by the whole Empire? If I am correct in supposing that the second hypothesis must be accepted, then why do the statesmen of the British Isles arrogate to themselves solely the methods by which it will be carried on?"

A few days later, when his temper and his lumbago had subsided, Borden cancelled the letter but he liked it well enough to include it in his memoirs twenty-five years later. It spelled out his assertion of a new status for Canada in the Empire and the war: henceforth she would be a junior but sovereign ally in the struggle, not a subservient colony.

From that, much would follow, but not right away. Through most of 1916, Borden was engulfed in the problems of war finance, bankrupt railways, the decay of Conservative support in the provinces, and, above all, rescuing the war effort from the tempestuous and terrifying Sam Hughes.

Nowhere was that effort more chaotic and embarrassing than in England. Some of the problems came from Canada. Scores of CEF battalions arrived only to be broken up, adding to the hundreds of surplus officers that had collected in England with the First Contingent. Battalions in France now preferred to fill vacancies from their own ranks rather than with colonels, majors, and captains who owed their rank more to politics than soldiering. Many such officers sacrificed rank and pay to serve; more helped expand the military bureaucracies that Carson, Steele, MacDougall, and lesser rivals created. In February 1916, when Alderson visited Shorncliffe in a hunt for men for the Corps in France, he found 1,476 officers and 25,085 other ranks — but only 75 officers and 2,385 men were even training to fight in France. Carson's staff in London had grown to 3,500 all ranks by the autumn of 1916.

By 1916, the War Office despaired of sorting out who was responsible for Canadian military administration in England. General Gwatkin, who understood that and most other problems, tried to let Borden know but the prime minister now regarded Gwatkin's messenger, the ancient Duke of Connaught, as a meddler. Twice Hughes left for England promising reform. In April, he was summoned back to face charges of double-dealing and profit-eering in his Shell Committee. Exonerated by a royal commission that dis-creetly loaded all the guilt on the unlovely J. Wesley Allison, Hughes was free to return in the summer of 1916 for another try. In both cases, his solution was a council of his aged cronies and dependants, with authority only to submit every decision to him.

By the end of September, when Hughes returned to Ottawa, he was as cer-tain as ever that a little bullying would make Borden accept his latest scheme. He was wrong. For one thing, the riot at Camp Borden in July, while Hughes was inspecting "his boys", not only underlined administrative failures, it dis-pelled the belief that the troops adored their minister. For another, his old enemy, Sir George Perley, had spent the summer in Ottawa. For more than a year Perley had pleaded for reform. With the war giving Canada a new influ-ence, he had warned, "it is especially necessary that we should just now impress people here that we are both sane and capable in the management of our own affairs". Ships carrying Perley and Hughes had passed in mid-Atlantic. Borden had made up his mind. On October 27, Hughes learned how. A new Minister of the Overseas Military Forces of Canada (OMFC) would be based in London, with the powers of a Minister of Militia and more. Hughes was outraged. He would lose all control over "his boys". Then, more slyly, he suggested a nominee: Max Aitken. No, it would be his enemy, Perley. Again Hughes exploded. For once, Borden was firm. A final abusive letter from the militia minister was too much. On November 9, Hughes was fired.

Borden had never fired a minister before, and he feared huge wellsprings of popular support for Hughes from Orangemen, Tories, and, above all, from the troops. He knew the secrets a furious Hughes would reveal and the lies, which would be believed. In the long run, he was right. For the moment, only Hughes's enemies rejoiced. "I do not like to kick a man when he is down," wrote Colonel J.J. Creelman, an artillery officer in France, "but I am willing to break nine toes in kicking Sam." The public posturing, the political offi-cers, and, above all, the Ross rifle had ended any Hughes identity with "his boys". In time, he would find defenders. Nationalists took pride in his pug-naciousness. Canadians yearn for larger-than-life figures; victims of his bul-lying, from the prime minister to permanent-force officers, should have stood up for themselves. Their failure made them wrong. Military red tape, his pro-fessed target, remains unpopular. Hughes's reputation will live as long as mountebanks are admired. That guarantees his historical longevity.

Sir George Perley had to clean up the mess. If he had known how much there was, he later told Borden, he would never have accepted the job. Perley found chaplains fighting each other, the Army Service Corps embedded in graft, and the Veterinary Corps in a mess. Surplus officers were everywhere. In France, there were 2,526 Canadian officers for 105,640 men; in England there were 7,420 for 128,980. Thousands of the men freshly arrived from Canada were unfit for service. The nastiest legacy was a report on the Canadian Army Medical Corps by a Hughes-appointed colonel. Dr. Herbert A. Bruce, founder of Toronto's Wellesley Hospital, was already a bitter critic of the overseas Director of Medical Services, Major-General G.C. Jones, when Hughes invited him to investigate medical matters overseas. After six weeks, Bruce had seen enough to blast Jones for toadying to the British. Canadian wounded had been sent to improvised English hospitals that were nothing more than "matrimonial agencies". Canadian hospitals had been sent to the Mediterranean where there were no Canadians. Too little was done to hurry Canadian wounded back to the front or to treat VD cases with severity. Some medical officers were even "drug fiends or addicted to alcoholism". A delighted Hughes had fired Jones, put Bruce in his place, and now used the report to attack Perley, who sympathized with the much-abused Jones.

Perley's strategy was to let proven officers from France run his Overseas Ministry. General Turner reluctantly gave up his division to come to London. Byng, delighted to be rid of an inadequate commander, gave the vacancy to General Harry Burstall, a permanent-force gunner. Perley faced his first crisis when Borden, anxious to pacify Sir Sam, demanded the vacant division for Garnet. A compromise was found by giving Garnet the new 5th Division, now designated, because of the lack of men from Canada, to be held for the home defence of Britain.

Once in England, Turner rapidly solved old problems. The seventy unused CEF battalions became twenty-four reserve battalions, linked to battalions in the Corps and soon to regions and provinces in Canada. Men from the same town would serve together. To Canadianize the Corps staff, the British agreed to provide vacancies in their staff courses. Carson, MacDougall, and Steele were eased out. Sir Max Aitken — now Lord Beaverbrook as a reward for helping Lloyd George into power — continued with the Canadian War Records Office but left Perley alone. In France, Colonel Manly-Sims would manage liaison with GHQ but, symbolic of a new regime, he soon had twenty-six pages of instructions to guide him.

The medical mess, Perley found, was "the most serious and difficult of all the many troubles here". Nothing would be more devastating to home-front morale than allegations that wounded heroes had been maltreated or neglected. At the same time, Bruce's exaggerated allegations so enraged the great Canadian physician Sir William Osler that he quit the game in disgust.

Just as furious and closer at hand were prominent ladies, from the Duchess of Connaught to Lady Perley herself, whom Bruce had impugned for their charity work in the hospitals. Perley promptly arranged for a report by Sir William Babtie, a prominent British army surgeon. When it criticized Bruce's snap judgements, General Jones was briefly restored and the senior medical officer with the Corps, Major-General G.L. Foster, was summoned as a permanent replacement. Bruce's fury would echo for a generation and at least some of his complaints were justified, but the Canadian Army Medical Corps was restored to relative calm.

Canadians had little idea why the OMFC was created. The government had no wish to advertise the mess. Front-line soldiers have a legendary contempt for the "bomb-proof" jobs at base, and Argyll House, the OMFC's London headquarters, soon became a soldier's shorthand for the insulated arrogance of a remote staff. The government, too, cautiously avoided publicizing the change of status that the Overseas Ministry represented. By reaching across the Atlantic to establish a department to control Canadian troops in England and on the continent, Ottawa had softly but firmly asserted that Canadians were no longer "part of the Imperial army in every sense of the word". "The Canadian Force," Perley explained to the War Office, "is an entity irrespective of where parts of it may be situated or serving...." It had not been so in 1914; it would be so in 1917.

Vimy Ridge

The Canadian Corps that emerged from the winter of 1917 was different. On their shoulders men now wore "Somme Patches", big flannel rectangles in red, blue, grey, and green for the 1st, 2nd, 3rd, and 4th divisions, with other patches to distinguish infantry battalions. The voices were different too: the Old Originals and the Second Contingent, with their British accents, had been swept away at the Somme; flatter Canadian accents now dominated. Most battalions had been rebuilt; a few from Quebec and British Columbia showed the impact of Canada's recruiting crisis. When Colonel Tremblay returned to the 22nd Battalion from five months in hospital, such was the state of discipline because of unsuitable men from the depots that he felt obliged to approve three death sentences. Manitoba and British Columbia battalions, too short of replacements, were transferred to Ontario or New Brunswick where recruits were still adequate in number.

The bitter winter weather had brought frozen hands and feet. Veterans remember hot food freezing in their mess tins. Soldiers showed unusual enthusiasm for kitchen fatigues, with their shared warmth. But men who

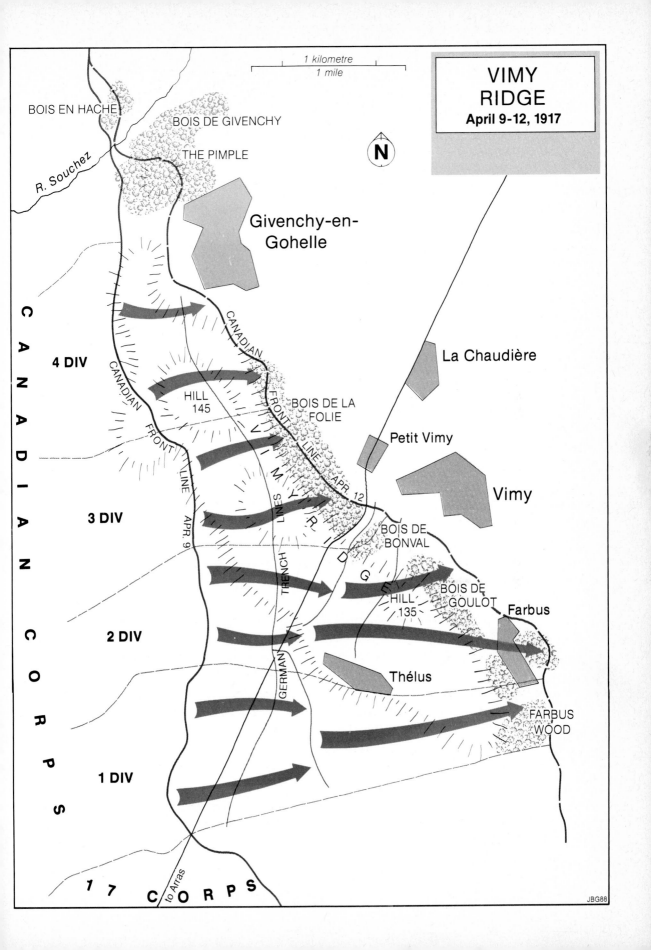

BOIS EN HACHE

BOIS DE GIVENCHY

THE PIMPLE

R. Souchez

Givenchy-en-Gohelle

N

VIMY RIDGE
April 9-12, 1917

1 kilometre
1 mile

4 DIV

CANADIAN

CANADIAN FRONT LINE

HILL 145

CANADIAN FRONT LINE APR. 9

BOIS DE LA FOLIE

FRONT LINE APR. 12

V I M Y   R I D G E

La Chaudière

Petit Vimy

Vimy

3 DIV

TRENCH

GERMAN LINE

BOIS DE BONVAL

HILL 135

BOIS DE GOULOT

Farbus

2 DIV

Thélus

FARBUS WOOD

1 DIV

to Arras

1 7   C O R P S

C A N A D I A N   C O R P S

JBG88

remembered Flanders in 1915–16 rejoiced in the dry, well-drained trenches and the dug-outs the French had left them. Vimy had been a quiet sector, dominated by a German-held ridge, running four miles north-west from Farbus Wood to the west of Givenchy-en-Gohelle, with an added hill in the Bois de Givenchy that soldiers christened "The Pimple". To the west, Canadians faced a gentle slope rising to two heights at opposite ends of the ridge, Hill 135 and Hill 145; to the east, the slope fell steeply, into thick woods. At 450 feet above sea level, Vimy Ridge would have been unremarkable elsewhere, but in flat country it dominated the landscape.

Twice in 1915, the ridge's German defenders had thrown back Foch's best troops; they had learned from the experience, creating a dense network of trenches, tunnels, concrete emplacements, wire, and dug-outs. One was so big it could hold a battalion. The German forward defences included three successive lines, and a second zone behind the crest was just as strong. Hills, farmsteads, and a couple of villages had been turned into small fortresses. Guns and mortars were hidden in the woods behind the ridge. Three divisions from General Freiherr von Falkenhausen's Sixth Army, two Bavarian and one Prussian, shared in defending Vimy Ridge, and they knew it was vital ground.

In February, British pressure on the Somme and Nivelle's approaching offensive convinced von Ludendorff that it was time for Operation "Alberich": a retreat to the Hindenburg Line after such systematic devastation of the intervening 2,000 square miles of France that the enemy could not pursue. After four days, March 15 to 18, the operation was complete. Not until April 5 could the Allies establish their new lines. The Somme salient, a key to Nivelle's plan, was gone. French politicians and generals invited him to reconsider his offensive. He threatened to resign. They gave way. The Germans had not abandoned his objective on the Chemin des Dames Ridge nor the objectives he had assigned to Haig: Arras and Vimy Ridge.

From November, General Byng had known that his Corps would be attacking Vimy though it was only on January 19 that he knew that the Canadians would have to do the job alone. If they failed, the British Third Army attack along the Scarpe River from Arras would be in serious danger. In six months Byng and his men had seen a lot, and they liked each other. "This is a soldier," wrote Andrew Macphail, now a medical officer, "large, strong, lithe, with worn boots and frayed puttees. He carries his hand in his pocket and returns a salute by lifting his hand as far as the pocket will allow." Canadians liked that.

Byng was slack about salutes but not about preparations. Since Nivelle seemed to have discovered the secret of attacks, he sent Arthur Currie to Verdun to find out. Currie came back skeptical of some French theories but with some important new ideas. Instead of attacking in line and in waves, as the British had insisted in 1916, assaulting troops should move as fast as they could, fighting their way forward in platoons, tackling resistance from the flank or in the rear. Maps and air photos belonged with front-line troops, not just with the staff. Remembering Regina Trench, Currie insisted that objectives should be obvious natural features men could easily find, not a map reference or a trench that might be obliterated or confused. And, above all, attacking units should be rested, fed, and happy. Other units should do the dirty work always assigned to the PBI — the "poor bloody infantry".

Perhaps the strongest image of the First World War is of bull-headed generals ordering their men into hopeless attacks. The memory of a generation was scarred by the sixty thousand dead and wounded on the first day at the Somme. Yet soldiers did manage to overcome barbed wire, machine guns, and artillery barrages — because generals and staff officers searched feverishly for weapons and tactics that could break the trench stalemate. Most of the devices offered by eager inventors were rubbish. Even the famous tank deserved most of the skepticism it collected from colonels and privates alike; it would not have survived without Haig's willingness to divert men and resources to the new arm. But artillery tactics were transformed by science and ingenuity, and the most dramatic changes have been the least understood. By 1917, when the Canadians attacked Vimy, troops fought in "platoons" of thirty or forty men. Specialist sections in the platoon carried a Lewis gun for firepower, bombs, and "rifle grenades". A Mills bomb on the end of a stick turned a soldier's rifle into a personal artillery piece to knock out a German pillbox or machine-gun post. At a horrifying cost, platoons of infantry could fight their way forward until they ran out of bullets and bombs. When victory eventually came, it was because soldiers — French and British as much as Canadian — learned, experimented, and learned again.

Byng had made other preparations as well. For three winter months, engineers and pioneer battalions — filled with men unfit for front-line service — built and repaired roads, laid twenty miles of light-railway track, buried twenty-one miles of signal cable, and laid sixty-six miles of telephone wire. Signal wires were "laddered" — separate lines with connecting links so that a single shell could no longer snap communications. Tunnelling companies burrowed eleven underground galleries to help infantry get to assault positions safely, wired them for lights, and added chambers for headquarters, dressing stations, and supplies. Just to water the fifty thousand horses needed to haul supplies and guns required forty-five miles of pipeline.

The key to success, Byng insisted, would be artillery. The Corps could count on 480 18-pounders, 245 howitzers and heavy guns, and 42,500 tons of shells, with new fuses that ensured that, this time, German wire could be cut. A young engineering professor from McGill, Lieutenant-Colonel Andrew McNaughton, had borrowed counter-battery techniques from the French and British and improved on them. Three groups of heavy guns, a squadron from the Royal Flying Corps under Major Charles Portal, and an elaborate network of spotters detected 83 per cent of the guns behind Vimy Ridge and targeted them for destruction.

Sir Edmund Allenby of the neighbouring Third Army had wanted two days of bombardment; Byng insisted on two weeks, doubling the rate of fire in the second week. German survivors, pinned in their dug-outs and starving because ration parties could not reach them, remembered it as "the week of suffering". At dusk on April 8, firing slowed. Germans emerged and then relaxed. Nothing happened. Far below them, gunners piled shells and fixed fuses for the next day. Infantry battalions, which had practised for days on a vast replica of the Ridge, filed past for the real thing. In assembly areas, men stopped for a hot meal and a tot of rum. It was bitterly cold.

In the black pre-dawn, men crawled from the forward trenches and waited on the frozen mud. At 5:30 A.M., April 9, Easter Monday, as a sudden storm of sleet and snow gusted from the west, almost a thousand guns opened fire. "Imagine the loudest clap of thunder you ever heard," Lieutenant E.L.M. Burns recalled, "multiplied by two and prolonged indefinitely." Sixteen battalions, eight thousand men, rose to move forward across cratered, debris-strewn ground. All four Canadian divisions advanced in line, from the 1st, opposite Thélus, to the 4th, facing Hill 145 and Givenchy.

Dazed Germans defenders emerged to face sleet and snow. Few of their own guns survived to support them. In the first couple of lines, only sentries and a few men stumbled out to offer resistance. Canadian assault troops hurried forward behind the barrage, visible now in the grey dawn with its white puffs of shrapnel and the oily black eruptions of high-explosive. Follow-up waves bombed German dug-outs or took the occupants prisoner. The third line was different. German machine-gunners sliced into advancing Canadians. Strong points had survived the awful barrage. Depleted platoons tried their new tactics. When officers and sergeants were gone, corporals and privates took over. Weary survivors struggled on to the next murderous battle.

At 7:00 A.M., the 1st Division was the first on its primary objective. The 3rd reported reaching the crest at 7:30 and the 2nd, with much heavier fighting, took another half-hour. For a few hours the attackers paused while supporting brigades moved up for the final phase. Currie's division was responsible for Farbus Wood; Lipsett's 3rd, with an attached British brigade to help, moved down the far slope to the woods below. Two battalions of the 2nd Division swarmed down the ridge with bayonets fixed to take 150 prisoners, including a German colonel. Captain Thain MacDowell of the 28th personally took two machine guns and, by bluff, persuaded 77 Prussian Guards to give up. The handsome university athlete won one of the four VCs earned that day. Of the four winners, he alone survived the war.

On the left, the 4th Division had some of the toughest objectives, made all the harder because two of its battalions had been almost destroyed in a disastrous trench raid on March 1. Watson's division faced Hill 145, the highest point of the ridge and the best defended. To help him, the colonel of the 87th asked the artillery to leave one German trench intact as cover for his men. Instead, the Canadians found it full of hard-fighting Germans. As the Canadian attack faltered, Germans to the rear had time to emerge. Survivors of the 102nd Battalion from northern B.C. got to Hill 145 and held on, but that meant that guns could not blast Germans without killing Canadians too. Watson had intended his reserve brigade to take The Pimple. It was sucked into the battle for Hill 145. It was after dark when a raw Nova Scotia battalion, the 85th, brought into the battle as a labour force, went up and took the German defences. The few Canadians who struggled as far as Givenchy were overwhelmed. For the moment, Watson could do no more.

By April 12, the Germans had pulled their line well back on the Douai Plain but they had thrown the Prussian Guard Grenadiers into the defences of Givenchy and The Pimple. Watson had given the objective to Brigadier-General Edward Hilliam, an Alberta rancher who had once been a British sergeant-major. With eighteen artillery batteries in support and driving snow and sleet behind him, the westerners of Hilliam's 10th Brigade attacked at 5:00 A.M. An hour later, though half of them were killed or wounded, the Canadians had won. Hilliam signed his report "Lord Pimple".

Vimy was a triumph: "Canada's Easter gift to France", wrote a Paris newspaper, with the ineffable assumption that the French were entitled to it. The King sent Haig his congratulations. Canadians then and later knew that they had done a great thing and that on such deeds nations are built. A victory so quick might also seem easy. At most, 40,000 Canadians shared the naked vulnerability of the infantry on April 9 and the days that followed. Almost all the Canadian losses — 3,598 killed, 7,004 wounded — came from that number. Most of the wounded would survive and many would return to their battalions but almost one in ten of those who fought at Vimy would live only as a name engraved on the soaring memorial that now stands atop Hill 145.

MILITARY SERVICE ACT

When the Canadian Corps scored its Easter Monday triumph, Sir Robert

Borden was in London, a hundred and fifty miles away. It was not by accident. Early in January, Lloyd George had announced to advisers that it was time to summon the Dominion premiers. "We want more men from them," he explained. "We can hardly ask them to make another great recruiting effort unless it is accompanied by an invitation to come over and discuss the situation with us."

The summons to discuss "great matters" at an Imperial War Conference was what Borden had wanted since 1915. The Canadian Parliament was summoned and adjourned within a month to free the prime minister for his historic journey. In London, ministers and lesser lights busied themselves with the conference while premiers and key advisers were closeted with Lloyd George in an Imperial War Cabinet. "When they are here," Bonar Law had warned his new chief, "you will wish to goodness you could get rid of them." Doubtless it was true when Borden, South Africa's Jan Smuts, and New Zealand's W.F. Massey led discussion into the future shape of the "Imperial Commonwealth" or the need for "an adequate voice" in foreign policy. Chiefly, though, the premiers learned of matters they had not read about in newspapers: the disastrous U-boat campaign, the collapse of Russia, the exhaustion of French and British manpower and, when the United States entered the war on April 6, the certain delay in American mobilization.

The message was clear: even if Russia recovered and the United States someday delivered vast armies, the brunt of fighting now fell on the Empire. To weaken was to lose. A prime minister who had preached earnestness needed no persuading. Tireless visits to Canadian wounded steeled Borden's heart: he saw men who would be sent again and again to battle until they were dead or too maimed to be used. Easter Monday and the news of Vimy Ridge brought reflected glory. Borden hurried to France to review the troops in pelting snow, to see the devastated field and to talk to officers. To keep the Corps up to strength required 75,000 men a year; there were 10,000 in England and 18,000 in Canada. Fewer than 5,000 had joined the CEF in March and almost none had chosen the infantry. In England, Lloyd George had asked him to match the five Australian divisions in France. That was impossible but, without men, could Canada even keep four divisions? When Borden returned across the U-boat–infested Atlantic in early May, his slow, systematic mind was made up.

No news in Canada would change it. National registration had failed. So had a last valiant effort by Pierre Blondin, the postmaster general, to raise a Quebec battalion. So had the attempt to raise a special home-defence force to release thousands of CEF men for the front. The efforts of Major-General Syd-

Cavalry and Tanks Advance at Arras, Alfred Bastien. Both the new and the old means of battlefield mobility proved vulnerable. The artist, a Belgian who served as a cyclist before being seconded to the CWRO, portrays an advance near the end of the war. (NWM 8092)

The Conquerors, Eric Kennington. This popular allegorical painting of a Canadian Highland battalion suggests that the war-weary English artist was struck by the CEF's ethnic diversity, as well as its vigour. (NWM 8968)

German Prisoners, F.H. Varley. The prisoners make their way along a muddy, water-logged track overshadowed by trunks of shattered trees. More than most Canadian war artists, Varley anticipated the angry disillusionment that would be the dominant intellectual response to the war. (NWM 8961)

The Red Air Fighter, J.A. Turnbull. Defiantly abstract in composition, this painting of a Fokker triplane evokes a pilot's perspective of a dogfight, with ground and sky inverted and bewilderment a constant. The most renowned red Fokker of the war was, of course, that of the "Red Baron", Captain Manfred von Richthofen. (NWM 8905)

Coming Home, Armour Heights, Franz Johnston. A Curtiss Jenny lands
at dusk in north Toronto. Johnston, who was commissioned to record
the work of Canadian flying personnel training for overseas service,
was among the founders of the Group of Seven, but dropped out almost
immediately. (NWM 8268)

"If ye break faith —
we shall not sleep"

BUY VICTORY BONDS

"Well, If you knows of a better 'ole, Go to it."

Above Dr. John McCrae's poem "In Flander Fields", sometimes cited as a prayer for peace, was in fact intended to mobilize public support for the war effort; the Victory Bond campaign was only one of many applications of his words. McCrae himself died of pneumonia in 1918. (NWM 56-05-11-022)

Left Bruce Bairnsfather's best-known cartoon added an expression to the language. "Old Bill" was a type who was as much a backbone of CEF battalions as of British units. Bairnsfather reused the phrase as the title of his 1916 play. He later lost his money trying to make war movies in Canada, in the 1920s. (Collection of D. Morton) ney Mewburn, aided in Quebec by Colonel Armand Lavergne, produced 200 men for a force intended to be 50,000 strong.

For months, even years, some Canadians had cried out for conscription: the Liberal lawyer J.M. Godfrey, the blind Boer War hero Colonel Lorne Mulloy, Manitoba's chief justice T.G. Mathers, a host of clergy, and the IODE. Clarendon Worrell, the Anglican archbishop of Nova Scotia, summed up their common argument: "Why men of infinite value to the community should be called upon to sacrifice themselves in order that a number of worthless and non-producing creatures may go on in their animal enjoyment is beyond comprehension."

Those were not Borden's arguments when he spoke to the Cabinet on May 17 or to the House of Commons on May 18. Nor was his argument based on Empire or on Britain's need. "I conceive that the battle for Canadian liberty and autonomy is being fought today on the plains of France and Belgium." The Canadian Corps had become "a new revelation of Canadian patriotism"; conscription was needed to fill its ranks and to keep faith with its members. "If what are left of 400,000 such men come back to Canada with fierce resentment in their hearts, conscious that they have been deserted and betrayed," he demanded, "how shall we meet them when they ask the reason?"

Liberals had answers. Conscription, they insisted, was being used as a popular issue to attract votes. Borden was trying to distract Canadians from the plight of the bankrupt railways. Anti-recruiting riots in Montreal on May 24 were another answer. A day later, Borden invited Laurier into a coalition of equals; he would vacate the prime-ministership if it helped. He would even defer conscription. On June 6, Laurier said no. He should have been consulted before Borden spoke on conscription, not after. It was now too late. If he joined, he would hand his province to Henri Bourassa and the *nationalistes*.

Laurier had other motives he could not share with Borden. A Liberal victory seemed imminent that spring. Conscription might not be so popular. Australia, more British by far than Canada, had rejected it in 1916 and would do so again. Farmers and trade unionists would oppose conscription, if more discreetly than had the Québécois. Borden knew the arguments, too, and he had no illusions of easy victory. On the goal he was clear; on the means he would be flexible and very patient.

Chief of the means was a Military Service Bill, drafted by Arthur Meighen, the coldly eloquent solicitor general, and modelled on the new U.S. selective-service law. Critics could note that young bachelors would be selected first, that there were exemptions for religious objectors, and that three layers of

appeal had been included, from two-member local tribunals nominated by
the opposing political parties to a Supreme Court justice. On June 11, the
long, bitter debate began. "Do not tell me this is Canada's war," cried David-
Arthur Lafortune, a Quebec Liberal. "Canada did not make war on anybody."
Laurier, seeking above all to hold his party together, argued for a referendum. Even some Liberals dismissed the idea of delay. Conscription, Laurier
declared, drove a wedge through the unit of Canada; it was "an obstacle and
a bar to that union of heart and soul" on which Confederation was based. The
listeners grew tired. Minds were made up. On July 6 the House voted. Nine
Quebec Conservatives joined Laurier; twenty-five Liberals deserted him. One
of them, the devoutly partisan Frank Carvell, had confessed to a friend:
"There is something within me which abhors the idea of throwing up my
hands when others are fighting my battles." He had to go home and think. He
switched. The Senate took longer, but on August 29, conscription was law. The
wedge had been driven. In a New York paper at the end of August, a future
prime minister, W.L. Mackenzie King, reassured Americans: "it is perhaps
not surprising that the rest of Canada sees in the Quebec attitude nothing but
disloyalty, and is more determined than ever to make certain that Quebec
shall not prevent the Dominion from doing its entire and splendid duty to the
men at the front."

HAIG'S OFFENSIVE

The Canadian triumph at Vimy Ridge on April 9 was the overture to Nivelle's
victorious strategy. Nivelle's ideas had contributed to the success: the massive bombardment, the care in destroying the German artillery, the flood of
troops in the first wave. Fortunately the Canadians had not believed everything the French general preached: they had not raced on beyond the range of
their artillery and they had discovered for themselves the weary, deadly business of dragging their guns, ammunition, and supplies across the cratered
morass that any heavy bombardment left.

On the same day, General Sir Edmund Allenby's Third Army had driven
south and west along the axis of the Scarpe River with almost comparable
success: in a week the British had captured 13,000 prisoners and 200 guns.
That was the help the British had promised. The rest was up to Nivelle — and
the Germans.

Nivelle's tactical brilliance was an article of faith, at least among the war-
weary junior officers and men of the French army. His strategic vision was
almost as persuasive, at least to politicians who wanted to believe. The Germans occupied a deep salient stretching to the Somme. For six months, the

British and French armies had drawn German divisions in and destroyed them. Now, from Arras in the north and Champagne in the south, the Allied armies would strike with irresistible force, bursting the salient like a bubble. The trouble was that von Ludendorff in March had neatly pulled his troops back into his *Siegfried-Stellung*, creating a wasteland barrier to any heavy attack and saving himself thirteen divisions, which he promptly moved south. After all, anyone with a Paris newspaper knew when Nivelle's offensive was coming and a trench raid had even given the Germans a copy of the plan.

The Germans also had a new defensive strategy that topography and local stubbornness had not revealed at Vimy. German commanders thinned out their front lines, leaving them to be pulverized by the enemy's guns. The attackers were then channelled onto the "killing grounds" Germans themselves chose, to be slaughtered by concentrated fire from artillery and machine guns. Then German counter-attacks recovered lost ground.

On April 16, behind the fire of five thousand French guns, Nivelle's men found out for themselves how the new strategy worked. With the courage and conviction of men who believed in victory, the French rushed forward into a massacre. German guns knocked out the new French tanks. German fighters concentrated overhead to drive the French planes from the skies. By nightfall, the gains of the first day were lost. Nivelle poured in more divisions. French army medical services, told to prepare for ten thousand wounded, planned for fifteen thousand and got ninety thousand. In ten days, the French had gained four miles. On April 28, Nivelle was fired. The hard-headed hero of Verdun, General Henri-Philippe Pétain, replaced him.

Next day, an exhausted battalion, reduced to a third of its strength, refused to go back to the attack. On April 30, the ringleaders were shot and the remnant obeyed orders. On May 3, a whole division refused orders despite appeals and promises. Mutinies spread. Soldiers elected committees, raised the red flag, and sang the Internationale. Staff officers, the *buveurs de sang*, made themselves scarce. By June, most of the French army had been affected. Pétain moved efficiently to end the crisis. He corrected grievances about food, leave, and quarters. Discipline returned. Courts martial convicted 23,385 mutineers, and sentenced 412 to death. Pétain ordered 55 mutineers shot and sent hundreds more to penal colonies. There was no softness but there was understanding. The French army would defend France and the most mutinous regiments proved it in the line but soldiers would no longer be sent like sheep to slaughter.

The British army was not so lucky. Throughout April, Allenby continued the drive up the Scarpe against ever-tougher resistance. Sir Henry Horne, with the Canadians as part of his First Army, joined in. On April 28, Currie's division captured the Arleux loop of trenches south-west of Vimy. Nivelle's plight forced the British on. On May 3, Allenby's army failed almost everywhere along its line of attack. Currie's men alone made gains, taking Fresnoy: "The relieving feature," commented the British official history, "of a day which many who witnessed it considered the blackest of the War." By May 8, when the British called off their struggle, Fresnoy had fallen to a counter-attack and the Scarpe battles had cost the British 158,660 casualties, far more than the official total of 137,000 French losses in Nivelle's attack on the Chemin des Dames.

Haig would have stopped the Scarpe battles sooner. Loyalty to Nivelle and Lloyd George's commitment of the British army to the common cause kept the losses mounting. Since 1916 and perhaps earlier, Haig had believed that Flanders was the right place for the British to fight. Ten miles beyond Ypres, at Roulers, he could cut the rail junction the Germans needed to supply their northern front. At Zeebrugge and Ostend, Admiral Jellicoe erroneously believed, were the submarines that were strangling England. Each Allied disaster, from Salonika to the French mutinies, was a fresh argument for action. In Russia, with brave folly, Alexander Kerensky had pushed Russia's army into a new offensive which, for a few days, succeeded and then failed more disastrously than any. Entire Russian divisions shot their officers and dissolved. In Italy, a tenth Isonzo offensive failed as tragically as all the others. Even the British suffered set-backs, in Palestine, where two battles at Gaza in March and April were so disastrous that General Allenby was sent to rescue the situation.

Haig's arguments for his offensive were defective. In early May, French and British generals had met at Paris and agreed that victory was impossible in 1917. When the French army crumbled, Pétain wanted his ally to take over more trenches, not to waste men. Even General Foch, passionate defender of the offensive almost anywhere, insisted that Flanders was not the place. Who, he demanded of Sir Henry Wilson, now the chief British liaison officer in Paris, was sending Haig on "a duck's march through the inundations to Ostend and Zeebrugge"? If it was Jellicoe, he was wrong: there were few German submarines on the Belgian coast. It was certainly not Lloyd George, yet the British prime minister was not protesting, either. He had been so wrong about Nivelle that his judgement was shaken. The prime minister had promised Britain a victory and Haig was eager to fight for it.

Even more, Haig delivered a triumph. On June 7, the roar of nineteen huge explosions under the Messines Ridge rattled windows in London. After almost three weeks of bombardment, British and Australian troops of Sir Herbert Plumer's Second Army swarmed up the ridge. There were more days of the inevitable shelling and counter-attacks but the Messines-Wytschaete ridge Canadians had known in 1915–16 was taken. For the first time, the casualty toll favoured the British: 17,000 to 25,000 Germans.

If Haig had wanted to fight in Flanders, the shattering victory at Messines should have been followed up. Instead, fighting stopped for a month. He needed to persuade Lloyd George again, at meeting after meeting. He had also promised his protégé, Sir Herbert Gough, that he would command the attack and it took weeks to move the Fifth Army headquarters north and to prepare plans while, on the spot, Plumer's headquarters waited in frustration. It was time the Germans did not waste; they tunnelled and dug and built yet more concrete pillboxes to hold the low ridges in front of Ypres.

On July 31, Haig's offensive began. For fifteen days, shells had pounded the earth to dust. As Gough's troops waited to attack, a gentle rain turned to a drenching downpour. For four days, before it literally bogged down in a sea of mud, the Fifth Army moved 3,000 yards at a cost of 31,850 casualties. Even the direction was wrong. Haig had wanted to move towards high ground; instead Gough had chosen to push north, and his commander had not interfered. The attacks resumed in a week as the rain kept bucketing down. Years of shelling had destroyed any natural drainage system. Roads, trees, buildings, all had been demolished, leaving a sea of mud marked chiefly by occasional ruins, derelict tanks and guns, and bottomless lakes over mine craters and shell craters. By the end of August, the British had lost 68,000 men to regain St. Julien and part of Pilckem Ridge.

At the end of August, Lloyd George might have called a halt; Haig probably should have. It was not in him to do so. There was no more talk of Ostend or Zeebrugge but there was insistence on a German army worn down at the Somme and now reduced to exhaustion. The French, too, must be spared, though a French diversionary attack at Verdun in August not only took 10,000 prisoners but showed the benefit of Pétain's nursing. Lloyd George came, saw what Haig's GHQ showed him — carefully selected, weedy-looking German prisoners — and returned to London.

There was an added reason for Haig's confidence. In September, the rain stopped, the ground dried, and Plumer, the best of Haig's generals, took over the attack. On the 20th, the attack began. A day's rain made no difference. As usual, Plumer's staff had watched the details. Tactically, the battle was as perfect as any in the war. Rolling barrages were timed to stay with soldiers floundering in mud. Infantry headed for fixed, visible objectives. Aircraft overhead kept in touch with movements. On September 20, the British had reached Menin Road; on the 26th, Polygon Wood; and Broodseinde, on October 4. The onslaught, von Ludendorff wrote, "proved the superiority of the attack over the defence". Australians, leading Plumer's advance, reported seeing German guns being dragged away. Beyond "were green fields and pastures, things of course we had never seen in the Ypres sector".

Then, on October 4, the rains returned, driving, drenching torrents that restored the churned soil to an endless sea of stinking mud, spotted with the bodies of horses, men, and all the detritus of war. Wounded drowned in it. When eight or a dozen stretcher-bearers were needed to move a single casualty, too few reached hospitals. For the first time, Germans found British soldiers eager to surrender and talking of killing their officers. The optimism went out of the British army, wrote Philip Gibbs, the former "Eyewitness". The generals and their apologists could explain Passchendaele as a series of climatic misfortunes. Posterity preferred Siegfried Sassoon:

> I died in hell —
> (They called it Passchendaele); my wound was slight
> And I was hobbling back, and then a shell
> Burst slick upon the duck-board; so I fell
> Into the bottomless mud, and lost the light.

Though you might not guess it from the signs, this is an anti-conscription procession in Montreal in 1917. Before television, crowds felt less need to placard themselves for the viewing audience.

Soldiers of the 22nd Battalion perform a soldier's commonest task: waiting. One man scans the skies, presumably for aircraft — a particular pest during operations at Passchendaele. Until the MSA, battalions like the 22nd had a difficult task in finding suitable replacements.

Canadians on the march in December 1917. In the absence of conscription, their professional fatalism took on a hard edge: even if they were wounded, they would still be sent back to the front again and again until army doctors agreed that they were too badly mutilated to be cannon fodder any longer.

Soldiering in wet weather. While the men spent as little as a sixth of their time in the trenches, most of them lived without much protection from the weather throughout their time in France. Here, a soldier ties down the flaps of a tent under a cold winter rain.

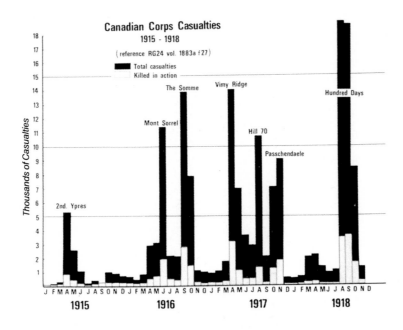

Canadian casualties occurred continuously but they soared to peaks during major battles, particularly in 1917. There was a relative lull during the first half of 1918, but the heaviest losses of the war came during the "Last Hundred Days".

A Canadian infantry company on the march. Soldiers carry their gas masks in the "ready" position. One man carries a Lewis gun, another a folded stretcher. On average, an infantry soldier carried 70–90 lbs. of kit, equipment, arms, and ammunition.

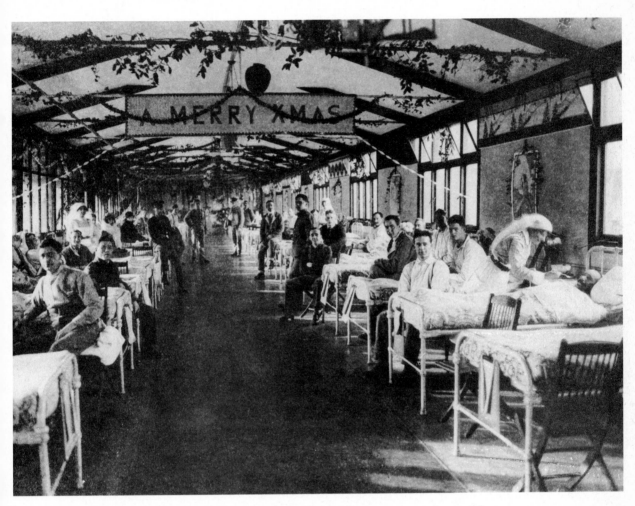

A Canadian hospital ward in France. Soldiers with serious wounds or sickness were evacuated to base hospitals. Without antibiotics, recovery could be a very slow process, but hospital death rates in the two world wars were surprisingly similar. One reason was that soldiers in the Great War were usually much closer to professional medical care.

Soldiers in the second or third wave advance on Vimy Ridge under puffs of German shellfire. Men carry duckboards, extra ammunition, and tools, as well as their own arms and equipment. Humans were the only dependable means of carrying supplies across the ruined expanse of captured ground.

A camp cooker heats the stew while its attendants wait for "cookhouse" to be called. In the line, battalion kitchens were moved up as far as safety permitted and ration parties carried big, insulated containers of soup or stew forward. This cooker belongs to a 2nd Division battalion, as the C-II device indicates.

Drivers on mules haul a supply train up a light railway to the front. The stable front allowed an extensive network of railways to be built, the secret behind the huge bombardments of the later years of the war.

Led by a tank, Canadian infantry advance towards Vimy Ridge. While this gives a useful impression of troops and ground, the neatly placed corpse and the tank suggest a posed photo. A little experience persuaded infantry to keep their distance from tanks because they attracted too much enemy fire.

A road near Lens. Notice the flat landscape and the dominance of a hill on the horizon. The shape of the land became a critical factor when all vehicles were reduced to the pace of a tired horse.

Sir Robert Borden and Sir Arthur Currie take the salute as infantry of the 4th Canadian Division march past along a dusty French road. Neither leader was much liked by the rank and file but both risked their careers for the sake of their fighting men.

VII
KILLING GROUNDS

LENS AND HILL 70

On June 6, 1917, a newly knighted Sir Arthur Currie was summoned to Corps headquarters and a week of rumours ended. Byng would replace Allenby in command of the Third Army and Currie would replace Byng. It all made sense. Vimy had proved Byng's competence. From Ypres to the recent vicious struggles at Arleux and Fresnoy, Currie had clearly emerged as the best of the Canadian generals. He was cool, innovative, with an instinctive eye for ground and tactics. A big, flabby real-estate promoter could also be a great field commander. Before Vimy, Currie and Byng had clashed angrily over trench raids, with the Canadian refusing to sacrifice his best officers and men. Currie remembered Byng circling him "like a cooper round a barrel", while he patiently explained why raiding hurt his troops, not the Germans. Currie had been right: his 1st Division, its battalions intact, had taken its objectives while the 4th Division, decimated by the raiding policy, had stumbled badly.

No set of Canadian appointments could be simple. Haig and Byng had forgotten that Perley now decided CEF promotions. In December, Turner had been promised the Corps if he went to London. On June 8 Colonel Manly-Sims arrived: "apparently wanted to suggest a dicker," Currie noted. It was not for Turner: promotion to lieutenant-general and status as senior Canadian soldier overseas sufficed for him. It was Sir Robert Borden who wanted to dicker: Currie must send a strong statement on conscription and he must give Garnet Hughes the vacant division to quiet old Sir Sam. The statement was easy but Garnet was unacceptable. Currie had already chosen Brigadier-General Archie Macdonell, a tough NWMP and cavalry veteran his men called "Batty Mac". In London, Currie and Hughes squared off in a three-hour shouting match. "I'll get even with you before I'm finished with you," Garnet finally shouted.

160

Perhaps he could. Back in August 1914, while Garnet had promoted Currie's virtues to his father, Currie had been busy paying off the worst of his business debts with a big government cheque intended to pay for his regiment's uniforms. For three years, Currie had hoped that his guilty secret was buried; meanwhile the regiment's creditors patiently tracked down their quarry. In June 1917, they succeeded. Just as Canadians learned that one of their own now commanded the Corps, the government got evidence that its new general was a thief. While Perley and A.E. Kemp, Hughes's successor as Minister of Militia, argued about what to do, Currie borrowed the missing money from Watson and General Odlum and paid back his old regiment. Whether or not the Hughes family knew Currie's secret, it could no longer blackmail Currie without implicating Sir Sam.

With a mind burdened by such problems, Currie returned to his new command and the war. His task, under Sir Henry Horne's First Army, was to hold German divisions that might otherwise stop Haig's Flanders offensive. From the first, Currie insisted on doing the job his way. Haig had ordered that attackers must hold any ground they took. To Currie, that meant exposing troops to needless casualties. His Canadians would raid, destroy, and return to their trenches before the Germans could catch them. In a series of carefully planned sorties, Currie showed how to hit without getting badly hurt. On June 8 and 9, brigades from the 3rd and 4th divisions drove deep into the German line south of Lens. The cost was 709 casualties, 100 killed, but the efforts paid off. Two weeks later, the Germans pulled back to Avion, well aware that their position was now hopelessly weakened.

What the British really wanted was Lens itself, a ruined coal-mining town that had defied them since the Battle of Loos in 1915. On July 7, Currie got his orders. On July 10, the Canadian replaced a British Corps in trenches that looked across at Lens and at the two hills, Sallaumines and Hill 70, that flanked it. Currie went out and climbed a hill behind the Canadian lines, the Bois de l'Hirondelle, and lay there for a morning, examining the ground. What he saw made him think. The Canadian troops could fight their way through the rubble of Lens but they and their supporting guns would be on low ground, easily commanded by Germans on the two hills. The smart answer was to seize one of the two hills, preferably Hill 70 to the north, and let the Germans waste their men trying to take it back. Corps commanders were supposed to obey orders, not change them, but Currie was different. To Horne, he explained his concerns: "if we were to fight at all," he insisted, "let us fight for something worth having." Haig was summoned, predicted that the Germans would not let the Canadians have the hill, and approved — provided the attack was under way by August 4.

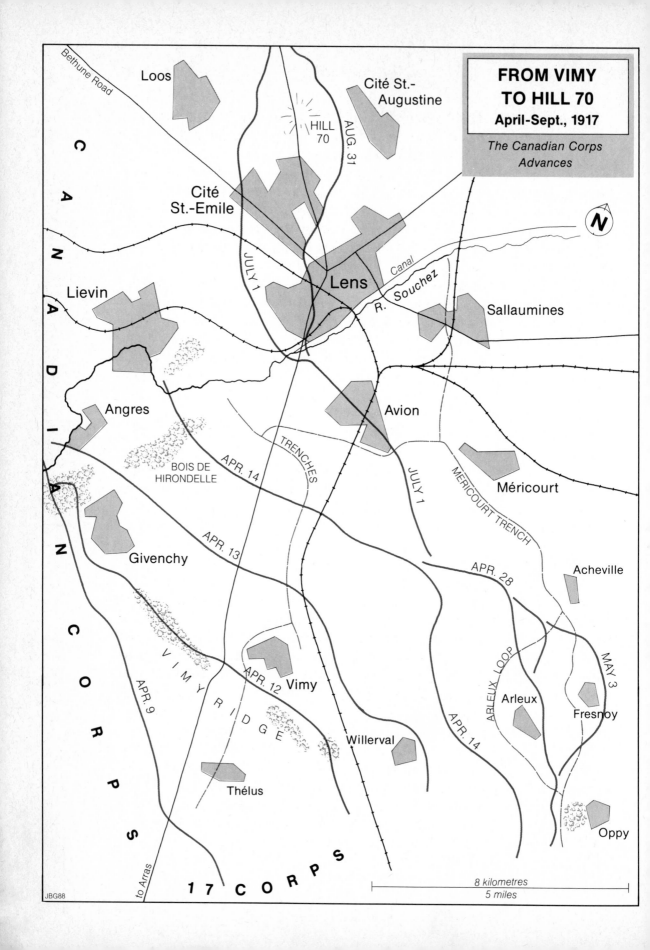

FROM VIMY
TO HILL 70
April–Sept., 1917

*The Canadian Corps
Advances*

Bethune Road

Loos

Cité St.-
Augustine

HILL
70

AUG. 31

Cité
St.-Emile

C
A
N
A
D
I
A
N

Lens

Canal

R. Souchez

Sallaumines

Lievin

N

Angres

A
D
I
A
N

BOIS DE
HIRONDELLE

APR. 14

TRENCHES

Avion

JULY 1

JULY 1

MÉRICOURT TRENCH

Méricourt

Acheville

APR. 13

APR. 28

Givenchy

C
O
R
P
S

VIMY RIDGE

APR. 12

APR. 9

Vimy

ARLEUX LOOP

Arleux

MAY 3

Fresnoy

APR. 14

Willerval

Thélus

Oppy

to Arras

17 C O R P S

8 kilometres
5 miles

JBG88

N

Haig had a point. Hill 70 was a bald knob of limestone the British had taken and lost in 1915. Clumps of miners' cottages on the slopes of the hill had given the Germans a perfect covered approach for their counter-attacks. The shell-battered ruins, with a maze of cellars, trenches, and tunnels, would now be even better cover. Currie had an answer. His new machine-gun companies would follow the assault waves, dig into the hard chalk surface, and wait for the counter-attacks. His artillery, better and heavier than anything the British had had in 1915, would be waiting for the Germans in a killing ground of his choosing, not theirs.

Currie had no illusion that Hill 70 would be easy. The batteries of British guns available at Vimy had moved north to Flanders. General Morrison knew that many of the remaining guns in the Corps heavy artillery were worn out and no longer accurate. Germans had introduced frightening new weapons in July — *Flammenwerfers* or flame-throwers that threw a jet of fire fifty feet or more, and a new gas that smelled of mustard and raised agonizing blisters wherever droplets fell, especially in the crotch, armpits, lungs, or wherever the skin was damp. Weather was a misery at Lens as much as in Flanders, and rain washed out Haig's deadline. To Currie, it was far more important that rehearsals and preparation be perfect.

So far as they could be, they were. At dawn on August 15, ten Canadian battalions rose from their trenches and walked into the barrage. In front of them, Hill 70 erupted in explosions of flame and dirt. The Germans, alarmed at the Canadian threat, had sent troops forward but a diversionary attack by Watson's 4th Division on Lens distracted them. Thick black smoke from five hundred blazing oil barrels spread as a screen over Hill 70, blinding German machine-gunners. Even blinded Spandaus spat out five hundred rounds a minute to kill and wound, but in twenty minutes the surviving Canadians were on top of Hill 70. Battalions from the 2nd Division wheeled south, into the mining villages on the slopes, while Macdonell's 1st Division pushed east and north. On the far side Brigadier-General F.O.W. Loomis's 2nd Brigade faced a huge chalk quarry and German defenders unshaken by the bombardment. British Columbians and Winnipeggers of the 7th and 8th battalions fought from shell-hole to shell-hole but it was early on August 16 before they were in position. Most men of the battalions were dead or wounded.

Then the real fight for Hill 70 began. As early as 9:00 A.M. on August 15, the Canadians fought off their first counter-attack. Attacks kept coming. In the intervals, infantry and machine-gunners hacked holes for themselves and their guns or cared for wounded comrades. Artillery observers used wireless for the first time to zero in on advancing German columns. Private Harry Brown of the 10th Battalion died of terrible wounds after struggling back with word of a massing German counter-attack. He won a vc. At Corps head-quarters, intelligence officers had calculated how long it took German reserves to reach points along the road into Lens. Long-range artillery shells met the Germans as they marched. Aircraft spotted the results. Certainly the Canadian artillery suffered heavily. German mustard-gas shells lobbed at the gun positions cost two artillery brigades 178 casualties after gunners had yanked off their masks to see what they were doing. Somehow, the survivors kept the batteries firing.

Hundreds of Germans got through the storm of shrapnel and high explosives and hurled themselves forward with grenades, rifles, and the terrifying flame-throwers. Canadians fought back, sometimes hand to hand. Sergeant Fred Hobson wielded a Lewis gun until it was jammed, tossed it to a private to repair, and fought off Germans with his bayonet until it was back in action. His body was found surrounded by fifteen dead Germans. Major Okill Learmonth of the 2nd Battalion, desperately wounded, led his men from the parapet, catching German grenades and hurling them back. Both Hobson and Learmonth earned a posthumous Victoria Cross. In all, Canadians won five vcs at Hill 70.

At dawn on August 18, Learmonth's men stopped the twenty-first and last German counter-attack. The battle for Hill 70 was over. Taking the Hill cost the Canadians 3,527 men; holding it cost 2,316 more, including the hundreds of gunners who had suffered from German mustard gas. Currie's strategy had paid off: five German divisions had been thrown into the battle at a cost of 20,000 men: they could not go to Flanders. For Currie, it was "altogether the hardest battle in which the Corps had participated" but years later, he remembered it as his proudest. Like Plumer at Messines, Canadians had cost the enemy far more than they had paid and, in his first battle, Currie had shown the British professionals that he was a shrewder tactician than they were.

Hill 70 did not end the fighting for Lens. To clear Germans from more of the mining villages on the slope, Currie ordered a fresh attack on August 18. Ketchen's 6th Brigade ran into a German counter-attack and was stopped. So was part of Hilliam's 10th Brigade, but two of his battalions got forward, inspired by an ex-Russian army bayonet instructor, Corporal Filip Konowal, who took three German machine guns. Ahead lay the wreckage of a pit-head and a slag heap called the Green Crassier. To take them, Hilliam sent in a badly depleted 44th Battalion. The Manitobans relived their bad luck at the Somme. They moved forward, took both positions in bitter fighting, and found themselves facing two German battalions. In a few hours, the 44th lost 354 dead or missing and 87 prisoners of war — almost all the men who had gone forward. It was a grim, local tragedy of war.

Lens and Green Crassier stayed German and the Canadian Corps headed into an even uglier, more encompassing tragedy.

PASSCHENDAELE

On October 3, without prior notice, Sir Douglas Haig showed up at the Canadian Corps headquarters. Currie had been half-expecting his message: the Canadians were needed at Passchendaele. The reasons, at least to Haig, were sadly obvious. He had pushed his British and Australian divisions to the limit, and the Germans still held the ridge and the symbolic smear of brick dust that gave the battle its name. Currie protested. Like other Canadians, he knew the Ypres salient and hated it. Nothing good had ever happened there to Canadians or to the Allies' cause. Canadians, he warned, would lose sixteen thousand men they could not afford. Haig was firm: "some day I will tell you why," he told Currie, "but Passchendaele must be taken."

No British lieutenant-general could make terms with a field marshal but the Canadian Corps was no longer British. Currie had conditions. He would not serve in General Gough's Fifth Army: the Somme and Gough's mindless orders to attack hopeless objectives were not forgotten. Instead, the Canadians would replace the Australian Corps under Plumer. They must also have time to make thorough preparations. Well aware that delay had already cost him too many chances that year and eager to end the battle, Haig begrudged any added days but he agreed. Then the two men went out to meet the divisional commanders and Haig explained it all again — including Currie's protest and his conditions.

Currie had no illusions about the Corps's reactions; few of his men would know that he opposed the new commitment. He sent Lipsett and Odlum to look at the battlefield: it was, if possible, even worse than they expected. Odlum later recalled: "all you could see was shell holes with a group of men in them, and you could look perhaps two hundred yards over and see the Germans in the same position. Both sides were just finished."

While the British occupied the vast bog created by a creek called the Ravebeek, the Germans occupied slightly higher and drier ground. Their heavy artillery reached every part of the salient, from men huddled in shell holes to the reserves, resting under sodden canvas shelters in the rear. German defences were based on scores of circular concrete pillboxes with walls five feet thick, impervious to any available artillery and located for interlocking sup-

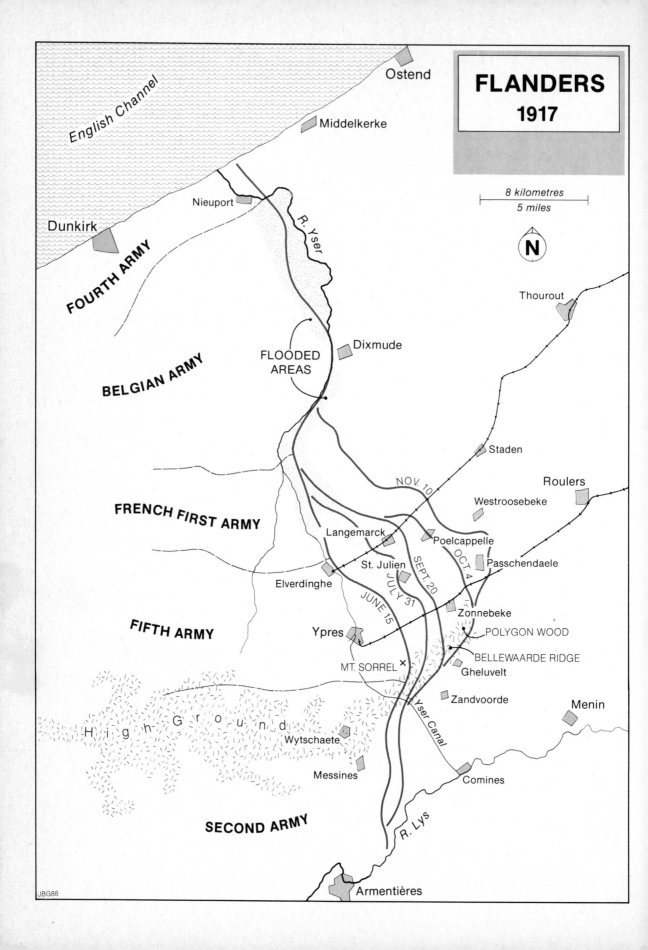

English Channel

Ostend

Middelkerke

Dunkirk

Nieuport

FOURTH ARMY

R. Yser

Thourout

BELGIAN ARMY

FLOODED AREAS

Dixmude

Staden

FRENCH FIRST ARMY

NOV. 10

Roulers

Westroosebeke

Langemarck

Poelcappelle

St. Julien

SEPT. 20

OCT. 4

Passchendaele

Elverdinghe

JULY 31

JUNE 15

Zonnebeke

POLYGON WOOD

FIFTH ARMY

Ypres

BELLEWAARDE RIDGE

MT. SORREL ×

Gheluvelt

Zandvoorde

Menin

H i g h   G r o u n d

Yser Canal

Wytschaete

Messines

Comines

SECOND ARMY

R. Lys

Armentières

FLANDERS 1917

8 kilometres
5 miles

N

JBG88

port. Only two roads led up through the salient to the front and the British had been forced to concentrate their artillery in dense clusters beside each of them, one for field guns, another farther back for the heavy guns. For lack of hard ground, engineers had built wooden platforms that became, in effect, rafts in the mud. To save time and the awful labour of moving guns, General Morrison agreed to take over the Australian Corps artillery where it sat. Canadian gunners reported that of the 250 Australian heavy guns they were supposed to take over, only 227 could be found and 89 of them were out of action. Barely half the 306 field guns farther forward were usable. A staff officer at Plumer's headquarters suggested that Currie submit a proper indent for the guns according to procedure. The Canadian general exploded: he could not kill Germans with indents. The paperwork was forgotten and the guns were brought forward.

There was everything to do. Brigadier-General W.B. Lindsay, the Corps chief engineer, a jumbo-sized man of proverbial resoucefulness, organized twenty-one companies of engineers and nine battalions of pioneers for the task of rebuilding roads, carving drainage ditches, constructing new gun platforms, and collecting supplies, all just a little faster than German artillery could destroy his work. Lindsay's men suffered almost fifteen hundred casualties before the fighting had even begun. The Germans, from their high ground, had easy targets. Men who fell off the roadways or the narrow duck-board tracks that snaked forward to the infantry positions risked drowning in the mud. Wounded men sank for ever in the foul soup. At Passchendaele, scores of German aircraft bombed and strafed troops and camps. Big two-engine Gotha bombers, designed to attack London, were diverted to the battle. Never had Canadians been hit so hard from the air. The dreadful weather provided one small compensation: German bombs and shells buried themselves in the deep mud, doing far less damage than on normal ground.

Currie's plan was simple: a succession of limited advances well within the range of his supporting artillery. At each stage, while the infantry consolidated, guns could be dragged up for the next advance. When he saw the ground for himself, Currie made another change. Traditionally, attacking troops rested in the rear, moved up just before zero hour, and advanced while they were still fresh. No man would be fresh after struggling through yards of knee-deep mud and there was no real rest anywhere in the salient. Currie's men would come up a couple of days before their attack, recover from exhaustion as best they could, and be ready to move when the barrage came down. Wireless, tried at Hill 70, would be used again to make sure that the shelling did not move beyond the floundering attackers. It was faster than

carrier pigeons and telephone wire rarely survived enemy shells. It was all
Currie could do for his troops.

The first attack was planned for October 24. Because preparations were so
painfully slow, Currie postponed it to the 29th and then, at Haig's insistence,
brought it back to the 26th. For ten days the weather had been dry; on the 25th
it broke and, at dawn on the 26th, men of the 3rd and 4th divisions faced a sea
of mud and flooded craters that blocked half their frontage. For two days and
nights, Canadians struggled forward under German fire. A few valiant men
discovered that the German pillboxes could be tackled if they could be isolated from supporting fire. The narrow slits, with thick walls, gave the
defenders little visibility and the Germans did most of their fighting from
trenches to the rear. The struggle depended on sodden, shivering heroes,
coated in twenty or thirty pounds of slimy yellow mud, crawling close enough
to lob grenades at an enemy who was in no hurry to give up or run away. By
the night of the 28th, the attacking battalions had lost 2,481 men. Three
Canadians had earned the vc. One of them, Private Tom Holmes, twice ran
forward with bombs under heavy fire, to blast a German pillbox. Finally, 19
Germans surrendered to him.

At 5:50 A.M. on October 30, fresh battalions tried again. This time the
weather was cold and clear; the shelling was harder and a thousand more
yards cost 1,321 in dead and wounded, among them Major Talbot Papineau of
the PPCLI, whose dismay at the conscription crisis had persuaded him to leave
a safe staff job. He was blown to pieces by a shell. Another casualty was George
Pearkes, an ex-mountie and a major in the 5th Canadian Mounted Rifles (CMR).
He was hit in the thigh as he emerged from cover but he knew that his men
would go back if he did. He clambered to his feet and plodded painfully forward until only a handful of men from his and an adjoining British battalion
remained. Since it didn't seem to make sense to go back, Pearkes stayed,
ignoring shells, counter-attacks, and the failure of attempts to rescue his tiny
force. Late on the 30th, 200 men of another CMR battalion finally got through
to relieve Pearkes and 35 survivors. Pearkes won the vc, as did three others
that day.

Another officer did not survive. Meyer Cohen, a Toronto Jew, had not been
welcome in the 42nd Battalion — the posh Royal Highlanders from Montreal
— until he showed fellow officers that he could fight with his fists. At Lens in
September, he took out a patrol, captured three Germans, waited, and captured three more. General Archie Macdonell came in person to congratulate
him and to tell him that, henceforth, he was MacCohen. At Passchendaele, he
took his platoon to take Graf House, a ruined farmhouse that had thrown back
attack after attack. Cohen and his men took the post after dark and held it

until only five men remained alive. Cohen was not among them. There is a tiny Star of David in the Royal Highlanders' memorial window in a Montreal Presbyterian church.

The 3rd and 4th divisions, exhausted and decimated, gave way in the first days of November to the 1st and 2nd divisions. The wounded, when they could be found alive, required twelve men in relays of six to struggle through the mud. There were not many German prisoners to help. The dead stayed where they were, adding to the special horror of Passchendaele. On November 6, Canadians launched their third attack. The sky was clear, the ground was higher and drier, and the barrage, which, despite precautions, had moved ahead of earlier attacks, had barely passed the Germans when the Canadians were among them with bayonets and grenades. A new German division should have provided a tougher resistance; instead the hand-over seems to have confused the defenders. Still, the Germans fought almost as relentlessly as ever, and Canadians in the open were still easy targets for shells and machine-gun bullets. The 31st Battalion reported double jeopardy. Its men had left their heavy greatcoats in long lines when they moved up to attack. German airmen mistook them for a line of troops and strafed the coats mercilessly. The real losses were 2,238 men, 734 of them dead. One of them, Private James Robertson, had gone out twice to rescue wounded under furious German fire. An unlucky shell got him on his second trip.

By noon, the 27th Battalion had overwhelmed the pillboxes that were all that remained of Passchendaele but Haig still needed the top of the ridge. On November 10, two Western Canadian battalions, the 7th and the 8th, opened the final attack. Conditions were vile but they got to their objective only to find that the adjoining British attack had utterly failed. The 10th Battalion, mostly Calgarians, took over the front line late in the afternoon. It was a narrow point, jutting deep into the German positions. "If the Canadians can hold that," an Australian observer commented, "they are wonderful troops." German guns hammered the Canadians from three sides. Fighters strafed anything that moved. Mud erupted in a storm of shells but the Alberta soldiers grimly endured. At dusk, counter-attacks faded and the line held.

For the Canadians, Passchendaele was almost over. On November 14, British divisions began to move into the Canadian trenches. By the 20th, Currie was once again in command of the Lens-Vimy sector. He had been right about Passchendaele. Canadians lost 15,654 dead and wounded in the battle, a thousand of them buried for ever under the Flanders mud. In Paris after the war, Haig did explain to Currie, as he had promised. The French mutinies and the German submarines were reasons, of course, but Haig's real concern was the spreading peace movement in London and Paris. Only a clear Allied victory in

1917 could stop the rot. The Canadians had done their part but, by mid-November, hardly anyone seemed to care.

On the way down the line or in billets behind the line, soldiers lined up to fill out a ballot in Canada's thirteenth general election. They wondered if it would make a difference.

UNION GOVERNMENT

In June 1917, Currie had cheerfully paid part of the price for his new command. Borden had wanted public support for conscription; Currie had provided it. Six months later, not a single conscript had appeared. Frustrated and feeling used, Currie felt very far from home.

In Canada, remote from the mud and the fear, the government played by political, not military rules. "Our first duty," Borden told his supporters, "is to win, at any cost, the coming election in order that we may continue to do our part in winning the war and that Canada be not disgraced." Without a mandate, there would be no conscription.

In England that spring, Lloyd George had offered an amendment to the British North America Act if Borden wished to prevent a wartime election. The Canadian had refused. Laurier, in turn, had refused a coalition but Borden did not stop with him. For years, while he played the political game, Borden had privately yearned for a government without the mean, corrupting squabbles of party politics. The conscription crisis had cracked party lines; might it unite all Canadians who saw the war as a national crusade — excluding the corrupt Bob Rogers as much as the unrepentant Liberal vote-mongers? Borden now had allies, among them the deaf but powerful Sir Clifford Sifton; his Winnipeg newspaper, the *Free Press;* and its respected editor, John Wesley Dafoe.

Coalition would not happen easily. Potential Liberal defectors were nervous, undecided, emotionally tied to their "plumed knight", Sir Wilfrid Laurier, and still hopeful of an election victory. In August, Borden turned back to Parliament and his Tory majority. A new Military Voters Act allowed men and women in uniform to vote for either the Government or the Opposition. Those without close links to a constituency in Canada could choose their own. Both parties, as the Minister of Justice gently explained, would want to persuade soldiers to put their votes where they would do the most good. No one doubted how soldiers would decide. Arthur Meighen, as a Manitoba minister, knew the rising Liberal strength among European immigrants: "to shift the franchise from the doubtful British or anti-British of the male sex," he suggested, "and to extend it at the same time to our patriotic women would be in my judgement a splendid stroke." Liberals howled, the *Vancouver Sun* called it a "Steal the Election Act", but closure and Conservative votes pushed Meighen's Wartime Elections Act through. Citizens from enemy countries, naturalized since 1902, lost their votes; the wives, mothers, and sisters of CEF members would be able to vote. The "patriotic women" would understand what conscription meant for their men.

Both laws had their effect. Liberal confidence faded. During the summer, hard-boiled Grit partisans had met in Toronto and Winnipeg to cheer for a leader who would bring them back to power. Now they had doubts. Frank Carvell, Newton Rowell, and others, to whom both Liberalism and the war were moral crusades, remembered how alienated they had felt by Laurier's perpetual concern for Quebec. By staying with him, were they not guilty of a corrupt "partyism" when the war called for sacrifice above self?

On October 6, Parliament was dissolved; Canadians would vote on December 17. On October 12, weeks of rumour and negotiation ended: Borden presented a Union government backed by every provincial premier but Quebec's Sir Lomer Gouin. Led by Newton Rowell, nine Liberals and a plump trade unionist, Gideon Robertson, joined twelve Conservatives in the biggest Cabinet Canada had yet seen. Outside Quebec all but a handful of Liberal papers endorsed the new regime. A delighted Tory confessed that he would match Borden against Job in a patience contest any day.

Now more than ever Borden needed patience. Tory ministers remembered the old bitter attacks from new colleagues. Rowell felt compelled to claim that a new purity had entered a once-corrupt regime. In scores of constituencies across Ontario and the West, nomination battles loomed between Conservatives and freshly converted Liberal Unionists. On October 18, the Unionists announced their platform. Some planks were predictable: full commitment to the war, reorganization of the railways, a crusade against political patronage. Other reforms were more controversial, though by 1917 their time seemed to have come: votes for all Canadian women, a total ban on the production and sale of liquor. On the tariff — a bitterly divisive issue between prairie farmers and most Tory supporters — the program was discreetly silent. Even Stephen Leacock, who despised women's suffrage as much as he cherished his whiskey, would hold his tongue.

To French Canada, such reforms were as much an anathema as conscription. They symbolized the Unionist rejection of the Canadian duality. Pierre Blondin had gone to England with the rump of his battalion; Albert Sévigny, who remained as almost the lone French-Canadian minister, needed police protection in Quebec. Few in the rest of Canada seemed to care what Quebec thought. "It is certainly not the intention of English Canada," warned *Satur-*

day Night magazine, "to stand idly by and see itself bled of men in order that the Quebec shirker may sidestep his responsibilities." No one asked, of course, whether Quebeckers had insisted on assuming those responsibilities.

In October, victory for the Unionists seemed easy. Laurier was shattered by the defection of life-long English-speaking colleagues. The Liberal organization was in ruins. Trusted party fund-raisers did not answer their calls. Then, as weeks passed, Unionist confidence began to ebb. In Nova Scotia, New Brunswick, and parts of the West, promises of Liberal backing proved worthless. In British Columbia, Liberals and Conservatives refused to co-operate. Soon both sides mistrusted the high-minded Rowell.

Liberals took heart. Candidates emerged, including Mackenzie King, oddly confident of victory in North York, the constituency of his rebel grandfather. An ailing and weary Laurier ventured west. Large, cheering crowds were a tonic. In Edmonton and Calgary, party organs had stayed faithful. If elected, Laurier told audiences, he would "increase, double and quadruple the output of all that may be necessary for marching and fighting armies". Conscription, he insisted, would be put to the people in a referendum and he would "carry out the wishes of the nation as thus expressed". Critics answered that Laurier's pledge was no more than Bourassa's policy of trying to get rich from war production but Unionists soon began to wonder if they would win a conscription plebiscite. At Kitchener, an anti-conscription crowd howled Borden from the platform for the first time in his political life. General Sydney Mewburn, the Hamilton Liberal who was now Minister of Militia, warned that Ontario farmers planned to vote for Laurier to keep their sons at home. Hurriedly, the government announced that farmers' sons would be exempted from conscription. So were the brothers of serving soldiers: ageing parents would not be robbed of their only breadwinner.

Desperation fuelled one of the ugliest election campaigns in Canadian experience. Laurier, Henri Bourassa, and the Kaiser were linked in speeches and cartoons. Quebec, declared George Allan, a Winnipeg Unionist, is "the plague spot of the whole Dominion". Clergy fed the hysteria. "Henry Bourassa is the real leader of Quebec," insisted Toronto's Archdeacon Henry Cody, "and I ask if that Province led by him, shall have the domination of the rest of this free Dominion which has sacrificed and suffered." The *Mail and Empire* warned on election day that a vote for Laurier was a vote for Germany, the Kaiser, von Hindenburg, and the sinking of the *Lusitania*.

Overseas, Sir Arthur Currie's neutrality was exceptional. Whatever their military limitations, surplus officers had political skills and they used them to organize military voters. The "Old Originals" of 1914 were promised a furlough home. The 5th Division at Witley was promised that it would stay together, perhaps even go to France. In France, Brigadier-General Manly-Sims abandoned GHQ to organize the Unionist campaign. There was no Liberal opposition. In England, Laurier's sole agent was an out-of-work patronage-seeker notorious in Ontario Liberal ranks as "Hug-the-Machine" Preston. His allegations of political manipulation were well founded, though his own record hurt Preston's credibility. Besides, any manipulation was irrelevant. Canadian troops needed no persuasion. Australian soldiers had rejected conscription because it would pollute their ranks with pressed men; Canadians had no such scruples. They were ready to share death with slackers. Yet, even overseas, government supporters wondered whether their efforts would pay off.

The early returns on December 17 justified the worst Unionist fears. Every seat in Prince Edward Island, nine of the twelve in Nova Scotia, and half the seats in New Brunswick went Liberal. In Quebec, Unionists clung to only three English-speaking seats in Montreal. Ontario farmers, targets of the special Unionist campaign, swung back but Borden's majority before polls closed in Western Canada was only eighteen seats. It was the West that gave the Unionists their victory, and the soldiers' votes when they were reported six weeks later. Military voters in Canada changed two seats; the overseas votes added a dozen more. In all, the civilian margin for the Unionists was a mere 97,065 of 1,650,958 votes cast; the CEF gave 215,849 votes to the government and only 18,522 to Laurier. Though the government's overseas organizers, with the full connivance of sympathetic officers, had done what they could to distribute loose votes where they were needed, the chief returning officer, the indispensable W.F. O'Connor, set aside the more fraudulent ballots. Liberals (and some historians) preferred to believe that the scandal had proceeded unimpeded.

Born in a mixture of opportunism and idealism, the new Union government had all the authority it needed to run a deeply divided Canada. Recognition was not its goal. For a generation, prominent English-speaking Canadians had called for an end to party politics. Others had condemned the compromises and concessions needed to conciliate the French-Canadian minority. Still others had pledged that a Canada in which women could vote and no one could drink would enter a new age of social justice and moral purity.

On December 17, 1917, their wishes had come true. Now they could live with the consequences.

STAGGERING LOSSES

Haig had been right in October in believing that the Allies desperately needed a victory. Morale among Allied leaders and followers was bad. Ironically, if Haig had ended Passchendaele in August, he might have delivered the necessary triumph.

Since the spring, British generals had planned an assault opposite Cambrai. In October, Haig finally authorized Sir Julian Byng to revive the plans for his Third Army. That was where Currie wanted his Canadians to be in November and he was right. Cambrai was a leap into the war of the future. At 6:20 A.M. on November 20, virtually without warning, hundreds of British aircraft roared over the German line, blasting trenches with bombs; 378 tanks thundered forward, flattening barbed wire; and the infantry of five divisions followed on a five-mile front. A thousand hidden guns opened fire for the first time, inundating preregistered targets with shells and poison gas. Tanks dropped fascines (huge bundles of wood) into trenches and craters, and crunched across. Six thousand Germans, many of them shell-shocked survivors of Passchendaele, surrendered without resistance. By evening, the British had advanced three to four miles.

But some of the Germans fought back. A single field gun knocked out sixteen British tanks. By nightfall, half the British tank force was broken down, ditched, or smashed. German machine guns ended the hope that the Cavalry Corps would finally break out into open country. A single squadron of the Fort Garry Horse filed across a lock gate at Masnières, cantered into the fields beyond, and came back hours later with 40 survivors and 16 prisoners. The surviving officer, Lieutenant Harcus Strachan, got a VC. In Britain, church bells rang for victory but, by November 23, the advance was over. Byng's eight divisions were exhausted and he had no more to send when the Germans took back Bourlon Wood on the 27th. Passchendaele had devoured Haig's army. He could send no help. On December 1, led by low-flying planes under an ace named Manfred von Richthofen, the Germans counter-attacked. It was the German turn to deluge British defences with shells and to harry them with aerial strafing. It was the British who surrendered or died. In three days, most of the gains were lost. Cambrai was not great as battles had gone — the British lost 44,000 men to the Germans' 41,000. Hopes had been raised too high on the 23rd and now they were dashed too low. Cambrai devastated British morale like no other setback of the war.

There was another reason why Byng had no more men. That fall, von Ludendorff had sent six German divisions to Italy. On October 24, they and the Austrians struck. The Italian line crumpled, steadied at the Tagliamento, and collapsed again. Foch, the French chief of staff, had foreseen the disaster and made plans. Six British and seven French divisions were rushed south, though it was Italian courage and pride and a new general, Armando Diaz, that finally stabilized the line on the Piave. Lloyd George's persistent dream of winning by way of Italy now had an ironic ring.

Lloyd George had tamed the Admiralty, so he boasted, when he marched across Whitehall on April 30 and forced Jellicoe to adopt the convoy system. In fact, the awful statistics were argument enough. So was experience when, in May, merchant ships left Gibraltar in a convoy and arrived intact and two days faster than if they had travelled separately. By the end of 1917, half of the shipping to Britain moved in convoy and losses had fallen dramatically. Fears of collision at sea and jam-ups in port proved groundless. Lloyd George's self-confidence grew while Haig's reputation fell. Perhaps the field marshal had too many powerful friends but there was no such backing for Haig's loyal ally, the ex-ranker, Sir William Robertson. As a devout "Westerner" and the sole source of military advice to the government, Robertson was the stubborn obstacle to Lloyd George's strategic insight. To each of the prime minister's arguments, "Wully" replied that "he'd 'eard different". The Italian disaster provided the occasion to break his grip.

On November 5, Allied leaders met at Rapallo in the midst of the Italian crisis. Now was the time, Lloyd George insisted, to co-ordinate Allied strategy. The French, Italian, and British prime ministers — and Colonel House for the United States if President Wilson let him — would form a Supreme War Council, with military advisers who must not, Lloyd George insisted, be chiefs of staff. All agreed.

Sir Henry Wilson, hopeless as a fighting soldier but a consummate conspirator, with a fascinating resemblance to a praying mantis, became Lloyd George's general. The faithful Robertson resigned when Haig made it clear that he would not risk his position to save him. Divine guidance told the field marshal that his own position in the field was more important. He may have been right.

It took faith to believe in the Allied cause that winter. In September, the Germans took Riga on the Baltic, with a mixture of devastating artillery and infantry tactics devised by Colonel Max Hoffmann. They would use the techniques again. When a Russian general tried to seize Petrograd, Alexander Kerensky, leader of the Provisional Government, armed the workers as a Red Guard. The general gave up. On November 6, Kerensky tried to crush the Bolsheviks. Instead, Lenin and Trotsky turned the Red Guard on the Winter Palace, seat of the Provisional Government. Six guards died. Kerensky fled. The futile liberal era in Russia was over. Vladimir Lenin and Leon Trotsky were in power. On November 8, they announced an armistice, and released all the embarrassing secret treaties the Allies had signed to bind themselves into the war effort. All over Europe, war-weary soldiers and workers realized that, somewhere, peace was breaking out. Lord Lansdowne finally revealed his own fear for civilization in the *Daily Telegraph*, organ of the British conservative middle class. Peace, he insisted, was the only way to preserve the old order. In the War Cabinet, Lord Milner suggested Germany be bribed out of her western conquests by being given a free hand in Russia. In France, the socialists quit the government to be free to consider peace. Ex-premier Caillaux at last had a following. This was the crisis that helped send the Canadians to Passchendaele.

In Paris, it was peace or war. President Poincaré made his decision: he turned to his old enemy, Georges Clemenceau, a man of seventy-seven who had never forgotten 1870. "You ask what are my war aims?" Clemenceau told the Assembly. "They are very simple: Victory." The compromisers and defeatists, Caillaux and Malvy, were seized, charged with treason, and locked away. Democracy, compromise, idealism were put away for the duration. When Woodrow Wilson, on January 8, 1918, sought to rally idealism with war aims summed up in Fourteen Points, Clemenceau scoffed; "Why fourteen? The Good Lord only had ten." The French would fight.

So would Lloyd George but not, if he could help it, in France. By now, Britain was conscripting eighteen-year-olds and "combing out" war industries. The manpower crisis was desperate. No belligerent found more jobs for women, but almost half of Britain's vast army was tied up in the "side-shows" Haig and Robertson had deplored. The victory Haig had failed to provide came on December 11 in Palestine, when Allenby's army, reinforced with men Haig wanted in France, out-manoeuvred the Turks and marched into Jerusalem. This belated restaging of the Crusades was complicated by a pledge from Lloyd George's foreign secretary, Arthur Balfour, that the Holy Land would be returned to the Jews. It was just as well that the vast Arab revolt, engineered for Allenby by the handsome, romantic T.E. Lawrence, was not kept fully informed.

Somewhere, somehow, Lloyd George believed, "knocking the props" would bring down Germany. Sir Douglas Haig would continue in command but he would have no more men. British divisions, depleted of men, were simply cut from twelve to nine battalions of infantry. With a Lewis gun in each platoon for added firepower, it was mathematically possible to prove they could fight as well as ever. Gough's Fifth Army, restored to the southern flank, took over another twenty-five miles of French trenches. Pétain and Haig, though not on good terms, agreed to share their reserves. With Russia out of the war, they knew that the initiative belonged to Germany.

Germany could look back on 1917 with more satisfaction than her enemies. The nightmare of a two-front war ended with a Russian armistice in Decem-

A War Record, Stanley F. Turner. By 1917, Canadians were beginning to see many disabled soldiers on their streets. Turner based this scene on the corner of Yonge and Davisville in Toronto, not far from the city's main military hospital. The civilians seem to regard the mutilated soldiers as curiosities — but how long would it be before the curiosity wore off? (NWM 8907)

An allegorical Miss Canada, suitably armoured and draped, was a reminder that food was one of the vital munitions of the war effort. While Canadian war art supported a powerful flowering of modernism, propaganda relied on more popular artistic traditions. (Erindale College collection)

Whatever the women of France were doing, few Canadians would have contemplated hauling a plough. Victory Bond campaigns mobilized the best available talent in Canadian commercial art — but while the resulting revenues transformed the country's public finance, high interest rates and exemption from income tax did more than pictures to attract savings. (NWM 56-05-11-023)

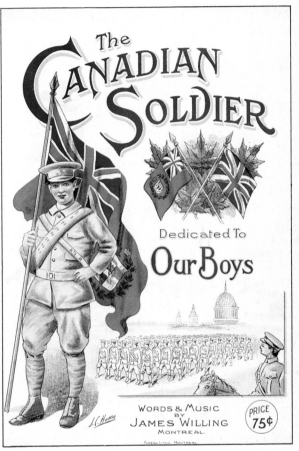

This recruiting poster for the 230th Voltigeurs is a somewhat primitive collection of symbols that most young Quebeckers could cheerfully ignore. Battling for a martyred France or the Union Jack was not high on people's list of priorities. (Erindale College collection)

The war generated a lot of unmemorable music, as well as a few durable favourites. This song by James Willing was clearly directed at a home-front audience, with its sentimental image of Canada's "soldier-boys". (Collection of J.L. Granatstein)

Over the Top, Alfred Bastien. The depiction of the 22nd Battalion's assault on the Drocourt-Quéant Line in August 1918 is among the best-known of Canadian war paintings. By the end of the battle, every officer of the battalion was dead or wounded, including a future governor general. (NWM 8058)

Soldiers of the Polish Army in the YMCA, C.W. Jefferys. The popular illustrator for the *Toronto Daily Star* went to Niagara-on-the-Lake in 1918 to record the training of a nascent Polish army, largely recruited in the United States. He found them in the cast-off red tunics and blue trousers of the peacetime Canadian Militia. (NWM 8225)

No Man's Land, Maurice Cullen. A shell explodes in the distance but humanity is invisible in Cullen's painting of a stretch of France in the late winter of 1917. Better than a photograph, the painting shows the drab reality of most of the Western Front. (NWM 8149)

Canadians outside the Depot, Siberia, Russia, Louis Keene. Keene accompanied the Canadian expedition to Siberia to share the harsh 1918–19 winter. A Canadian guard forms up outside the barracks in Vladivostok while a truckload of firewood is delivered. (NWM 8334)

Armistice Day, Toronto, J. Ernest Sampson. News of the
November 11 Armistice came to Canadian cities before dawn,
and the streets were soon packed with cheering people. Sampson
reduced Toronto's ecstatic throngs to suitable insignificance
under the city's towering buildings and cloud-streaked sky. (NWM
8795)

In 1922 France handed over to Canada in perpetuity 250 acres of Vimy Ridge, where over 3,500 Canadians had died. In 1936 the stark marble monument was finally unveiled. Three years later, Canada was embarking on a second world war. (Dept. of Veterans' Affairs)

ber and, after unsuccessful Bolshevik grandstanding, a triumphant peace at Brest-Litovsk in March. In theory the vast farmlands and resources of Poland, the Ukraine, and the Balkans would support the German war effort for ever. Victorious armies were already streaming westward in late December, though hundreds of thousands of troops remained as a *cordon sanitaire* against the Bolshevik bacillus. Even if the Americans arrived — and the creation of their army was slower than anyone had expected — Germany could hold on indefinitely in the West until peace movements forced Paris and London to seek terms. Wilson's Fourteen Points already suggested that the Americans themselves wanted a negotiated settlement.

That was not exactly how Germany's leaders saw matters. The German generals were as appalled as Haig at the prospect of a war ending short of a palpable victory. Riots, labour unrest, even a small naval mutiny suggested serious internal strains in Germany. The agricultural potential of Germany's eastern conquests lay strictly in the future. Regions that had fed most of Europe were now ruined and starving in the wake of marauding Russian, German, and Habsburg armies. Half the cattle in the Austrian Empire were gone by 1918; the swine population had fallen from 7.7 million in 1914 to 214,000 by the summer of 1918. In Germany 800,000 people would die prematurely from malnutrition during the war. Britain's blockade, barely noticed in accounts of battles and battleships, was in fact among the most effective Allied weapons of the war. The German generals knew they could not wait; they must win.

On November 11, von Ludendorff met his key generals at Mons. The war, he declared, would be won in a single, decisive blow, as early in 1918 as possible. Other German leaders, even von Hindenburg, were not consulted. It was still the General Staff's war. The weapons would be mass and surprise, the tactics tested at Riga. The best men in the army, elite storm-troopers — *Stosstruppen* — were concentrated in assault divisions. Lesser soldiers would suffice elsewhere. Under a storm of high explosive and poison gas, storm-troopers would bypass defences, heading for headquarters and gun positions. Operation "Michael" would fall on the British. So would a second assault, when "Michael" had succeeded. The French, a German staff officer predicted, would not "run themselves off their legs" to help the British.

While the Germans massed their troops for the coming 1918 offensive, Haig was forced to extend his line southward to relieve the exhausted French. As their own response to the German U-boat blockade, British (and Canadian) soldiers spent February clearing and planting vegetable gardens and grumbling at reduced rations.

That winter everyone knew that the Germans would attack, but when the blow fell on March 21, it caught the British by surprise. The generals claimed that they had planned defence in depth on the German model but too many troops were in the forward positions, caught under a hurricane of fire from 2,500 guns. German artillery searched out headquarters, gun positions, and crossroads, shattering command communications before a last, savage pummelling of the front lines. Gough's Fifth Army, still weary and under-strength from Passchendaele, was the victim. Dense late-winter mists, as well as smoke, artillery fire, and poison gas, masked the assaulting Germans. Storm-troopers ignored strong points and pushed deep into British territory. Bewildered defenders simply surrendered or fell back, looking for the familiar line of defence. In three days, Germans had recaptured all their losses at the Somme. British battalions disappeared; divisions dissolved. Elated, von Ludendorff poured in more troops. Now he was convinced that he could split the British from the French and roll up Haig's army against the English Channel. On his side, General Pétain seemed ready to co-operate with the German design. As he cautiously fed his reserves to the British, Pétain made it clear to Haig that the French army would swing back to defend Paris.

Sir Douglas Haig, as unshaken by this disaster as he had been by the tragedy of Passchendaele, knew that co-ordination was no longer enough. He took the initiative. At Doullens, on March 26, French and British leaders met and settled the issue. General Ferdinand Foch, the original co-conspirator of the Anglo-French alliance, emerged from the meeting as the effective Allied generalissimo and commander-in-chief. The title and the details followed in days.

A conference would not stop the Germans. On March 28, six British divisions astride the Scarpe halted thirteen German divisions on their drive to Arras. To the west and south, Germans pushed through towns British soldiers had known for years — Péronne, Albert, Noyon, Montdidier — to the edge of Villers-Bretonneux. Then, exhaustion, hunger, and the terrible casualties the storm-troopers had suffered from a shattered but unbeaten British army took their toll. Supporting battalions stopped to loot British supplies. Like the British at Cambrai, the Germans found that an enemy with railways could still move faster than attackers on foot. On April 5, Operation "Michael" petered out. The Allies had not been split but united. They had lost 77,000 French and 163,500 British troops but the German losses were staggering too — 239,000 *Stosstruppen*, the very best of their fighting men. Had von Ludendorff finally thrown and lost?

Major Talbot Papineau and one of a series of pet dogs. A descendant of the rebel of 1837 and a cousin of Henri Bourassa, Papineau was largely Anglicized, but that did not end his sense of identity with French Canada or his fear for English-French relations after the war. He gave up a safe staff job and rejoined his battalion for Passchendaele, well aware that death was the likely result.

Troops carrying ammunition pause in a communications trench for the photographer. Trench warfare could be appallingly cold and wet, but in the summer it could be hot, too — and the army did not provide warm-weather uniforms.

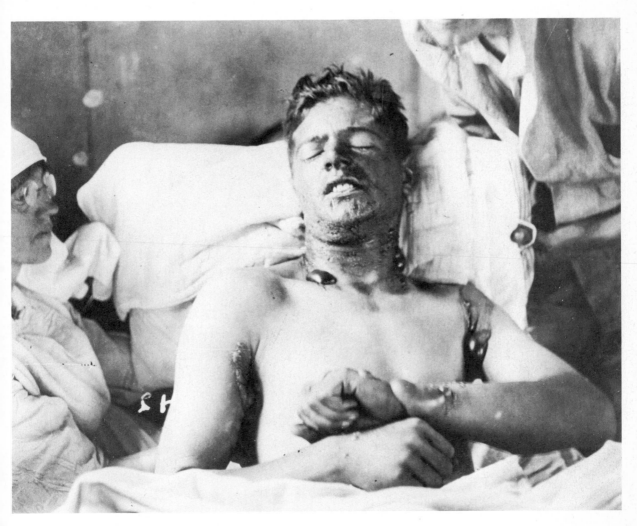

A casualty from mustard gas. The gas was rarely fatal unless breathed into the lungs, but it undermined morale because of the anguish of the sufferers, and the resources needed to care for them. Modern war was becoming an assault on an enemy's spirit.

The election campaign in 1917 affected soldiers more directly than other
Canadian voters — except, perhaps, for those "other men" who would be
conscripted. By 1917, both wounded men and scrap were being "recycled" for the
cause.

Election propaganda in 1917 was as unrestrained as in any campaign in Canadian history. Other Union Government cartoons portrayed the Kaiser's approval of Laurier's policies. English Canada was asked, "Shall Quebec Rule?", with the detested Henri Bourassa as the symbol of French-Canadian dominance.

SOLDIERS AND NURSES FROM ALBERTA !!

You will have TWO VOTES at the forthcoming
Election under the Alberta Military Representation Act.

GIVE ONE VOTE TO THE MAN OF YOUR CHOICE AND
THE OTHER TO THE SISTER.

LOOK   LOOK

FOR   FOR

No. 14   No. 14

ON YOUR   ON YOUR

BALLOT PAPER!   BALLOT PAPER!

Miss ROBERTA CATHERINE MacADAMS,
Lieut., C.A.M.C., Ontario Military Hospital,
Orpington, Kent.

SHE WILL WORK NOT ONLY FOR YOUR BEST INTERESTS BUT FOR THOSE
OF YOUR WIVES, MOTHERS, SWEETHEARTS, SISTERS AND CHILDREN
AFTER THE WAR.

Remember those who have helped you so nobly through the fight.

The first woman ever elected to a Canadian legislature was Roberta MacAdams, a
nurse chosen as one of the overseas members in the Alberta Legislature in 1917.
Well aware that soldiers tended to be Conservative, Liberal governments in
Alberta and Saskatchewan hived military voters into separate constituencies. For
the same reason, the federal Conservatives designed the Military Voters' Act to
allow soldiers to vote in their home ridings — and to choose where their votes
would do the most good.

Men of a Canadian machine-gun company shelter in shellholes at Passchendaele. It is easy to see why Currie wanted his men to rest after reaching their jumping-off positions; just getting there was half the misery.

Lieutenant Harcus Strachan leads the remnants of his squadron of the Fort Garry Horse near Cambrai. Strachan's feat, charging a German artillery battery at full gallop, delighted those who hoped, against all evidence, that cavalry was not obsolete, and earned the Scottish-born Canadian his Victoria Cross.

The battlefield at Passchendaele. A light railway track ends in a shellhole. A shattered tank provides a rare landmark in the sea of mud and a shell throws up mud and water. The Canadian Corps carried a dreadful battle to its conclusion over Currie's objections, and at a cost he had grimly predicted.

German prisoners and Canadian stretcher-bearers carry back wounded. As many as eight men were needed to haul a stretcher through the mud and few of the seriously wounded survived the wait or the lurching, agonized journey. Under the Geneva Convention, prisoners could be compelled to make one journey carrying casualties under fire.

Above An officer, petty officers, and ratings of the Canadian Royal Naval Volunteer Reserve at Quebec City in 1917. These men provided crews for the drifters and armed yachts that guarded the approaches of Halifax and the St. Lawrence against German u-boats.

Right Sir Robert Borden (front row, fourth from left) at the Imperial War Conference in 1917. While the representatives from the dominions and India learned no more than Lloyd George wanted them to, the principle of consultation was finally conceded by Britain. The 1917 meeting became the foundation for just enough imperial federalism to prove, even to Borden, that his dream would not work.

Above An obviously embarrassed Sergeant-Major Robert Hanna allows an admirer to see his Victoria Cross. An Irish-born member of Vancouver's 29th Battalion, Hanna won his VC at Hill 70, personally capturing a German strong point which had beaten off three attacks; he was reported as bayoneting three Germans and braining a fourth.

VIII
THE WEARIEST YEAR

HARDSHIPS OF WAR

In the winter of 1917–18, the war came home to Canadians in ways more tangible than the deceitful official communiqués or the long lists of casualties, with their tiny half-column photographs of sons and husbands who would never return. In Canada war now meant shortages of fuel and food, shrill exhortations to save, and endless regulations enforced by patriotism and the fear of snooping neighbours. There was a sour vengefulness in the air as Canadians looked on profiteers, "slackers", foreigners, Bolsheviks — or all of them together — as a source of their misery.

Halifax, garrisoned, fortified, and the seaport from which most soldiers departed, had always been closer to the war than the rest of Canada. Nothing could have prepared its 50,000 people for December 6, 1917. At 8:00 A.M., in mid-harbour, two battered cargo ships collided in a screech of metal and sparks. The crew of the *Mont Blanc* saw smoke rising from a hold and raced for their lifeboats and the Dartmouth shore. They could only imagine what a cargo of 3,000 tons of TNT would do. So could the British and Canadian sailors who raced against time to put out the fire. They never found out. At 9:00 A.M., the *Mont Blanc* blew up. Halifax experienced the biggest man-made explosion to that time. The blast levelled the working-class end of Halifax. Wooden clapboard houses collapsed. Farther away, as people rushed to their windows, the back-blast shattered the glass. Hundreds were blinded. Survivors, horribly maimed and bleeding, struggled away from the devastation in fear of fire. That night, a savage blizzard blanketed the city in snow drifts. Freezing rain followed. Rescuers found 1,630 dead and thousands of injured. Help poured in. Boston sent a hospital ship, Ottawa created a Relief Commission, the British sent a million pounds. The U.S. Congress promised $5 million — but forgot to vote on it.

Halifax struggled back to life. It had to. The city was at war. Convoys sailed for Europe every eight days. The Admiralty had belatedly demanded Canadian help in protecting coasts and sea lanes. Long-range U-boats were on their way. Ottawa had sent Captain Walter Hose to Halifax with the crew and guns from the *Rainbow*, commandeered yachts, and built tiny trawlers at a score of shipyards. By the summer of 1918, Hose's Halifax Patrol boasted two thousand men and a hundred small vessels, most of them able to carry a 6-pounder gun and a couple of depth charges. None of them encountered the two German submarines that surfaced that summer, destroyed a few schooners, and vanished. The U.S. Navy despatched a squadron of flying boats to Dartmouth under the command of Lieutenant Richard Byrd, a future Antarctic explorer. An infant Royal Canadian Naval Air Service sent its would-be pilots to train at the Massachusetts Institute of Technology in Boston.

For most Canadians, 1918 meant hardship, resentment, and a special anxiety for those who might receive the cold official death notices from Ottawa. Across Canada that winter, lack of fuel forced schools and factories to close. In February and March, Ontario homeowners observed "Heatless Mondays". Westerners grumbled when the government-appointed fuel controller, C.A. Magrath, tried to force them to use their own brown lignite instead of scarce imported anthracite. W.J. Hanna, the food controller, had tried exhortation and the licensing of grocers and restaurants to stop hoarding and cut consumption. It was, said the political scientist J.A. Corry, like trying to turn off a garden hose by sitting on the sprinkler. A new Canada Food Board replaced Hanna in 1918 and focused on production as well as consumers, but with no better luck. Prices kept rising; bad harvests and a lack of labour cut farm output. An "anti-loafing law" — a regulation under the War Measures Act compelling all men and boys over the age of sixteen to prove they were usefully employed — was a Food Board inspiration. Borden and others were delighted by it — a good law in war, he called it, and perhaps a good law in peacetime — but the effect was insignificant. By the autumn of 1918 Canadian shoppers bought "war bread" with 20 per cent flour substitutes and limited themselves by "honour rationing" to a pound and a half of butter and two pounds of sugar a month. Sir George Foster sourly noted that none of the ladies of his acquaintance in Ottawa seemed to be stinting.

As in most elections, voters had backed Borden on December 17 with contradictory and unspecific expectations. Most wanted to win the war; many expected reforms; a few expected to abolish politics. The new ministers certainly were busy. Within a week of the election, a new Canadian government railway system was announced, incorporating the Canadian Northern. Large increases in freight rates came too late for even the Grand Trunk. Liberals in the government boasted that patronage was dead: hiring for all forty thousand jobs in the public service was handed to the Civil Service Commission, and the War Purchasing Commission took over all government buying. C.C. Ballantyne, the Montreal industrialist who became Minister of Marine, announced plans to build forty-three ships in Canadian yards. He did not mention that they would cost twice as much as British-built ships. An advisory committee on scientific and industrial research busied itself on projects as varied as salmon-spawning to feed the hungry and flax-production to provide linen for British aircraft fuselages. By early January, the War Measures Act abolished even the mail-order traffic in liquor in the name of food conservation. Only a doctor's prescription could authorize the purchase of alcohol. Hardened drinkers had to pursue a sympathetic physician for a "per".

Sir Robert Borden spent a post-election holiday in Georgia and called on the White House on his return. The Americans, he proudly reported, "expressed the view that the resources of the two countries should be pooled in the most effective co-operation and that the boundary line had little or no significance in considering or dealing with these vital questions." It was a change for a man elected in 1911 on the slogan: "No truck nor trade with the Yankees". Lloyd Harris, a vigorous Brantford businessman, went to Washington to head a Canadian War Mission and to support the Imperial Munitions Board search for contracts. A War Trade Board was created to work with the U.S. War Industries Board.

On March 18, the new House of Commons met in the Victoria Museum, as parliaments had since the Parliament Buildings were destroyed by fire on February 3, 1916. There were the usual stale jokes about fossils and dinosaurs but much was new. Unionists could rejoice over prohibition, civil-service reform, and the railway reorganization. Soon, Canadians would experience Daylight Saving Time, an electricity-conservation measure urged by a new power controller. Free-traders took what comfort they could from a budget that removed the tariff from tractors. Though Quebec Liberals raged that the laws of history, religion, and biology would be undone, on May 24 the Unionist majority extended votes to all Canadian women. The reservations of Unionist misogynists were buried in the caucus.

Reforms were one thing, the war was another. Every Unionist supporter had expected the new government to make conscription work, especially in Quebec. In May 1917, Borden had pleaded the desperate need for men but, until January 3, 1918, thanks to his promise to await the election, not a single man was compelled to serve. An "engine of tyranny" had so many apparent safeguards that it was unworkable. In October, the government had called on Class I — single men and widowers aged 20–32 — to register: of 401,882 who appeared, 93.7 per cent sought exemption. Their cases passed through 1,253 local tribunals and 195 appeal courts to a single central appeal judge, Mr. Justice Lyman Duff of the Supreme Court. Duff was strict. Most farmers and their sons were exempted because the government had promised it. Catholic novices were in holy orders and exempt; Protestant divinity students were not. Pacifism was integral to the faith of Mennonites and Doukhobors; for Jehovah's Witnesses and Plymouth Brethren, it was incidental and they could serve without being expelled from their faith. No judge could have worked faster but how many judges faced 42,000 cases in five months?

Quebec was a special case. French Canadians had lost the election but they could try passive resistance. By the end of February, Quebec tribunals had settled only 2,000 of 32,000 appeals. French-speaking applicants were given blanket exemption but, claimed Duff, "they applied conscription against the English-speaking minority with a rigour unparalleled". Few of the men ordered to appear turned up; local Quebec police were unhelpful. The tiny Dominion Police, normally used to guard public buildings in Ottawa, did its best. At Quebec City on March 28, a riot exploded when federal police tried to arrest defaulters. A mob burned the Military Service Registry office, including its records, and pillaged English-Canadian businesses. Municipal officials stood by. General Lessard, summoned by Ottawa, used troops to restore order. On April 1, soldiers from Toronto, trapped by an angry crowd, opened fire. Four civilians were killed. The coroner's jury blamed Ottawa for tactless enforcement of the Military Service Act but the violence had shocked the province. Clergy ordered the faithful to obey the law; politicians cooled their language.

A week before the Quebec riots, on March 21, the long-awaited German offensive had struck. Not even official communiqués could conceal the disaster. The Canadian Corps would soon be in the desperate struggle. From London, Perley's successor, Sir Edward Kemp, cabled for 15,000 infantry reinforcements. Mewburn had only 4,800 available. For Borden the time had come to end the exemptions farce. On April 12, a divided Cabinet reluctantly agreed. A week later, in the drama of a secret session, MPs endorsed the decision by a margin of forty-nine votes, including four Liberals. Single men, aged 20 to 22, perhaps even men 19 to 23, would be taken without exemptions.

There was an explosion of anger. Quebec and Ontario farmers made common cause in demonstrations in Ottawa. They exploded again when journalists sneered at "hayseed profiteers". Western farmers were more restrained but an Alberta appeal court ruled four to one that the government had no right to alter a parliamentary statute. For two weeks in July the Alberta judges tried to enforce *habeas corpus* for the benefit of a conscript while the Supreme

Court in Ottawa shuffled its docket to settle a comparable Ontario case. On July 20, the Court ruled, four to two, that the War Measures Act took priority over the Military Service Act with its exceptions and that Parliament, after all, had given its consent.

The decision may not have been great law but Supreme Court justices reflected a national mood that, outside Quebec, no longer had much patience with dissent. Egged on by local Protestant clergy, military police raided the Jesuit Novitiate at Guelph. Edward Grey, whose case the Supreme Court had decided, was sentenced with nine other conscientious objectors to life in prison. Another man, J.E. Plant, was sentenced to be shot. The sentences were commuted to ten and fifteen years. In Winnipeg, Jehovah's Witnesses were beaten and soaked in icy water to make them submit. One went insane. By the war's end, 117 conscientious objectors were serving prison terms.

When it could, the government resisted the pressure to oppress. "When are the hangings going to start in Quebec?" demanded a prairie voter. "Shooting is too good for them." Of 24,139 defaulters under the Act by November 1918, 18,827 were in Quebec but the government made no serious effort to find them. To reassure farmers, MSA officials were directed to take city dwellers. In the West, 23.3 per cent of eligible farmers were conscripted and 39.3 per cent of non-farmers. The government had promised to find 100,000 soldiers under the MSA; by the end of 1918, 99,561 "MSA men" were in uniform, more than half were overseas, and 24,132 had joined CEF battalions in France.

CANADA'S VOICE AND STRENGTH

By 1918, Borden and his key ministers were as war-weary as any Canadians. The prime minister's closest friend, Sir Thomas White, insisted that he must resign or die. Instead, Borden sent him to California for a rest. Borden would have gladly followed. Once, he had dreamed that a coalition would end the personal and political squabbling he detested. Patriotic ministers would get on with the war. Instead, his ministers jockeyed for post-war advantages. Rowell and Carvell publicly contrasted the morality of the new regime with the evils of the old. New ministers fumbled their responsibilities; ex-ministers took malicious delight. Bob Rogers, excluded by Borden, sniped from the sidelines. So did Sam Hughes. In every Cabinet dispute, Borden alone was the trusted arbiter.

Borden also had to patch up a divided Canada. On January 19, a Liberal member of the Quebec assembly, J.N. Francoeur, proposed that Quebec leave Confederation if "in the view of the other provinces, it is believed that she is an obstacle to the union, progress, and development of Canada". For all the resentment over conscription, imperialism, and Regulation 17, not a single member spoke for separation and no one spoke more eloquently for Canada than Quebec's premier, Sir Lomer Gouin. Borden had his own olive branch: when he cancelled exemptions in April, he emphasized that single men must go so that married men could stay home. In no province did men marry earlier. In May, Gouin and Borden met for dinner. The conversation was easy. Henceforth, Borden suggested, Gouin would be consulted on contracts and appointments in his province. There was no need to spell out Gouin's side of the bargain: he would keep Quebec quiet for the rest of the war.

To Borden, that was necessary but minor political work. The prime minister's real task was to give Canada a voice in the Empire's policies on war and peace. On June 8, he reached London on his third wartime visit. Borden had much to learn.

When the Allies somehow stopped the German advance at Amiens, von Ludendorff had switched his offensive to the north. On April 9, a fresh tornado of artillery had dissolved an already demoralized Portuguese division. Some of them fled on bicycles left by a Canadian cyclist-battalion sent to plug the hole. In a day, all the gains of the Passchendaele offensive were lost. German troops penetrated almost to Hazebrouck and Ypres before they were held. On May 27, it was the turn of the French on the Chemin des Dames. Fifteen German divisions stormed across the Aisne. Pétain formed his line at the Marne and, for the first time, two U.S. divisions joined a major battle at Château Thierry. A huge German gun, nicknamed "Big Bertha", began lobbing shells at Paris. Allied losses were enormous.

Yet there was good news for Borden, too. He might not believe the perennial claim from generals that the enemy was exhausting himself, but it was true. It was certainly true that the Allies had somehow managed to hold their line and that Canadians had helped. Brigadier-General Raymond Brutinel's Motor Machine Gun Brigade, so far a mildly embarrassing element in the Corps, had found a major role in shoring up the crumbling Fifth British Army. One of its batteries had held off a German division for a day until only one gun and five men remained. At Moreuil Wood, all three regiments of the Canadian Cavalry Brigade had helped drive back the German advance on Amiens. A squadron commander, Lieutenant G.M. Flowerdew, had won a posthumous vc for leading his men in a glorious, if hopeless, charge. Battalions of Canadian railway troops, caught in the German offensives, had fought and died as infantry.

Best of all, the Canadian Corps had escaped the devastating impact of the German assaults. When he met Borden, Sir Arthur Currie had an explanation for Canadian immunity: during the winter, his men had worked hard to improve defences and strengthen the wire entanglements while British generals had built tennis courts. That was not fair. It ignored the exhaustion of British manpower, Lloyd George's deliberate policy of starving Haig of troops, and the extended line the British had accepted from the French. It also reflected Currie's growing nationalism and the mood of the Corps. On March 23, struggling to stem the German tide, Sir Douglas Haig had removed the 1st and 2nd divisions from the Canadian Corps. On the 26th, he called for the 3rd and 4th divisions as well, leaving Currie's headquarters with nothing to command. For a normal army corps, with no fixed complement of divisions, this was routine. In the March crisis, the Australian Corps accepted the arrangement but not Currie. Canadian divisions, he insisted, fought best under a headquarters that knew them. Not only did Currie let Haig know, he also warned Kemp in London. The plump and pompous new Overseas Minister took his concerns to the War Office. In the midst of the battle, Haig was directed to restore the Canadian Corps. By April 8, all but the 2nd Division were back under Currie's command. The British commander was furious. Currie, Haig grumbled, suffered from a swollen head.

Perhaps he did. Currie had earlier won an even more difficult struggle with his Canadian political superiors. When the British cut their divisions to nine infantry battalions, they assumed that the Canadians would follow suit. So did Canadians. Since conscription would soon relieve the CEF of the kind of desperate manpower shortage faced by Britain, a dozen extra battalions from the Corps and six from the 5th Division in England would allow two extra Canadian divisions in France, one more than the Australians. In turn, that would mean two Corps headquarters and perhaps a small Canadian army headquarters too: ten new headquarters in all, counting the new brigades — a boost to national pride and more than enough jobs for ambitious generals and surplus colonels. In December, Garnet Hughes offered to bet Currie any money he wanted that he would soon be in France. The British would be delighted to add a couple of new divisions when their real strength was shrinking, and Sir Edward Kemp could rejoice at Canada's enlarged status in the conflict.

Currie absolutely disagreed. The Corps, he claimed, was already a balanced, experienced team, which no one should break up. Where were the extra artillery and the supporting arms the new divisions would need? Well aware of Garnet Hughes and the surplus officers in England, Currie explained that many of the new staff positions would have to be filled by seasoned British officers. First General Turner and then Kemp heard the arguments. From Ottawa, Borden added his own warning. If the British insisted, the expansion could go ahead but, by September, Canada might not have enough men for the new organization. The British generals did not insist: they had no enthusiasm for weaker divisions. Currie's officers gave him an extra argument: adding six battalions would increase fighting strength by about 3,600 rifles but if a hundred men were added to each of the existing forty-eight battalions, fighting strength would rise by 1,400. If reinforcements grew scarce, it would be easier to cut back the extra men than to eliminate whole battalions and divisions.

Kemp was persuaded. When Garnet Hughes made a last bid, getting Lord Beaverbrook to involve Lloyd George, the answer was blunt: "Our cock won't fight." Instead of going to France, Garnet was out of a job. The 20,000 men of the 5th Division, held in England throughout the manpower crisis of 1917, became the manpower reserve that carried the Canadian Corps into the autumn of 1918.

Early in May, Haig pulled the Canadian Corps out of the line to rebuild for the coming battles. Sir Arthur Currie had ambitious plans for Canada's role in the war. He wanted Canadian squadrons in the Royal Flying Corps. "I am a good enough Canadian to believe, and my experience justifies me in believing, that Canadians are best served by Canadians," he had told Turner in November 1917. The government balked at the cost and complications, but in March 1918 it agreed to form a Canadian tank battalion. In April, Currie expanded the new machine-gun battalions in each division from sixty-four to ninety-six guns. At Passchendaele, he remembered, weary infantry had been forced to labour as road menders. That was wrong, and in May Currie used his pioneer battalions and men from the 5th Division to give each division a brigade of three battalions of engineers and a bridging company. Engineers, he foresaw, would be essential if the Corps was to keep mobile in the new conditions of open warfare. Infantry men built up their strength with route marches and practised the new German tactics of infiltration. "Maps to section leaders" had been a Currie slogan; now he had time to make sure that corporals and even privates would know what to do when their leaders were gone.

Currie, as his most recent biographer admits, was not loved by his men. His ponderous figure, stuffed in a general's uniform, looked ridiculous. When he inspected troops, he was pompous and fussy — "a regular Paul Pry", complained one gunner. Currie had an unfortunate gift for the ill-chosen phrase. "That's the way I like to see you," he told survivors of a battered unit, "all mud and blood." During the 1918 retreats, he had tried his hand at an inspiring message: "to those who will fall I say 'You will not die, but step into immortality'". The words brought jeers in dug-outs and billets. Canadians liked colourful, sympathetic officers: the fearless, friendly General Lipsett, the outspoken Archie Macdonell, and the cocky Dave Watson. Only generals themselves and the staff were aware of Currie's genuine openness to ideas and his patient pursuit of cheap routes to victory. What even privates could appreciate was Currie's remarkable technical competence and his determination to be liberal with materiel and conservative with lives.

In France, Currie was creating a Canadian army. In London, Kemp was determined to bring that army under Canadian control. Fresh from a Militia Department in which a politician was in charge, Kemp found that his predecessor had left matters to Sir Richard Turner and the generals. Kemp created an Overseas Council and presided over it. All the generals answered to him. So long as he served under Haig, Currie would be an exception but he did not command the small army of Canadians in France, ranging from tunnelling companies to field hospitals, which served outside the Corps. Canadian Railway Troops, 19,000 strong, played a major role in building and operating the British army's railways; 12,000 members of the Canadian Forestry Corps worked in French forests. By June 1918, Kemp had persuaded the War Office, Haig, and a very reluctant Currie that a Canadian Section at GHQ would oversee these troops and serve as the link between the Corps and the Overseas Ministry. The choice of Brigadier-General J.F.L. Embury, a former brigade commander, Saskatchewan Tory, and judge, won the confidence of both Kemp and Currie. "For matters of military operations," a War Office memo explained, "the Canadian Forces in the Field have been placed by the Canadian government under the Commander-in-Chief, British Armies in France...." Canada was now an ally, not a colony. Lord Derby had warned Haig about his troublesome subordinates late in 1917: "we must look upon them in the light in which they wish to be looked upon rather than in the light in which we would wish to do so".

AMIENS

From May until mid-July, the Canadian Corps enjoyed its longest respite from fighting. It did more than train and reorganize. On July 1, Dominion Day, fifty thousand Canadians gathered at Tincques, west of Arras, for the Corps sports championships. Engineers built a stadium and a platform for Borden, the Duke of Connaught, and the U.S. commander, General J.J. Pershing. On July 6, the 3rd Brigade's kilted battalions welcomed the entire British army to participate in Highland games. It was a time for pipes and drums, massed bands, twinkling brass, and polished boots. Then, on July 15, the Canadians went back to the line. They were part of a plan.

As Allied commander-in-chief, Marshal Foch had lost none of his old enthusiasm for the offensive. The British, he insisted, must attack near Festubert.

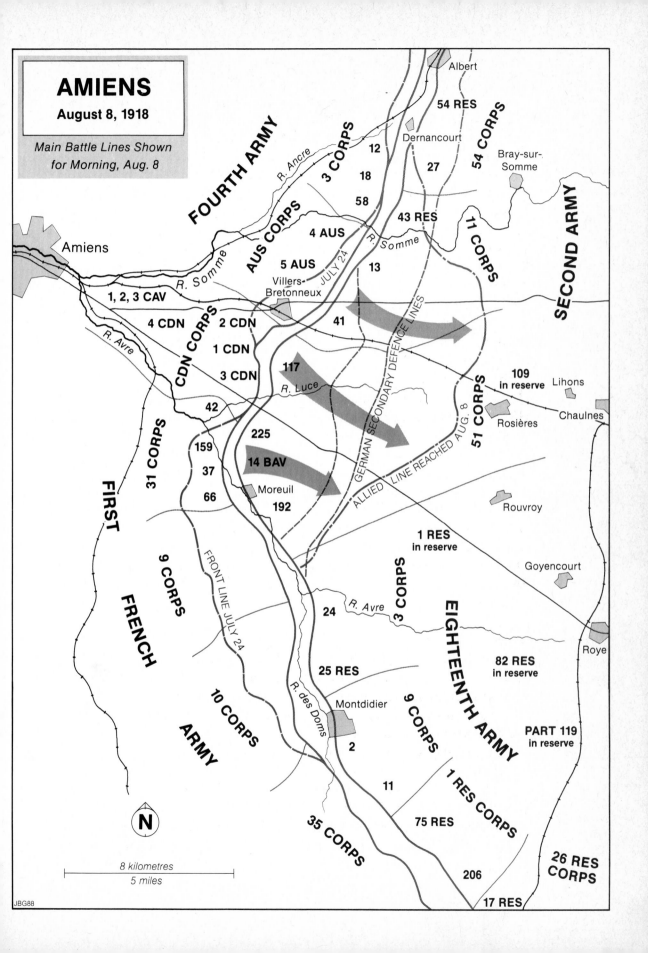

AMIENS

August 8, 1918

*Main Battle Lines Shown
for Morning, Aug. 8*

FOURTH ARMY

SECOND ARMY

R. Ancre

3 CORPS

AUS CORPS

Albert

54 RES

Dernancourt

54 CORPS

Bray-sur-Somme

12

18

27

58

43 RES

11 CORPS

4 AUS

R. Somme

Amiens

R. Somme

5 AUS

JULY 24

13

Villers-Bretonneux

1, 2, 3 CAV

4 CDN

2 CDN

41

CDN CORPS

1 CDN

R. Avre

3 CDN

117

109
in reserve

Lihons

R. Luce

Chaulnes

51 CORPS

GERMAN SECONDARY DEFENCE LINES

ALLIED LINE REACHED AUG. 8

Rosières

42

159

225

14 BAV

Moreuil

192

37

66

31 CORPS

FIRST

Rouvroy

1 RES
in reserve

Goyencourt

9 CORPS

FRONT LINE JULY 24

3 CORPS

R. Avre

24

FRENCH

EIGHTEENTH ARMY

82 RES
in reserve

Roye

10 CORPS

25 RES

ARMY

R. des Doms

Montdidier

9 CORPS

PART 119
in reserve

2

11

1 RES CORPS

N

35 CORPS

75 RES

26 RES
CORPS

206

17 RES

8 kilometres

5 miles

JBG88

For once, Haig rejected Flanders. He had another idea. On July 4, the Australians and sixty tanks had easily captured Hamel in a replay of the Cambrai tactics. Sir John Monash, the Australian Corps commander, was eager to try again on a bigger scale. The German salient at Amiens was the obvious place. The terrain was dry, unscarred, and ideal for tanks. German defences were ill-developed and the defenders were battle-weary and understrength. They could be shoved back from Amiens and perhaps farther. Foch was delighted. The French First Army would join in and, with Rawlinson's Fourth Army, the Boche could be shoved all the way to Roye.

Monash made a condition: his Australians deserved dependable troops on their flank. Canadians and Australians had not been friendly behind the lines but Monash respected Currie and the Canadian Corps was fresh, well trained, and backed by ten thousand reinforcements. The trouble was that the Canadians were thirty miles to the north and their sudden appearance at Amiens would warn the Germans of impending attack. Could a hundred thousand men, their guns and transport, be moved in secrecy? Currie hoped so. He continued the planning and rehearsals for the attack along the Scarpe that had been his original mission. Fresh orders about security were pasted in each soldier's paybook: "Keep your mouth shut!" they began. Two battalions, some medical units, and all the Corps wireless were sent north to Flanders. Currie kept his secret from his divisional commanders until July 31; the troops were told on August 6, two days before the battle.

Secrecy affected everyone. From August 1, GHQ ordered, all movement around Amiens would be at night. Dense columns of guns, wagons, trucks, and buses jammed the narrow roads. Canadian infantry were collected and delivered by buses to secret destinations in dense forests. In the damp undergrowth they slept or played poker. Overhead, planes of the new Royal Air Force tried to spot breaches of secrecy. A thousand guns and a hundred thousand tons of ammunition were hauled into place. As each Canadian field gun opened fire to test the range, an Australian gun fell silent. RAF bombers buzzed up and down the line to hide the sound of hundreds of tanks rolling into position. Assault troops were reminded, in their briefing, of the fate of the *Llandovery Castle*, a Canadian hospital ship torpedoed on June 27. Survivors had been machine-gunned in the water: only 24 of the 244 men and none of the 14 nursing sisters aboard were saved.

Currie had no time for elaborate plans or rehearsals. Secrecy dictated no barrage before zero hour but tanks would crush uncut wire on his front. The French corps on his right, however, had few tanks and depended on its guns to clear a path. That should take an hour; it could take for ever. Lipsett's 3rd Division would have to watch its flank. A tiny "international force" — a platoon each of Canadians and French — would move along the border. Across the Canadian front meandered the Luce, a river infantry could cross. What about tanks and guns? Could Currie's new engineer organization cope? Otherwise, the infantry would be all alone tackling the hundreds of hidden machine guns that formed the real German defences. Above all, had the Germans really been fooled? Were they planning to unleash a storm of fire on the waiting Canadians, packed in their thousands under the trees? At 3:30 A.M. on August 8, there was an explosion of German gunfire. Then it passed away. Soldiers slept, rolled in ground sheets. A few scribbled letters by hooded lanterns. "What I miss most about these months," Captain Fred Adams wrote to his wife, "is you and the sense that I am not seeing Charlotte or Betty grow up...all the babyish talk and the feeling that these are years none of us can live again."

At 4:20 A.M., in the eerie half-light of dawn, thick fog shrouded the ground. Suddenly, an inferno of sound made the ground shudder. The bombardment had begun. Smiling and joking at the power of it, infantry hoisted on their equipment and walked into the mist. It suddenly seemed easy. The German defences dissolved. Infantry threw duck-boards across the Luce and crossed dry-shod. Tanks were blinded and stopped by the fog but so were German machine-gunners. Many Germans simply surrendered. A few fought to a merciless end. Canadian platoons and sections were cut down. Survivors practised the tactics they had learned in the fields behind Arras. As usual, the officers and sergeants fell first but corporals and privates took the lead, pushing around or past resistance. A Black Watch corporal, Herman Good, rushed a German battery with only three comrades. For taking three guns and their shaken crews, he won the VC. So did two other Canadians that day. Both others died of their wounds. As the mist burned off, the tanks came forward to help — "one of the finest features of the day," the 18th Battalion diary remembered. Australians helped too, as their advance kept pace with the Canadians. On the right, as Currie had feared, the French lagged and Lipsett's division had a much harder time. The Royal Canadian Regiment took Mézières in the French sector so it could reach its own objectives.

Currie had expected the trouble, and the 3rd Division had the closest objective. The British 3rd Cavalry Division — including the Canadian Cavalry Brigade — came up behind Lipsett's men and passed through in hope that, finally, the horses would have their heads. Canadian horsemen took Beaucourt and Fresnoy but Germans drove them back from Beaucourt Wood. At 12:40 P.M. the 4th Canadian Division followed, two hours behind the cavalry. Watson had loaded his tanks with machine guns and infantry, with orders to rush four miles to the division objective and hold it. The experiment failed. Heat and fumes overcame the soldiers crammed into the rocking, noisy monsters. German guns in the French sector blasted ten of the tanks into smoking wreckage. Eleven surviving tanks reached their goal under such intense fire that most of them backed away. Troops who saw the carnage preferred to walk. Germans retook Fresnoy and, from the flank, mowed down the men of the 75th and 87th battalions in an open field as they headed for Le Quesnel.

It was the only real setback of the day. By dusk, the Canadians had swept forward eight miles and the Australians seven. The Corps had taken 5,033 prisoners and 161 guns at a cost of 1,036 dead, 2,803 wounded, and 29 prisoners. The French, at much higher cost, had covered five miles; the British corps on Monash's left flank had failed to go a mile. Across the front, the Germans had lost 27,000 men — half of them prisoners — and 400 guns. The Germans had not been entirely fooled: they had expected the attack but not so soon. Tanks and infantry might have done even better if they had known more about the ground and, as Brigadier-General George Tuxford of the 3rd Brigade complained, officers who could not keep a secret were unfit for command.

Both sides reacted to August 8 by instinct. The German Second Army sent in five new divisions; Rawlinson ordered the attack to continue, this time beyond the trench lines of 1916. No one in front pretended it would be easy. The new-style tactics sacrificed the aggressive risk-takers and wore down battalions even faster than the old. Rawlinson promised Currie a fresh British division, the 32nd. Then his staff countermanded the order, forcing Currie at the last moment to change plans, summon back the weary 3rd Division, and shuffle frontages for the 1st and 2nd divisions. Before dawn, the 4th Division took Le Quesnel but the rest of the Corps waited through the day as battalions took up position and batteries worked out fresh fire plans. Finally, between 11:00 and 2:00 P.M., brigades attacked piecemeal.

On August 9, the fighting got mean. Few tanks remained in action and they were sacrificed to German guns as the price of destroying machine-gunners. More than ever, courage and self-sacrifice made the difference. Battalions advanced behind the few men willing to tackle machine guns single-handed: Sergeant R.L. Zengel of the 7th Battalion and Corporal F.C. Coppins and Lance-Corporal Alexander Brereton of the 8th won VCs. Lieutenant Jean Brillant of the 22nd had been wounded on the 8th and he was wounded again when he led two platoons into Vrély to capture fifteen machine guns. Somehow he and the remnant struggled on to Méharicourt where he died capturing a German five-inch gun. He, too, was a posthumous VC. On the right, the 8th Brigade — the Canadian Mounted Rifles — fell victim to enfilade fire because the

French had barely moved. Somehow, by 5:00 P.M., they took Bouchoir and then Arvillers in the French sector.

August 9 took the Canadians to the edge of the old trench systems, an advance of four miles and often more, but there was little sense of triumph and the price was 2,574 dead and wounded — Captain Adams would never see his daughters again. The defence had been as disorganized as the Canadian attack but by evening thirteen German divisions faced Rawlinson's thirteen divisions and the fighting had moved into the rotted sandbags and rusty wire of the old trench line. That night Currie was finally given the 32nd British Division. He matched it with the 4th Canadian Division and ordered both to attack on August 10 to clear the old trench lines.

For Canadians exhilarated by open warfare, there was no pleasure in reviving the evil memory of uncut wire, sagging dug-outs, and collapsing traverses. German defenders no longer gave up; they counter-attacked. By now, the Canadian Corps was far ahead of the Australians and the French and its men could wonder what purpose their sacrifice served. As soldiers, of course, they had no choice. By the evening of August 10, the British and Canadian battalions had pushed their way past the old British trenches and into the German lines, but only at a heavy cost. On August 12, the 3rd Division replaced the British 32nd, and for three days it painfully pushed on, with platoons battling almost independently. One of them, led by a Danish immigrant, Thomas Dinesen, worked its way deep into the German line, adding about a mile of trenches. Dinesen, a private in the 42nd Battalion, earned his VC and a commission. On the same day, Sergeant Robert Spell of the PPCLI calmly sacrificed his life so that his platoon could escape a strong German counter-attack. His VC was posthumous.

Independently, Currie, Rawlinson, and Haig recognized that the battle was losing its point. The sweeping victory of August 8 would soon be forgotten as casualties mounted. In four days, Currie had lost 9,074 men to advance fourteen miles but the cost of each additional yard was soaring. Soldiers could be replaced but not leaders like Jean Brillant. Artillery, too, needed to be repaired and replenished. The tanks had been almost wiped out in two days of fighting; the surviving crews were utterly exhausted. It made no sense to continue. Rawlinson agreed. On August 11, he warned Currie not to drive the 32nd Division into heavy casualties and the Canadian took the hint: the general advance was cancelled. Only Foch was obdurate but he found that Haig, too, could be stubborn. "I spoke to Foch quite straightly," he recorded, "and let him know that I was responsible to my Government and fellow citizens for the handling of the British forces."

On August 15, the Amiens battle ended. On the night of the 19th–20th, Canadians began moving north again, to rejoin the First Army at Arras. They had won a victory but, like Ypres, Amiens was beginning to have unpleasant memories.

VICTORY IN 1920?

It might well have surprised Lloyd George, to say nothing of posterity, to discover Sir Douglas Haig defending the lives of his men from the Allies' new generalissimo, but 1918 was to be full of surprises and Canada was to share in them.

Borden had come to England in June to assert his claims as an Allied leader. He had kept his side of the 1917 bargain; had the British? Had they told him that Australians, New Zealanders, and Canadians would be dragged through the mud of Flanders? Currie's version of his grim experience had raised Borden close to the boiling point. "Mr. Prime Minister," he told Lloyd George, "I want to tell you that if there is a repetition of the battle of Passchendaele, not a Canadian soldier will leave the shores of Canada so long as the Canadian people entrust the government of their country to my hands."

Lloyd George was so pleased by the message that he persuaded Borden to repeat himself to the British generals. On June 20, he announced that the dominion prime ministers would begin meeting with him to review Britain's past and future military plans. At noon the next day, the new committee agreed that the dominions would have "a direct voice in the conduct of the war, and in the plans of campaign, so far as the War Cabinet had power to determine them." This was certainly progress from 1917, though the wily Lloyd George judged that he had created a forum of like-minded advisers to reinforce him against the folly of the generals or their political allies.

The war, by common consent, would not be over soon. Indeed, if the Russians could not be brought back into the struggle, the dominion prime ministers were soon persuaded, it might not end before 1920. Even more than the Germans, the Allies had been persuaded that a two-front war was prerequisite for German defeat. Getting the Russians to fight was an invitation to optimism and opportunism.

"Dunsterforce", a contingent of officers and other ranks (including forty-one Canadians) sent to Baku in the spring of 1918, was an example of both. Major-General L.C. Dunsterville had the task of recruiting Armenian levies, defending the local oil wells, and fending off Germans, Turks, Bolsheviks, and Jangali tribesmen. In September the enterprise collapsed when the Turks advanced, the Armenians fled, and the British escaped under Bolshevik guns.

Landings at Archangel and Murmansk were hardly more successful. Having welcomed the apparent British protection against a German advance, the Bolsheviks rapidly realized that their former allies were bent on renewing the war, or supporting counter-revolution or both.

A more substantial Allied hope was the Czech Legion, formed by Kerensky's government from Austro-Hungarian prisoners and deserters. By the spring of 1918, with its ranks swollen to sixty thousand, the Czech force was the most effective military organization in Russia and the only one eager to fight Germans and Austrians. The Bolsheviks grew alarmed. On May 14, they tried to disarm the Legion at Chelyabinsk. Instead, the Czechs seized the Trans-Siberian Railway from Samara to Irkutsk and set out across Siberia for Vladivostok to join the Allied cause. It was very convenient. So long as the Czechs disrupted the Russian railways, food and liberated prisoners could not get back to Germany. The Japanese, with an appropriate sense of self-interest, proposed to invade Siberia to rescue the embattled Czechs. President Wilson, alarmed at Tokyo's ill-concealed ambitions, insisted on an Allied presence. In July, Britain and the United States decided to send seven thousand men each; the Japanese, with no distractions, sent seventy thousand.

As Borden discovered, there was a price to be paid for belonging to the prime minister's committee. Having favoured every effort being made to revive the Eastern Front, Canada found itself invited to provide most of the British Siberian contingent. There might be other benefits too. Canadians also considered their interests. "Intimate relations with that rapidly developing country," Borden assured his colleagues in Ottawa, "will be a great advantage to Canada in the future." Trade with Siberia might follow the flag. On July 12, Militia Headquarters was ordered to create a force of five thousand. The CEF generated its last two battalions and, after a brief hunt for volunteers, Military Service Act men filled the ranks. A cavalry squadron from the Royal North West Mounted Police, a battery of artillery, machine-gunners, and supporting units left Vancouver in October, long after the Czechs had emerged from Siberia and barely a month before the war ended. A hundred more Canadians went to Murmansk to help organize and train local Russian levies and two Canadian field-artillery batteries, organized in England, left for Archangel in September to join a British, American, and French force under Major-General W.E. Ironside, formerly one of the British staff officers in the Canadian Corps. Canadian flyers with the RAF provided most of the air support for a largely French expedition to the Black Sea.

One may wonder why a country weary enough with fighting Germans would add Russian revolutionaries to their enemies. For Borden and many like him, the answer was simple: Bolshevism was a disease that had sapped

Russia's will to fight. With a little help, the patient would throw off the illness and rejoin the struggle. It was also an infectious disease. By leaving the war, even under the brutal conditions imposed by Germany at Brest-Litovsk, the Bolsheviks had encouraged the war-weary everywhere, including Canada. Bolshevism, with the savage atrocities committed in its name, might also be a warning to those who argued that Canada should emerge from the war into its own social revolution. In 1917, so conservative a thinker as Stephen Leacock had argued that "the government of every country ought to supply work and pay for the unemployed, maintenance of the infirm and aged, and education and opportunity for the children". Bolshevism showed the danger of such radical notions as the welfare state, pacifism, and social equality.

There were those, of course, who would brave such dangers. "If our masters force us to fight," declared Joe Naylor, president of the B.C. Federation of Labour, "let us fight for our own liberty and cast from our limbs the chains of slavery." Radicals, socialists, even liberals had welcomed Lenin's victory and argued for an end to war. Thousands of pre-war immigrants, fugitives from Tsarist oppression, had strong sympathy with Bolsheviks. They had little influence in Canada but they terrified or enraged those who had.

In 1918, there were more strikes in Canada than in the rest of the war years combined, and militancy spread from miners and machinists to municipal workers and even police. Inflation was the real reason, and the stubborn refusal of private and public employers to raise wages. It was "unpatriotic" to raise municipal taxes. Bolshevism was a more congenial explanation, particularly when labour leaders themselves talked of creating "soviets" and the irresistible power of the general strike.

Bolshevism became the excuse for a wave of repression that fed equally on conservatism and anti-alien feeling. C.H. Cahan, a Montreal Conservative, forced his services on the government on the strength of his claims that the country was riddled with sedition. The Dominion Police and the RNWMP, assigned to their respective ends of the country, found very little supporting evidence but orders-in-council in September banned a list of allegedly subversive organizations ranging from the Industrial Workers of the World to the Ukrainian Social Democratic Party. Months of pressure from veterans and patriotic organizations led to a ban on all publications in "enemy" languages. On the argument that minorities would be left with no information the ban was modified to require parallel translations into English. In October, the government simultaneously banned strikes and promised workers decent wages, the right to organize, and equal pay for equal work by women. None of these provisions was enforced.

Bolshevism, like war-weariness, was relative. In Canada, there was no comparison with the mood in Europe, where death and hunger had gone on too long. The German army had outlasted both its allies and its enemies. The Austrians had cracked in 1915; the Russians in 1916; the French, Italians, and even the British in 1917; but von Ludendorff had still found and trained the divisions for three great offensives in the spring of 1918. On July 15, he launched the greatest at Reims, the old cathedral town of France. West of Reims, the German guns crushed French defenders. To the east, the French had mastered German defence tactics. They kept back from the bombardment and smashed the assaulting storm-troopers when they were out of range of their own guns. With massed Renault tanks and no bombardment, Pétain ordered his divisions forward on August 7. French troops forced the Germans back to the Vesle.

A day later, on August 8, von Ludendorff learned of the battle at Amiens. What appalled him was the helpless crumbling of German resistance. Whole battalions had surrendered. Troops hurrying to plug the line had been met with cries of "War Prolongers", "Blacklegs", "Scab", by soldiers retreating from the line. It was, von Ludendorff wrote, *Die Katastrophe*, the Black Day of the German army. "Everything I had feared and of which I had so often given warning, had here in one place become a reality."

Germany was not beaten. Her army had 2.5 million men. Her conquests were intact. Her most powerful enemies were exhausted, as Canadians and Australians had painfully discovered at Amiens. What was gone was von Ludendorff's will to fight. That, like Bolshevism, was a communicable disease.

A British aircraft over Cambrai. While aviation historians tend to celebrate fighter combat and the air aces who emerged, the major contribution of aviation to the war was the monotonous, systematic collection of information, the direction of artillery fire, and the spotting of enemy preparations. Aerial surveillance forced front-line soldiers to work at night and rest, if they could, by day.

Vehicles of the Canadian Motor Machine Gun Brigade rest during the German offensives of 1918. While of limited use in most operations, the "Motors" played an invaluable role in stemming the German tide. Motorized firepower became an Allied advantage.

Save the Food and Serve the Empire !

The Average Canadian Family Wastes Enough to Feed a Soldier

"The Kitchen must help as well as the Workshop and the Trenches."
Lloyd George.

INTELLIGENT economy in the kitchen can do much to prevent the threatened world famine—can counteract the effect of high prices—and can replace growing debt with systematic saving.

Careful investigations show that before the war the average British family wasted 25% of their food—and we Canadians were even more extravagant.

This waste is not in a few big things, but in many little ones, each, we used to think, too small to bother about—such as careless peeling of vegetables and fruit—failure to make good use of dripping and "left-overs"—and such others as will occur to every thrifty housekeeper.

For the Empire's sake as well as your own, hunt up and cut out these leaks ! You'll be helping to relieve the food shortage—saving your own money—and putting yourself in a position to buy Canadian War Savings Certificates and help win the war.

War Savings Certificates are issued in denominations of $25, $50 and $100, to be repaid in three years at full face value. They cost $21.50, $43 and $86 respectively, at all Money Order Post-Offices and Banks, thus yielding over 5% Interest. Should you need it, you can get your money back at any time.   11

The National Service Board of Canada.

R. B. BENNETT,   C. W. PETERSON,
Director General.   Secretary.

By 1917 even Canadians were feeling the pinch of food scarcity; with experienced farm workers overseas, crop yields had fallen significantly. While government agencies produced floods of propaganda and some ingenious schemes for increasing the food supply and cutting consumption, rationing was rejected.

A Mark IV tank waits during the Amiens offensive on August 8, 1918. Canadians were delighted by the tracked monsters — but by the end of the day many had fallen victim to the enemy or to their own mechanical weakness. Never, until the end of the war, would as many tanks be available again.

Men of the 22nd Battalion bivouac on their way to the Amiens offensive. Years of experience had taught soldiers how to make themselves comfortable with their rifles and a couple of groundsheets.

One way to understand what a battalion meant is to see the officers of the 85th Nova Scotia Highlanders, proudly assembled in 1918 with their commanding officer, Lieutenant-Colonel J.L. Ralston, in their midst. A French liaison officer, in kepi and horizon-blue uniform, completes the group. A quarter-century later, in another war, Ralston would be Minister of National Defence.

Halifax after the explosion. The devastation flattened much of the working-class section of the city. The British cruiser *Highflyer* suffered only minor damage in the harbour, but clapboard houses ashore collapsed like cardboard.

Survivors of the Halifax explosion carry household treasures to safety. The city's black community, crowded into a working-class ghetto along Gottingen Street, suffered disproportionately from the devastation.

With food shortages a reality by the summer of 1918, the Canada Food Board did its best to inspire and then to frighten Canadians into buying only what they needed. But it was left to municipal authorities to enforce the regulations, and there is little evidence that many of them took a nearly impossible task seriously.

A 1917 cartoon in Toronto's *Saturday Night* relished the discomfiture of Sir
Joseph Flavelle, chairman of the all-powerful Imperial Munitions Board, when
his meat-packing company was discovered to have done very well out of the war.
That the charges were technically inaccurate did not restore "His Lardship's"
reputation.

Canadians and their allies on leave, visiting Versailles. By the end of the war, Paris had begun to rival London as a destination of choice. Men in the ranks averaged a week of leave each year; officers seem to have qualified for leave four times as often.

Top An irreverent cartoon of Sir Arthur Currie with Lindsay, his even stouter Chief Engineer, and an obese sergeant of the Veterinary Staff; compare Currie (front, centre) and Lindsay (behind him) in the photo below. The British staff officers flanking Currie, brigadier-generals Farmar and Radcliffe, should have much of the credit for the Corps's efficiency, but Currie deserved his reputation as a cool tactician who never believed that his men's lives were expendable.

Although by 1918 men no longer had the option of refusing to serve, wealth had to be persuaded to volunteer — through high-interest, tax-exempt bonds. In Regina, boy scouts joined civic leaders in promoting the 1918 Victory Bond campaign.

IX
ROAD TO VICTORY

On August 17, when Sir Robert Borden left for Canada, he still believed that the war might last until 1920. He had not consulted Haig or Foch. The Allied generalissimo had a simple message for his armies: "Tout le monde à la bataille." Haig agreed. "If we allow the enemy a period of quiet," he warned Winston Churchill after the Amiens drive, "he will recover and the 'wear-out' process must be recommenced." Politicians had heard the message too often to believe it but generals, including Sir Arthur Currie, still had faith. Co-ordinated attacks along the Western Front would also keep the Germans from concentrating their strength.

Foch wanted to attack everywhere and continuously. Like Pétain, Haig had learned moderation. All but his worn-out Fifth Army would have tasks. In the north, King Albert's Belgians and Plumer's Second Army would recover losses in Flanders. With the Australians as spearhead, Rawlinson's Fourth Army would drive the Germans back to the Hindenburg Line while Byng's Third Army would push for Bapaume and Cambrai. The Canadians would lead Sir Henry Horne's First Army in a drive up the Scarpe, through the Drocourt-Quéant Line and into the rolling country behind Cambrai. If they succeeded, the Hindenburg Line would be outflanked and useless.

The point had not escaped the Germans. In 1917, the British had lost 158,000 men trying to force their way up the Scarpe from Arras and it would be no easier in 1918. The hilly, wooded country was ideal for defence and the Germans had done their ingenious best to improve it. Attackers would have to fight their way through the old British and German trenches, past Monchy-le-Preux, where the Newfoundland battalion had been destroyed a second time in 1917, and two miles on to the Fresnes-Rouvroy Line. A mile farther was the formidable defence line the Germans christened *Woton-I-Stellung* and the

British D-Q, for Drocourt-Quéant. Down the slope was another line based on the unfinished Canal du Nord and beyond it, dominating the skyline, was the dark mass of Bourlon Wood. This was not Amiens, with worn-out divisions waiting in shallow trenches. It was the route Canadians would have to take to Cambrai.

There would be no surprises for either side. Currie had preferred the Arras front to the growing hopelessness of Amiens because the Corps had spent most of July preparing to take Monchy. The Germans were waiting too and they let the 31st Battalion take Neuville-Vitasse on August 24 because they wanted their strength where it mattered. Sir Henry Horne gave the Canadians two days to get ready; Currie demanded a third. Only two of his divisions were ready, the 2nd and 3rd. Horne lent him another, the renowned 51st Highland Division. The basic plan was simple. Each division would use up a brigade a day getting to the Fresnes-Rouvroy Line. On the fourth day, the 1st and 4th divisions would take over for the drive through the Drocourt-Quéant Line and, if possible, across the Canal du Nord. Guns were plentiful though many of them would be out of range by the second and third day if they could not be hauled forward. Tanks were scarce — only fifty were available — and experience warned the Canadians that, valuable as they were, there would be few in action by the second day.

That was the dilemma of trench warfare. Twenty years later, armies would have the mechanized equipment to get across the battlefield and support the infantry, but not in 1918. Generals could draw objectives on maps and historians later would draw arrows to show how troops attacked, but the reality was tiny clumps of exhausted, frightened men going forward amid bursting shells and machine-gun bullets. The advance depended on a few men who found a way through the wire or who wormed their way within grenade-throwing range of a German machine gun. If they had the luck to survive and the courage to go on, they and the handful of men who followed them were why battalions reached the goals marked out by staff officers' chinagraph pencils. There was nothing special about Canadians except, perhaps, something in their culture that told ex-clerks or farm boys not to wait for an officer to tell them what to do. Many of those officers were now ex-privates and corporals, picked out because a cool courage had made them natural leaders. When such men were dead or wounded, battalions faltered and the strain of going ahead became more than flesh and minds could endure. Then, if they could be found, fresh battalions took over or sometimes pride would push weary remnants of humanity just a little further beyond their limits.

That was the reality that waited for Canadians on August 26. Once the plan was made and the artillery barrages were planned, there was little more Cur-

rie or his generals could do to help, beyond adding a little surprise. The British always attacked at dawn, when first light from the east profiled the
German defences; Currie's attack began at 3:00 A.M., in hopes that the night
would be clear and the Germans would be dozing. In fact, that Monday, it was
drizzling and dark but most of the Germans were asleep. Burstall's battalions found little to stop them until dawn when they and their tanks were
blasted in the side from Monchy. Lipsett's 8th Brigade, the CMRs, found a concealed approach to the German stronghold and took it from a flank as field
gunners switched their barrage in an hour of hurried calculations — a feat
impossible a year earlier. Lieutenant Charles Rutherford, a big, cheerful officer from Colborne, Ontario, was far ahead of his troops when he boldly persuaded a German officer to surrender the remnant of his company. By day's
end, he had collected eighty prisoners and a VC. Beyond Monchy, the front
widened and both divisions needed two brigades against a German resistance that was even tougher than Currie had foreseen.

Next day, Tuesday, Currie had planned to reach the Fresnes-Rouvroy Line.
It was easier ordered than done. Fresh German divisions had rushed into
position overnight. Special companies of machine-gunners came with them,
and the terrain was full of hiding places for their deadly weapons. Canadians
faced a morning of pouring rain and slippery mud. The 5th Brigade waited for
its tanks and arrived late. The Quebeckers and New Brunswickers started at
10:00 A.M. and ran into the 26th Reserve Division, tough Württembergers. By
the time they got through Chérisy, the 22nd and 24th battalions combined had
only a few officers and a couple of hundred men. General Burstall settled for
a line just beyond the Sensée. His 4th Brigade and men of the 3rd Division
fought a murderous battle for Vis-en-Artois, a fortified village on the Cambrai
road. The rest of the 3rd Division did little better than push past the old German trenches.

Currie might have pulled out the skeleton battalions that remained but he
stuck with his plan. On the 28th, they must again face the German line. Lipsett spent the night reorganizing his units, concentrating those that remained
in the front line and organizing a barrage from all the heavy guns he could
muster. Burstall depended on the two brigades still in line. "Oh, it'll be all
right," Lieutenant-Colonel William Clark-Kennedy of the 24th reassured
Major Georges Vanier, the ex-lawyer who had just taken over the 22nd. The
two men knew the grim truth.

On Lipsett's front, the barrage crushed the German machine-gunners; from
Rémy to the Scarpe, battalions broke through. On the right, the barrage was
feeble, and weary soldiers, some of them eight days without sleep, made little
progress. Clark-Kennedy led his men into the German trenches but a counter-

attack drove them out. As he lay with a shattered leg, Clark-Kennedy inspired the survivors to another, more successful assault. He won the vc. Vanier also lost his leg, and Lieutenant-Colonel A.E.G. Mackenzie of the 26th New Brunswick Battalion was killed. So were most of the officers, including the Vandoo's medical officer, who rounded up men for a final attack. In all, the two divisions lost 5,801 men. On August 29, the German war communiqué gave special mention to the hard-fighting Württembergers.

Currie had extracted the ultimate sacrifice from Burstall's and Lipsett's men because taking the actual Drocourt-Quéant Line might be an even worse struggle. By dawn on August 29, three fresh divisions were in place, the 1st, 4th, and, on the left, the 4th British, a regular army formation. Brutinel's mobile force moved to the middle, ready to race down the Arras-Cambrai highway to seize bridges on the Canal du Nord. Currie insisted on three days' preparation. The 1st Division used the time to finish Burstall's work. Brigadier-General Griesbach's 1st Brigade worked out an ingenious artillery barrage, slipped two battalions through a British bridgehead in the Fresnes-Rouvroy Line, and took the key German strong point in Upton Wood by attacking from three sides. Of the two battalions of Württembergers, German accounts recorded, only fifty men escaped. The German 26th Reserve Division was pulled out the next night. On the 4th Division front, it was Germans who kept up the pressure, attacking at dawn on September 2, coinciding with Currie's assault.

The D-Q Line lived up to its reputation. So did the Corps. On the right, the 1st Division suffered because the adjoining 57th British Division lagged behind. Hardest hit was the 3rd Brigade and its 16th Canadian Scottish. When a company faltered, Lance-Corporal Bill Metcalf, an American, jumped to his feet and led a tank towards a menacing German machine-gun post. No one knew how he survived. Lieutenant-Colonel Cy Peck, of the 16th, a huge man, walked through the bullets and exploding shells, prodding his men, raging at a tank that lumbered off to safety, and personally bringing up reserves. Both men earned vcs. So did three other Canadians...and many others who would never see them. The Division's objective was two miles beyond the D-Q Line, a stretch of reserve trench called the Buissy Switch. Despite terrible losses, the Canadians made it through though it took until 11:00 P.M.

The 4th Division faced a shorter, tougher route. Beyond the D-Q Line lay Dury and, beside it, a bald knob of ground called Mont Dury. The 47th and 50th battalions got through the line to find the wire in front of Dury uncut. Brave men grabbed cutters to snip open a gap and the 46th Battalion went through. The 38th and 72nd went over Mont Dury and fell in swathes when machine guns caught them. Unaccountably there was no artillery support.

The survivors struggled through without it. Later they learned the reason: the guns had stopped firing to let Brutinel's cavalry and machine-gun trucks go through. The 10th Hussars, a British regiment, saw the carnage and took its horses home. A few fallen trees stopped the trucks. Brutinel's bright idea of driving across the battlefield — with Currie's endorsement — had cost a lot of Canadian lives.

On Monday, September 3, exhausted Canadian and British survivors got up and resumed the attack. It turned out to be easy. The Germans had retreated behind the Canal du Nord — one of the "disagreeable decisions", von Hindenburg recalled. In three days of waiting and fighting, the 1st and 4th divisions and Brutinel's units had lost 5,622 dead and wounded, near-annihilation for the ten battalions that bore the brunt of the attack. Yet they had finished a fight that General Watson for one, and even the over-optimistic Haig, had thought impossible. Canadian infantry had taken on the toughest of defence lines and some of the toughest German troops and they had prevailed.

CANAL DU NORD

The politicians were more worried about losses than gains that month. From London, Sir Henry Wilson passed a blunt warning to Haig that heavy casualties would cost him his command. Lord Milner passed by Currie's headquarters on September 14 to hint that if the war lasted to 1919, the Canadian might have Haig's job. In fact, Currie's men would help make sure that never happened.

By mid-September, there was fighting up and down the Western Front. On September 12, Americans began driving in the St. Mihiel salient. On the same day, Byng's men cleared Germans from Havrincourt. Six days later, Rawlinson launched a fresh attack. Horne got his orders on the 15th: he would take Bourlon Wood and cover Byng as far as Cambrai. The Canadians again would lead the way.

Currie had expected it. Far in the rear, Horne's chief of staff had already sneered that, with a little more energy and leadership, the Canadians could have seized the Canal du Nord. That was absurd. On the 4th, Currie had climbed a hill to make his own assessment of the problem. It was formidable. Opposite the Canadian positions, the canal overflowed its banks, creating a vast, impassable marsh. Farther along, though, a thousand-yard stretch of the ditch was dry. With ladders, infantry could get down one side and up the other, but they would then face a line of German machine guns and, a mile back, a solid defence system called the Marcoing Line. Above it, on a slope covered by old trenches and excavations, was Bourlon Wood, a vast stand of

prime oak that could hide a division. To the left the ground was open and bare
of cover except for a handful of fortified villages and the Marcoing Line.

On September 18, three days after his orders, Currie submitted his plan. It
broke most of the rules of sound generalship. A horrified Horne consulted
Haig and even Byng. What the Canadian proposed was to shift his front south
to the dry part of the canal, seize a narrow bridgehead, and then expand out-
ward, getting behind the German defences on the canal. It was so easy to see
what could go wrong. Three divisions jammed in a narrow defile would be a
German gunner's dream. If the advance stalled, troops behind would be
slaughtered. For Canadian artillery, the planning would be incredibly complicated, with barrages moving forward, back, and sideways. Failure would
hurt the chances of three British armies and possibly destroy the Canadian
Corps. Surely Currie should try something simpler. He was adamant. The
only alternative — a frontal attack — would be far more costly. Sir Julian
Byng was asked to review the plan. Currie was confident. His staff, his gunners, and his infantry would, in his favourite phrase, "deliver the goods". If
they didn't, Byng reminded him, "it means home for you".

Of course the Canadians needed time, and they had most of September to
get ready. Thousands of reinforcements filled the gaps left along the Scarpe;
many of them were now MSA men. There was little discrimination, though
colonels complained that the conscripts were poorly trained. Germans gave
them a baptism of fire: the weeks along the canal cost an average of one
hundred casualties a day. General Odlum was hit; so was Colonel Pearkes, so
badly that his intestines were exposed; tough as ever, he lived. On September
13, General Lipsett left, full of regrets, to take over the 4th British Division.
Currie might have insisted on keeping his old mentor — unquestionably his
best division commander — but another of the Ypres colonels, Major-
General F.O.W. Loomis, took over. Canadians now commanded all the divisions of their corps.

At dusk on September 27, platoons shuffled out of bunkers on the D-Q Line,
shivered in the cold, damp darkness, and set off down slopes that seemed alive
with troops. By midnight, clusters of men waited in the open, huddled for
warmth and reassurance. Harness squeaked and chains rattled as field guns
moved into position for the dawn rush. Engineers manhandled bridges as
close to the canal as they dared. Surely the Germans must know the huge,
helpless target in front of them. A few shells fell and there were losses, but not
many.

At 5:20, a dreary, overcast dawn, the barrage began. Smoke and high explosive edged the canal as infantry with ladders raced forward. The 14th Battalion, unaccountably unprovided, found it did not need them. The 10th Brigade

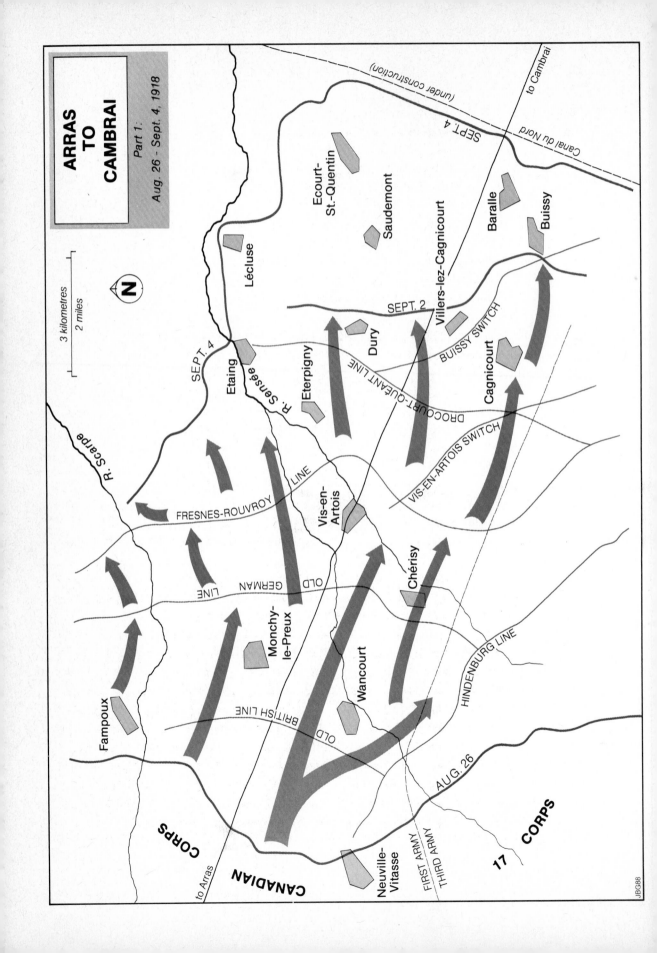

ARRAS
TO
CAMBRAI

Part 1:
Aug. 26 - Sept. 4, 1918

N

3 kilometres
2 miles

to Cambrai

(under construction)

Canal du Nord

SEPT. 4

Ecourt-
St.-Quentin

Saudemont

Baralle

Buissy

Lécluse

Villers-lez-Cagnicourt

SEPT. 2

BUISSY SWITCH

R. Sensée

SEPT. 4

Etaing

Eterpigny

Dury

Cagnicourt

DROCOURT-QUEANT LINE

VIS-EN-ARTOIS SWITCH

R. Scarpe

FRESNES-ROUVROY

LINE

Vis-en-
Artois

Chérisy

OLD GERMAN LINE

LINE

Monchy-
le-Preux

Fampoux

Wancourt

HINDENBURG LINE

OLD BRITISH LINE

AUG. 26

FIRST ARMY
THIRD ARMY

CANADIAN CORPS

CORPS

Neuville-
Vitasse

to Arras

17

CORPS

JBG88

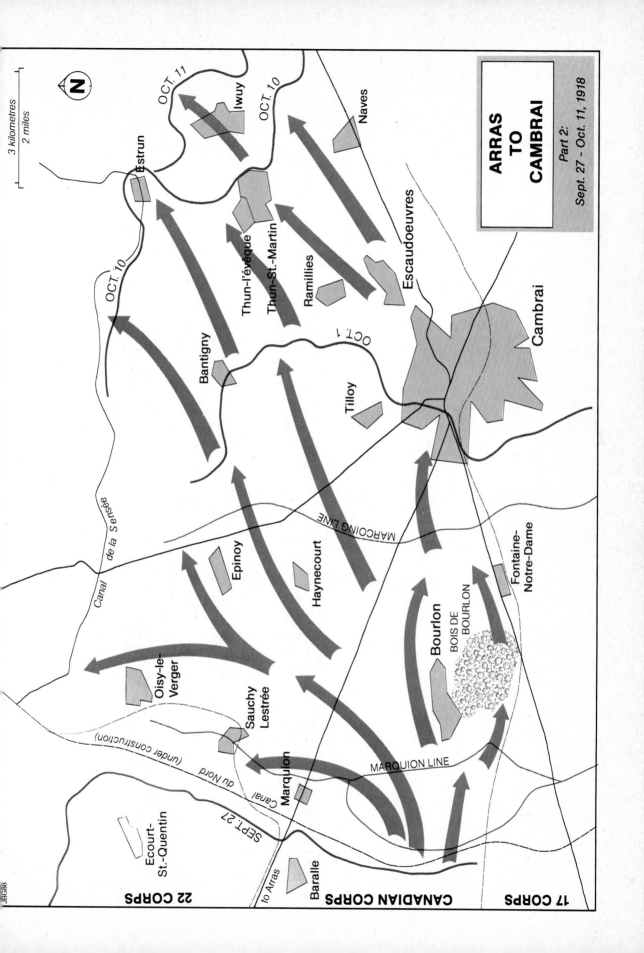

ARRAS
TO
CAMBRAI

Part 2:
Sept. 27 - Oct. 11, 1918

N

3 kilometres
2 miles

OCT. 11

Iwuy

OCT. 10

Estrun

Naves

OCT. 10

Thun-l'évêque

Thun-St.-Martin

Ramillies

Escaudoeuvres

Bantigny

OCT. 1

Tilloy

Cambrai

Canal de la Sensée

Epinoy

Haynecourt

MARCOING LINE

Bourlon

BOIS DE BOURLON

Fontaine-
Notre-Dame

Oisy-le-
Verger

Sauchy
Lestrée

Canal du Nord (under construction)

Marquion

MARQUION LINE

Ecourt-
St.-Quentin

SEPT. 27

to Arras

Baralle

22 CORPS

CANADIAN CORPS

17 CORPS

JBG88

cleared the bridgehead and rushed the Marcoing Line. The 1st Brigade pushed north to Sains-lez-Marquion and Marquion. Brigadier-General Tuxford stolidly stumped along with his men, pausing to take some prisoners. As Canadians cleared the canal the 11th British Division crossed and pushed through open country to Oisy-le-Verger and Epinoy. The rest of the 1st Division flanked them, battling through Haynecourt and to the edge of the Marcoing Line, where barbed wire and deadly machine-gun fire stopped them at dusk. The 4th Division faced a tougher fight as the 12th Brigade struggled up the slope to the village of Bourlon and the 11th Brigade attempted to surround Bourlon Wood. The 54th Battalion did more than its job, penetrating almost as far as Fontaine-Notre-Dame east of the forest, but on the south side, the 102nd Battalion was isolated by a lagging British attack and dug in for its own survival. Two officers, lieutenants S.L. Honey and Graham Lyall, won VCs for their leadership, their battalions won the right to oak-leaf badges for their heroism amid the trees of Bourlon Wood. Lyall lived; Honey died.

Except on the right, where a tired, understrength British division had failed, the day was a complete victory. Currie had gambled on the professionalism and courage in his corps and won. Those who had condemned his massive engineer organization could reckon with its success in starting the flow of guns, tanks, and supplies within three hours of the first assault, despite German snipers and artillery. Tuxford's brigade had been helped by barrages moving in every direction, including backwards. At nightfall, the Germans abandoned Bourlon and fell back to the Marcoing Line. The diarist of the 188th Regiment, the Bourlon garrison, recalled the 27th of September: "on this day we buried all our hopes for victory".

After the impossible, anything else should be easy. Cambrai, the first real city the Canadians had seen behind German lines, seemed an easy prize. Loomis's rested 3rd Division was brought into line between the British XVII Corps and the 4th Division, with the city a bare two miles away. A continuous, relentless drive seemed the only sensible tactics. Success seemed certain.

Yet experience repeated itself: the second day at Amiens, the second day on the Scarpe. Being victorious was no compensation for exhaustion, the loss of key leaders, the lack of tanks, and the impossible task of dragging guns and ammunition across the battlefield to set up effective fire support. The Canadians could not keep advancing at night into unknown obstacles but the Germans could bring up fresh divisions and supply them from shortened supply lines. Cambrai was too vital to be sacrificed.

At dawn on September 28, the 9th Brigade took Fontaine-Notre-Dame for the British but when it moved east it found the RCR and the PPCLI pinned down by the same tough Württembergers who had stopped the 4th Division almost a month earlier. Captain George Little, filling in for his dead colonel, pulled the remnants of the PPCLI back to a dip in the ground to face his brigadier. "What we have, we hold," said the general. "We didn't have any," replied the captain. On the left, Lieutenant Milton Gregg of the RCR found a tiny gap in the wire and crawled through with a few men. Twice he was wounded, once he went back for grenades but Gregg and dozens like him broke the Marcoing Line. The 10th Brigade, which had led the Corps across the Canal du Nord the day before, struggled through the German line at Raillencourt with men "mowed down like grass". The 46th Battalion, men from south Saskatchewan, got through to the road; the 44th — now from New Brunswick — had 112 men left next day after a night of counter-attacks in front of Sailly. The 1st Division and the British 11th made almost no progress. The 10th Battalion, already trapped in a salient of dense barbed wire, reluctantly obeyed orders for a hopeless attack and lost 100 men, half of them when the Canadian artillery barrage landed in its own positions.

September 29 was hardly better. Brigades attacked at intervals, in hope that this time their guns could offer better support. The Germans were waiting. The 116th — the once-raw Umpty-Umps from Ontario — left two companies dead in swathes; the two others took Ste. Olle. Behind it the 2nd CMR fought its way into the suburb of Neuville St. Rémy. Survivors remembered it as their cruellest fight of the war. The 42nd and 49th battalions got to the Douai-Cambrai road. The Highlanders cut their way by hand through dense thickets of wire. The Germans waited patiently until the Canadians were fully entangled and then opened fire. Most of the 42nd were killed or wounded. Bodies hung from the wire, twitching as bullets struck them. The remnant grimly kept on cutting; when they were done, they avenged their comrades.

In contrast, the 72nd Highlanders of the 4th Division broke through easily, took Sancourt, and sent a six-man patrol to Blécourt to collect 80 prisoners. Then the Canadians found they had been led into a trap: the shallow valley was a German killing ground. The survivors ended up back where they had started. In turn, that contributed to a disaster for the 8th Battalion. Sent into an attack without flank support, the Winnipeggers were decimated. A corporal brought back one company. The day cost the Corps 2,089 men, including the 1st Division's beloved senior chaplain, Canon Frederick Scott, painfully wounded as he tended casualties near the front.

By now, Currie was worried. The fighting was far tougher than he had expected and casualties were heavy. On September 30, the PPCLI got over a defended railway embankment and took Tilloy but that was the day's only real success. Farther along the embankment, Germans crushed an attack by the 11th Brigade. The 75th Mississaugas took 467 into action; 78 walked back.

Next day, October 1, Currie planned a co-ordinated attack by all three divisions in the line. The 11th British Division promised three battalions; as worn out as the Canadians, they sent three companies. Currie described it as an "absolute betrayal". So it proved for the 3rd Brigade, which forced a way up the valley from Sancourt to Blécourt and to Bantigny and Cuvillers only to be isolated from north and south when a 4th Division attack also bogged down. The Canadians fought their way out, using German rifles when their own ammunition ran out. By nightfall, the 14th Royal Montrealers had 92 men left; the 16th Canadian Scottish had 78. It was after dark when the 102nd Battalion reached Cuvillers, at a cost of 177 men. Hardest hit was the 9th Brigade, which took the high ground east of Tilloy only to run into a storm of fire on the forward slope. Dazed survivors simply dug in amidst their own dead and wounded.

That afternoon, Horne sent word to Currie to hold his ground. The Corps could do little more. The 2nd Division had yet to fight but Currie knew that Burstall's shaken battalions were far from ready for serious battle. Instead, they replaced the 1st and 4th divisions and dug in from Tilloy to Cuvillers. Cambrai remained just out of reach. Staff officers counted 7,000 prisoners and reassured Currie that the death rate for casualties since Amiens was unusually low — one in seven compared to one in two or three at the Somme or Passchendaele. Machine-gun bullets left clean wounds. The carnage in the 75th Battalion was a little more tolerable since only 25 of the 389 casualties were killed.

Men who had lost friends in hopeless, unsupported attacks were not consoled. If victory was now imminent, it was all the worse to die. Soldiers grumbled that Currie was a glory-seeker, demanding the bloodiest tasks for his corps. Australians in Rawlinson's army made the same bitter charges against Sir John Monash. Currie's anger at the 11th Division on October 1 was his own version of inter-Allied friction. So were complaints by British generals that dominion troops got too much credit for the progress all along the British front. Beaverbrook, now in charge of Lloyd George's propaganda, took care of his own, and both Currie and Monash needed victorious reputations if Lloyd George was to give them command of the British armies in 1919. Around Cambrai, as the cold October rain pelted down, there was anything but a mood of triumph.

PURSUIT TO MONS

If the Canadians felt exhausted and resentful of their thirty thousand casualties since August 8, that was exactly what von Ludendorff had intended by his hard-fought withdrawal to the Hindenburg Line. Without conscription to fill its ranks and with minor mutinies erupting in exhausted battalions, the Australian Corps was pulled out of the line on October 5. British divisions, cut to nine battalions, lacked fighting endurance, as the Canadians had learned to their cost, but, taken as a whole, Haig's armies were in far better shape than Pétain's. The American drive into the Argonne forest in October turned into a near-disaster because of staff inexperience and logistic breakdown.

That was not how it looked to the Germans. All along the front, their gains from the spring offensives had vanished. In the Argonne, the Americans and French had moved seven miles in seven days. British and Belgian troops took Passchendaele and the Messines ridge in two days. On September 27, Byng's army broke the Hindenburg Line south of Cambrai. After Amiens, von Ludendorff had urged that Germany negotiate an immediate armistice — preferably on the basis of Wilson's Fourteen Points. On September 28, he found to his fury that nothing serious had been done. Next day at Spa, he and an unhappy Field Marshal von Hindenburg demanded an immediate armistice. That night von Ludendorff learned that Rawlinson's Fourth Army, with a couple of American divisions, had again broken the line and pushed three miles beyond it. The German army seemed to be collapsing.

Nor was there comfort from anywhere else. General Louis Franchet d'Esperey, relieved of his army during the German offensives, arrived at Salonika with Clemenceau's permission to restore his reputation. On September 15, he sent his French, British, and Serbian troops up the Vardar and the Bulgarian army, ragged and starving, collapsed. By the 29th, King Ferdinand had asked for an armistice and "the gardeners of Salonika" were free to threaten both Vienna and Constantinople. Turkey was lost. A British army advanced from Baghdad to the oil wells of Mosul. In Palestine on September 19, Sir Edmund Allenby began the envelopment and destruction of three Turkish armies in the battle of Megidoo — the biblical Armageddon. By the end of the month, he had 70,000 Turkish and 3,700 German prisoners and the road to Damascus was clear.

Everywhere, an unexpected actor played a part: a pandemic of acute influenza which the French blamed on Spain but which seems to have had its origins in India. Such pandemics were not new: doctors remembered the mass outbreak of 1890 when the old and middle-aged had sickened and died; this time it was young adults who seemed to be most susceptible, an ironic yet appalling ally to war as a killer of the young. Both virology and antibiotics were unknown in 1918. The disease swept through Europe in the spring and summer and returned, with even more virulence, in the autumn, adding to the exhaustion, bereavement, and despair of four long years of war.

Influenza could not be allowed a role in diplomacy or strategy. Haig was winning his war and, albeit with little gratitude, the politicans had to let him do it. The Germans, too, had to fight because, as von Hindenburg warned his generals, the armistice terms would depend on how well their armies held together and what damage they could inflict. Behind the Hindenburg Line, prisoners and deportee labour struggled to build a *Hermann-Stellung* from the Dutch border through the old fortress town of Valenciennes to the Oise River. Air reconnaissance told the Allied generals what to expect. The more time they gave the Germans, the tougher the next fight would be. The Canadian respite was over.

On October 6, Currie got his orders. The Corps would take Cambrai and link up with the Third Army. Burstall's battalions would seize crossings over the Canal de l'Escaut. For the operation he called "Peace Proposal", Burstall chose a night attack. Canadians were not fond of them but they made sense after the 3rd Division's experience of attacking down the same forward slope from Tilloy on October 1. Poison gas, dumped in the valley between Blécourt and Batigny, discouraged any German flank attack. At 1:30 A.M. on the 9th, the barrage began. Men of the 6th Brigade started forward. They caught the Germans getting ready to withdraw. By mid-morning, the 5th Brigade was fighting for the canal crossings, as teams of engineers hunted feverishly for demolition charges to defuse. At Pont d'Aire, Captain Charles Mitchell of the Canadian Engineers had to stop dismantling German explosives and fight off German defenders. He won his corps's first VC. The 25th Battalion took Escaudoeuvres; the canal was crossed.

In Cambrai, men of the 4th and 5th CMRs crossed the canal on partly demolished bridges and made their way gingerly through a city undefended except by German snipers and occasional shells. Engineers followed to repair bridges, clear streets, and fight the fires deliberately set by the retreating enemy to destroy the old city. As General Loomis entered at 11:00 A.M., his men encountered the first British troops entering the far suburbs. That afternoon the Corps's cavalry regiment, the Canadian Light Horse, tried its hand at chasing a retreating enemy; German machine guns hit a dozen men and forty-seven horses, and the pursuit ended. The Germans were not in flight. Burstall's men faced hard fighting on the 10th and 11th as they battled their way north-east along the canal. The 20th Battalion, sent past Iwuy with the 21st Battalion to seize high ground, lost three hundred men from enfilade fire. One of them was Lieutenant Wallace Algie, who had earned a VC by rushing two machine guns. As the Canadians moved down the far slope a soldier cried: "My God, look at them houses moving". They were German tanks. The Canadian infantry and nearby British troops fled back up the slope until a battery of Canadian field guns galloped up and disposed of the threat. The shaken infantry were content to hold their ground.

The capture of Cambrai changed the Canadian mood. Now they felt victorious and, when they saw what German occupation had meant for the French, they were angry too. Civilians were hungry; their homes and cities had been pillaged, and mines and factories had been systematically destroyed. They were also cautious; who wants to die on the eve of victory? General Lipsett, scouting in front as usual, was killed on October 14, after only a few days in his new command. Currie and men of Lipsett's old battalion, the 8th, went to Quéant on the 15th for the funeral. It seemed a waste but men might also wonder what place a good general would have in a post-war world. Horne shuffled his army, putting the Canadians in the middle, between the VII and XXII corps, along the Canal de la Sensée. Beyond a morning barrage and a few patrols, the front was quiet. On the 17th, there was no reply; the Germans had gone. The pursuit was on.

Some Canadians had already joined in. On October 8, near Le Cateau, the Canadian Cavalry Brigade helped advancing infantry from the Fourth Army. While dismounted men from the Fort Garry Horse held the front, the Strathconas and Royal Canadian Dragoons swept around on horseback in successful flanking attacks while the Royal Canadian Horse Artillery provided support. At a cost of 168 men and 171 horses, the cavalry finally showed the little that was left to them by 1918. Haig and his fellow cavalry generals were delighted.

For the most part, the war of movement advanced at an infantry pace of three miles an hour. Thanks to their engineer brigades, the Canadians outmarched their neighbouring corps, but everything seemed to conspire to hold them up. The Germans had emptied the country of food, demolished every bridge, ripped up every railway, and mined every road. The crowds of civilians who cheered the Canadian infantry and gunners desperately needed food and medical care. The Corps's trucks, worn out from months of hauling heavy shells, faced a sixty-mile turnaround on roads that, at their best, usually were limited to one-way traffic. Soldiers, footsore and weary from forced marches, cursed the staff for late and inadequate supplies; Currie, in turn, raged at "Higher Authorities" who had failed to plan.

Four days on the road brought the Canadians to Valenciennes, an industrial city of 36,000 people that was the key to the new German defence line. Five divisions, admittedly understrength, guarded the city. Two of them faced the Canadians across acres of flooded land, the Canal de l'Escaut, and a well-fortified city. Three of them defended Mont Houy, a 150-foot hill that dominated the southern approach. Horne ordered the 51st Highland Division to take Mont Houy. Currie's 4th Division would move through it to the high ground east of Valenciennes and the rest of the Corps would then cross the Escaut, avoiding the city and its population as much as possible. Currie sent Brigadier-General Andrew McNaughton, now commanding the Corps heavy artillery, to offer the British his help. He was rudely rebuffed. On October 28, the 51st Division sent a single battalion to take Mont Houy: it took the hill only to be thrown off with heavy losses.

First Army staff were upset: the defeat might interfere with the general advance Haig had ordered for November 3. The Canadians must take over and do the job. Currie refused. He remembered St. Eloi in 1916, when Canadians had also inherited a mess. Either the 51st Division would take the hill or he would do it his way. On the 29th, the Army headquarters grudgingly agreed. Then they told McNaughton to economize on shells. The Canadians refused. This might well be their last barrage of the war and they would do it well. McNaughton sent officers to beg, borrow, and salvage all the shells they could. At dawn on November 1, he had 108 heavy guns and the field artillery of three divisions. With the aid of old French maps and new air photos, gunnery staffs prepared an elaborate fire plan: box barrages, rolling barrages, even a reverse barrage to give German defenders the illusion they were being hit by their own guns.

At 5:15 A.M., Mont Houy exploded in a deluge of fire. A single battalion, the 44th, walked up the hill behind a wall of fire. Other battalions passed through on the other side. Not until they reached the suburb of Marly and a demolished steel plant did they meet tough resistance: the remnants of the German 8th Division. Sergeant Hugh Cairns, an ex-apprentice of twenty-one from Saskatoon, led his men through three machine-gun nests. He was arranging for sixty Germans to surrender when their officer shot him. Few of the Germans survived. Canadians that day were in an ugly mood. Too many Germans surrendered, complained the diarist of the 50th Battalion, but "some very useful killing was also achieved".

That night patrols of the 3rd Division crossed into the city and by dawn the Germans had left. On the 2nd, the British had taken the steel works and the Hermann Line was history. Including Cairns, the last Canadian VC winner of the war, 80 men had died and 300 were wounded. Burial parties counted 800 German dead. McNaughton boasted that his guns had fired 2,149 tons of shells, not much less than both sides had used in the South African War.

From Valenciennes, the Canadian route lay to the Belgian border and Mons. It was a country of hills, rapid streams, hedges, and dense forests, ideal for tough rearguard fighting. Rain poured down on marching troops on every day but one. As transport lagged behind, weary infantry had to carry all they needed, from spare ammunition and grenades to extra rations. Engineers concentrated on keeping three brigades of heavy artillery up with the Corps as back-up for any rearguard battle. On November 5, at the Aunelle River on the Belgian frontier, Watson's division ran into a stiff rearguard fight. After a brief set-back, the 85th Battalion forced a passage. On the 6th, the 2nd Division took over the advance. On the left, the 3rd Division ran into the German rearguard at Vicq on November 4. Soon, its men were in Belgium too, noticing, like all Canadians, that there were young men in the crowds, goods in the stores, and no devastation. Belgians had fared a lot better under the Germans than the French.

By November 9, the 7th Brigade reached Jemappes, outside Mons. To the south, Burstall's battalions had to fight their way through the densely clustered villages and coal tips of Belgium's best mining district. Air observers and deserters warned of a real battle at Mons. On the 10th, both Canadian divisions found hardening German resistance. Fighting through the coalfields south of Mons, with German machine-gunners hidden at every tip, cost 350 Canadian casualties, only a few of them killed. The 3rd Division, in the approaches to Mons, spent the day cautiously probing its way around the west side of the city, losing 116 men to machine guns and a few shells. Late that night, companies of the RCR and the 42nd Highlanders moved cautiously into the city. The Germans were gone. Excited soldiers woke the residents by clattering their bayonets along the grilled windows. The 5th Lancers, a British regiment that had retreated from Mons in 1914, rode through the streets and out towards Nimy. To the south, the 2nd Division advanced as far as St. Symphorien, and battalions of the 6th Brigade sent patrols as far as the Canal du Centre. At 10:55 A.M., a German sniper spotted Private George Price of the 28th Northwest Battalion and shot him in the chest. By 11:00 A.M. on November 11, he was dead, the sole Canadian killed that day.

The Armistice

Von Ludendorff's anger had worked. At the suggestion of the high command, a new chancellor with a liberal reputation, Prince Max of Baden, was appointed, a few social democrats were invited into the government, and, on October 4, President Wilson was invited to offer an armistice based on his Fourteen Points. Wilson was taken aback. Were the Germans serious? Would they evacuate all conquered territory? They must do so before he would act. On October 12, Prince Max eagerly agreed. On the same day, a German U-boat torpedoed the s.s. *Leinster* in the Irish Sea and 450 passengers, some of them

American, drowned. Wilson and the Americans were indignant. The deal was off. Military commanders would have to settle any armistice.

Prince Max tried again. So did Wilson. On October 23, the American president told the Allied commanders to arrange the cease-fire. The commanders were not equally pleased. Pershing wanted more battles to give his soldiers victories. The French wanted a lot more than the Fourteen Points; they wanted the Rhineland. Admiral Sir Rosslyn Wemyss, Foch's British deputy, wanted the German battle fleet. Haig was the moderate. A badly weakened German army should survive, if only as bulwark against the Bolsheviks. American voters had an influence too. In the November mid-term elections, Republicans won a commanding lead. Their policy was simple: win the war, bring the boys home, and let Europe settle its own affairs.

The war was certainly being won. On October 30, Turkish delegates signed an armistice with a British admiral and his fleet sailed through the Dardanelles, four years too late. Allenby had reached Damascus. Franchet d'Esperey reached the Danube. From Vienna, Emperor Karl also asked Wilson for a peace based on the Fourteen Points but the American president had already promised self-determination to Czechs, Poles, South Slavs, and even Romanians. Most of the Habsburg Empire could switch from vanquished to victors by proclaiming independence. Only Hungary and the Austrians were too late. On November 2, Hungary recalled its troops from Italy. The Italian armies advanced in the glorious and nearly bloodless battle of Vittoria Veneto and took 300,000 unresisting prisoners.

On October 26, the Kaiser dismissed von Ludendorff, who prudently withdrew to Sweden. His successor, General Wilhelm Groener, had managed Germany's industrial mobilization and worked closely enough with union leaders and social democrats to have their confidence. Otherwise, the hapless Kaiser and his commanders hardly knew what to do. On the 29th, the Kaiser went to army headquarters and refused to leave. The admirals decided that they would wreck the armistice talks by sending the High Seas Fleet to sea. Their sailors mutinied. By November 3, they had taken over the dockyards. By November 9 revolution had reached Berlin. Groener, the son of a Swabian sergeant, was given the unpleasant task of telling the Kaiser that the army would not fight for him. Von Hindenburg and the more aristocratic generals had spared themselves such embarrassment. On the 10th, the Kaiser crossed the Dutch border after tiresome haggling, and never returned.

There were no generals on the German armistice commission, chiefly because they might have made trouble. Matthias Erzberger, leader of the Catholic Center Party, had that dirty job. Foch and Admiral Wemyss met him in a railway carriage in the Forest of Compiègne on November 8. The Germans, Foch announced, must hand over their war materiel, fleet, and sub-marines. They must withdraw from all invaded territory and Alsace-Lorraine. The treaties Berlin had signed with a defeated Romania and Russia were annulled. The Allies would occupy the west bank and bridgeheads for fifty miles beyond. Erzberger was appalled but, by the time he could report, the Kaiser was gone and an ex-saddlemaker and socialist, Friedrich Ebert, had replaced Prince Max. He must sign. Erzberger returned on the 10th, pleaded in vain for the Allies to lift their blockade on Germany, and at 5:00 A.M. on November 11, he signed. "A nation of seventy millions of people suffers," said Erzberger, "but it does not die." "Très bien," said Foch, and left without shaking hands.

Around the world, people had watched the collapse of the Central Powers with astonishment and a realization that other problems were already pushing for attention: Bolshevism, starvation, and the killer influenza. In Canada, the disease had arrived in mid-September, at a Polish army training camp at Niagara-on-the-Lake. Other cases spread up the St. Lawrence from ships docking at Quebec and Montreal. Troopships, loaded with conscripts, carried it back across the Atlantic. The *City of Cairo* lost 32 of its 1,057 soldiers and crew, the *Victoria* lost 40 of 1,549. Across Canada, one in six fell ill and 30,000 to 50,000 died. A third of the people of Labrador died, including half the Inuit. There was no treatment or cure, or even an understanding of the cause, until 1933. By October, schools and theatres were closed, coal production fell, and railways were disrupted. Alberta made gauze masks compulsory. Since people of military age were often the hardest hit, military hospitals in Canada overflowed, only months after the Army Medical Corps had taken them over from the civilian-run Hospitals Commission. A public indoctrinated in the legend of Florence Nightingale knew whom to blame.

A country that was prone to sickness, shortages, and displays of wartime wealth could fear Bolsheviks and foreigners — and the two were easily linked. Government responded with fresh regulations and restrictions. The only escape would be peace and, for a moment on November 7, it seemed to have arrived. Reports of an armistice spread from New York, bringing joyful crowds into the streets. Within hours, the people learned that it was all a rumour.

On November 11, the armistice was no rumour. The timing let Canadian newspapers lay out their biggest headline type for the early editions. Canadians awoke to the news and went out on a cold grey morning to celebrate. In small towns, they decorated carts and trucks and fire engines and staged impromptu processions. In the cities, people thronged the main streets, jamming traffic. On Parliament Hill, the sober Methodist Newton

Rowell sought to lead Canadians in solemn thanksgiving. Elsewhere, Canadians broke into whatever stock of liquor prohibition had left them, to celebrate the peace.

In London and Paris and Rome, there were cheering crowds, too. In Trafalgar Square, Canadian soldiers lit a bonfire by Nelson's Monument that left marks that are still visible. At Canadian bases at Witley and Bramshott, celebrations boiled into attacks on the neighbouring "tin towns", the shops on the edge of camp where merchants had spent a profitable war, separating Canadian soldiers from their pay. At Mons and along the front, no one remembered cheering. News of the armistice reached the Canadian Corps at 7:00 A.M. but it took two hours to spread the order that all shooting would stop at 11:00 A.M.

In Mons, the 42nd Battalion sent its pipe band to play through the city at 7:00 A.M. and General Loomis invited Currie to stage a triumphant entry at 11:00 A.M. He had a reason. A week earlier, the mayor of Valenciennes had invited the Canadians to celebrate its liberation. Sir Henry Horne had intervened to insist that British troops also be honoured and that he would take the salute. Currie was even angrier when the British troops took precedence over Canadians in the parade. Currie rode into Mons with an escort of the British 5th Lancers but the 1,500 troops drawn up in the Grand Place were all Canadians. General Horne bore no grudge. "The Capture of Mons at the last moment," he wrote to Currie, "is a splendid crowning achievement on the part of the Canadian Corps. It is, I think, just about the best thing that could have happened."

The Canadians had ended their war where a younger Brigadier-General Henry Horne had begun it in August 1914.

A Canadian howitzer is readied to fire as dawn mist rises from the gunpit. The target is the German line east of Arras as the Canadian Corps launches the second phase of its "Last Hundred Days". Infantry carried the brunt of the fighting, but effective artillery support made their advances possible.

A German prisoner surrenders near Cambrai. While prisoners were a staple for war photographers eager to assure civilians that enemy morale was cracking, Canadians attacking at Cambrai in 1918 found their German opponents to be as tough, ingenious, and relentless as ever.

Sir Douglas Haig congratulates a Canadian battalion as the men stand easy by the side of a road. Haig had no deep affection for his obstreperous colonials, but by the autumn of 1918 the Australians and Canadians were among the best troops he commanded.

German prisoners captured in the Canadian advance look as young as the raw
Canadian reinforcements waiting to move up. Cavalry, one with a drawn sabre,
serve as escort — their most common operational role after the first few months
of the war.

Bridging the Canal du Nord. The photograph, taken from the German side, shows the obstacle the Canadians faced at dawn on September 27, and why Currie insisted on launching his assault across the narrow but dry section of the canal.

A German victim of the Canadian assault on the Canal du Nord. Shellfire was probably the means of "neutralizing" this machine-gun post.

A Canadian gunner attempts to feed and comfort a Belgian orphan whose mother was killed at the end of the war by a stray German shell. Contemporary accounts suggest little of the live-and-let-live spirit between Germans and Canadians, and none at all when Canadians saw for themselves the effect of German occupation on civilian populations.

The burning ruins of Cambrai. The fight to capture Cambrai was the bitterest and most costly part of the long autumn struggle by the Canadian Corps. Here, a Canadian patrol pauses to find its direction in the rubble-clogged streets.

Crowds celebrating the Armistice in Vancouver on November 9. Unfortunately they were two days early, misled by a rumour that may have originated in New York.

The pipe band of the 42nd Battalion marches through the crowd in the main square at Mons on the morning of November 11. Currie was later condemned by his enemies for rushing to capture the town where the war had begun for the British Army in 1914. In fact, the Canadians took Mons without casualties, and most soldiers felt a sense of dramatic fulfilment. Others merely enjoyed the hospitality.

X
COUNTING THE COSTS

SETTLING THE PEACE

An armistice only interrupted the conflict. Neither the war nor the fighting was over. Two of Currie's divisions, the 1st and 2nd, rested a few days and then set out on a long, wet march through Belgium and Germany to the occupied bridgeheads at Bonn and Cologne. Far away, at Tulgas, south of Archangel, the infant Red Army had chosen November 11 to attack Canadian gunners and American infantry. By the spring, twenty-four Canadians would be dead or wounded in north Russia. Four thousand more Canadians waited at Vladivostok. In Belgium, there were some Canadians who would have fought on. "We have them on the run," wrote General Andrew McNaughton. "That means we have to do it over again in another twenty-five years."

Borden was on the *Mauretania*, a day out of New York on November 11. "The world has drifted far from its anchorage," he noted a little sadly, "and no man can with certainty prophesy what the outcome will be." For Canada, he intended that outcome to include international status and recognition. When Lloyd George had summoned the dominion prime ministers on October 27, to develop a British Empire position for the peace conference, Borden made his point firmly: "The press and people of this country take it for granted that Canada will be represented at the Peace Conference." That did not mean, he repeated in London, sharing one of the five British seats with one of the other dominions or India. He had other views too. Putting the Kaiser on trial — a popular theme in the British election campaign in December — Borden found repugnant. So was the grab for German colonies by Australia and South Africa. Such behaviour, he warned, would anger Americans. An Anglo-American accord, he insisted was "the best asset we could bring home from the war".

246

President Wilson, Borden soon discovered, was just as offended at Lloyd George's efforts to get seats for the dominions; it seemed to the Americans just another scheme to enhance British influence. Besides, the conference would be crowded enough. A score of nations had hopped on the winning side in the last months of the war. Perhaps one seat each would suffice. Borden was furious. Canada would not settle for less representation than Belgium or Portugal; she had "lost more men killed in France than Portugal had put into the field". In the end, after a reminder that seats carried no votes, Wilson gave way. India, Canada, Australia, and South Africa would each have two seats, like Belgium and Portugal; New Zealand would have one; and Newfoundland would have none at all.

In January, Borden and the remaining premiers and their delegations moved to Paris. It was soon apparent that seats made no difference; the issues were settled in a Council of Five (or Ten, when foreign ministers attended) with only the United States, France, Britain, Italy, and Japan represented. In practice Wilson, Clemenceau, and Lloyd George decided most things. The results were imperfect but, given their exhaustion, their personal differences, and their incessant domestic interruptions, it is a marvel that there were any results at all.

Of the three, the U.S. president had come farthest. The first president to leave the United States during his term, Wilson left a hostile Congress and restive citizens. To the throngs gathered to cheer him, the tall, bespectacled Wilson seemed to promise a fresh idealism and a respect for small nations. In fact, Americans had ended their involvement in the financial and transportation problems of the Allies on November 11, and most of them wanted to go home. Wilson believed he would have to fight for his dream of a League of Nations. To his surprise, he found his allies eager to embrace it. The British had even worked out a detailed scheme, which Wilson, lacking his own, largely adopted. Indeed, Wilson found that his allies wanted to do more than he did. The Japanese proposed to make racial equality part of the covenant. The French wanted a league militant enough to protect it from German vengeance. Australia, South Africa, and New Zealand found that a league "mandate" gave respectability to their seizure of German colonies.

With the league and mandates settled and the German fleet safely under guard in Scapa Flow, the British, French, and Americans could settle down to decide the terms of peace. The Germans now felt confident of a reasonable settlement: the Kaiser and his ministers were gone, socialists were in power, and there could be no victors or vanquished in President Wilson's world. They were wrong. Allied propaganda had insisted that there were no "good" Germans. In a triumphant election campaign, Lloyd George and his followers had

talked of squeezing Germany "til the pips squeaked". At the end of the Napo-
leonic wars a century earlier, aristocratic leaders from all sides had met at
Vienna and, amidst balls and receptions, easily become reconciled. Democracies were less forgiving, and their leaders knew it. They also knew that
their democratic armies had largely melted away with demobilization. What
remained to pressure Germany was a blockade that reduced the enemy to
such a state of hunger that thousands died prematurely.

France dictated the terms, with minor modifications imposed by her major
allies. Germany would be disarmed — no air force, tanks, submarines, or
dreadnoughts. France proposed a peacetime German army of only two
hundred thousand conscripts; Wilson and Lloyd George insisted that a small
professional army like their own was less militaristic and Germany was
allowed a hundred thousand professionals. France wanted the Rhineland;
Lloyd George insisted instead on demilitarization and a fifteen-year occupation of the Saar as compensation for German sabotage of French coal mines.
France, of course, got Alsace and Lorraine and the Belgians got a few villages.
In the East, the Poles and Czechs got most of what they wanted from Germany, with warm French support. The biggest issue was reparations. In 1871,
Germany had imposed a five-billion–franc indemnity, confident that it would
cripple the French economy for generations. France remembered. Leaders, if
not their voters, might admit that Germany could hardly bear the whole cost
of the war but she had been wholly immune from damage while large regions
of France, Belgium, and Italy had been devastated. South Africa's Jan Smuts
reminded delegates that war pensions might also be financed from reparations. The details would be complicated. The solution, Allied leaders agreed,
was to force Germany to accept her full guilt for starting the war and leave the
specifics to a commission of experts.

The German delegates first saw the Allied terms in May. They were
appalled. They were permitted to object in writing. As a modest concession to
self-determination, the people of Silesia were allowed a plebiscite on their
fate. Nothing else would be altered. Germany would be disarmed in the middle of its enemies. Millions of Germans would live under Polish, Czech, or
French rule. The war-guilt clause was a national humiliation few Germans felt
they deserved. The German national assembly, meeting at Weimar to debate
a constitution for the new republic, paused to consider renewing the war.
President Ebert asked von Hindenburg for an opinion. Once again, the low-
born General Groener was left to tell politicians the truth: Germany was def-
enceless. There could be no more war. Ebert accepted the facts as he heard
them. He did not have to be reminded of the starvation and the disorder.

On June 28, 1919, Paris society followed the Allied delegations to the Hall of Mirrors at Versailles where, in 1871, the German Empire had been proclaimed. Now the delegates of the German republic were escorted in to sign, as their triumphant conquerors waited. Then it was the turn of the conquerors. Under Great Britain, but slightly indented at the insistence of James T. Shotwell, one of Wilson's aides, the dominions were listed. Then the guns fired salutes, the fountains danced, and the Germans withdrew to reflect on their own special bitterness.

Borden was not at Versailles; nor was Sir George Foster, though his face appears in Sir William Orpen's painting of the occasion. A.L. Sifton, the former Alberta premier, and C.J. Doherty, the Minister of Justice, signed for Canada. Canadians took little interest in the other treaties that, in the following months, ended wars with Bulgaria, Austria, Hungary, and Turkey. Most wrote themselves, with exchanges of territory and reparations that were never paid. Only Versailles really mattered. In the end, Borden and his colleagues had had little to do with the tone or the details. They were more concerned with the League Covenant and its Article X, requiring that the "High Contracting Parties undertake to respect and preserve against external aggression the territorial integrity and existing political independence of all State members of the League". Such a clause, warned Doherty, meant that Canada, though no longer willing to be involved automatically in Britain's war, would be forced to defend France, Italy, and someday even Germany. The Canadians could protest but discreetly, because for Borden it was even more important to belong to the league and its first subordinate body, the International Labour Organization, than to fuss about details.

Did Canadians agree? Borden insisted that Canada's Parliament would ratify the treaty even if the British had to wait. A day after the special session opened, on September 2, Borden presented the treaty. It was, for him, the climax of a five-year ordeal and he sought, in his own fashion, to instruct Canadians on the importance of his diplomatic role:

On behalf of my country I stood firmly upon this solid ground: that in the greatest of all wars, in which the world's liberty, the world's justice, in short, the world's future destiny were at stake, Canada had led the democracies of both the American continents. Her resolve had given inspiration, her sacrifices had been conspicuous, her effort was unabated to the end. The same indomitable spirit which made her capable of that effort and sacrifice made her equally incapable of accepting at the Peace Conference, in the League of Nations or elsewhere, a status inferior to that accorded to nations less advanced in their development, less amply endowed in wealth, resources, population, no more complete in their sovereignty and far less conspicuous in their sacrifice.

As so often on such occasions, party rancour clouded the significance of the occasion. Liberals split on whether Borden had wickedly separated Canada from the Empire or whether he had surrendered her sovereignty to a new league. Bringing the peace treaty to Parliament, claimed William Fielding, Laurier's old finance minister, was "a colossal humbug, designed to impose upon an innocent Parliament and to bamboozle a too-credulous people". Quebec Liberals deplored Article X. So, privately, did Borden, but a nation newly emerged in the world had to accept worldly imperfection. Without division but with far less enthusiasm than Borden would have hoped, Parliament ratified the treaty on September 12.

The U.S. Senate did not. Three times it refused. Among the arguments hurled at President Wilson was the provision that allowed votes to Britain's colonies. To Washington, at least, Canada remained a British dependency. The war itself dragged on in law, if not in practice, until midnight on August 21, 1920, a fact trivial to all but pension claimants.

DEMOBILIZATION

Like her allies, Canada did not wait for the peace treaty to demobilize. Within days of the armistice the Imperial Munitions Board cancelled its contracts, put its factories up for sale, and laid off 289,000 workers. By death or discharge, more than a third of the 619,636 members of the CEF had left before November 11; at the end of July, another 321,188 officers and other ranks of the CEF had been released.

Many, of course, would not return. In all, 59,544 members of the CEF had died during their service, 51,748 by enemy action, 51,346 of them in France or Belgium. The tiny Canadian navy recorded 150 deaths from all causes but there was no count of the Canadians who died with the Royal Navy, as reservists or volunteers with the British army, or in the Allied forces. A painstaking search of Royal Air Force records allowed the Canadian official historian to report that 1,388 Canadians died as aircrew with the British flying services out of a British total of 6,166. At the war's end, 43,000 patients lay in British or Canadian hospitals overseas. During the war, 154,361 men reported wounds, though many soldiers were wounded several times and there was no record of those whose mental or emotional damage went undiagnosed. In all, 3,846 Canadians were taken prisoner, of whom 3,478 returned from German camps. Many of them had survived appalling brutality and exploitation in German mines and labour camps; most had little to report but boredom and malnutrition.

Planning for returned soldiers had begun in the summer of 1915 with the formation of the Military Hospitals Commission. Its secretary, Ernest Scammell, devised his own policy in the absence of better guidance and no one altered its fundamentals. The state, he insisted, owed disabled soldiers more than a pension; they must also be restored and, if necessary, retrained for a suitable job. "There must be a minimum of sentiment and a maximum of hard business sense," Scammell warned. A Toronto engineer, Walter Segsworth, created a no-nonsense vocational-training organization that began with female ward aides teaching occupational therapy to the bedridden and culminated in "scouts" who found job placements for retrained veterans. Courses were limited to men who could not go back to former occupations. Retraining, insisted Segsworth, was a need, not a right.

Scammell's policies also meshed with a military-pension system specifically designed to spare Canada the bloated pension burden of the post–Civil War United States. Widows' pensions depended on good behaviour; their offspring were expected to support themselves at age sixteen for boys and seventeen for girls. The disabilities of sick or wounded veterans were examined by a medical board and assessed in Ottawa by a pension examiner, using a French-inspired "Table of Disabilities". Loss of both legs, both arms, or both eyes was 100 per cent disability; a missing eye or lower leg was 40 per cent. Though reproductive organs hardly affected earning power, a burst of Gallic sentiment valued them at 60 per cent. The scheme made generosity cheap. No more than 5 per cent of Canadian pensioners ever earned the rate for total disability.

By 1918, the Hospitals Commission and an independent Board of Pension Commissioners could boast that Canada had the most logical, efficient, and generous repatriation program of any of the Allies. Pressure from the Great War Veterans' Association (GWVA), formed at Winnipeg in 1917, helped persuade Parliament to keep Canadian pension rates even higher than in the United States, mainly by levelling up the rates for lower ranks until by 1920 a totally disabled private received as much as a lieutenant, $900 a year. Hospitals, training programs, tuberculosis sanatoria beds, even a government-run prosthetics factory in Toronto, bespoke a country eager to do its duty by disabled veterans and their families.

Like most veterans, the disabled defied stereotype. Most suffered from illness, not wounds. By the end of 1919, military hospitals had treated 8,508 cases of tuberculosis or referred them to sanatoria. Grants and building by the MHC doubled sanatorium accommodation during the war and introduced x-ray and other modern equipment. The CEF also recorded 2,000 insane, many of them victims of tertiary syphilis. Among the wounded, 127 men had been blinded and 3,461 men and one woman had suffered amputation of a limb. A black soldier, Curly Christian, was the lone quadrilateral amputee to survive; three others had lost three limbs. Shell shock, in the opinion of the official medical historian, was "a manifestation of childishness and femininity" and, as such, best cured by offering no pension, no encouragement, and no medical record. No count of psychological victims was kept until long after the war.

Planning to bring soldiers home began in 1917. Staff prepared forms, devised procedures, and explored a British plan to release soldiers in occupations specially necessary to restart a peacetime economy. A questionnaire administered in October 1918 revealed an unexpected enthusiasm for taking up farming. Unfortunately, the November armistice interfered with the official plans. So did the soldiers. The imminent winter meant slumping employment, ice-bound ports, and bad weather on the Atlantic. Worn-out railways more than shipping shortages limited Canadian ports to thirty thousand men a month. Business, unions, even the GWVA urged the government to postpone demobilization until spring. Sending two Canadian divisions to help occupy Germany was an added complication.

The government wanted early repatriation: it wanted to cut its costs. Soldiers, too, wanted to come home. If they could not do so at once, "first over, first back" was the only fair way. Mutinies by British soldiers ended schemes to release "pivotal men" and "demobilizers". Sir Arthur Currie also had his ideas: he wanted his battalions returned intact, to be welcomed by the cities and towns that had sponsored them. To politicians terrified that war had turned soldiers into homicidal barbarians, he had a powerful argument: only in cohesive units, under their own officers, would soldiers observe discipline. The Overseas Ministry compromised. Men outside the Corps would return in drafts, with married men having priority. Disgruntled soldiers disembarking from one of the first troopships to reach Halifax brought another directive from Ottawa: only the best ships would do for returning heroes.

In an England afflicted by cold weather, shortages, strikes, and influenza, the Overseas minister, Sir Edward Kemp, and his officials did their best. "You cannot blame the soldiers for kicking and complaining," he reported to Borden. "You are living in paradise in Canada as compared with this place." At Kinmel Park, a Canadian transit camp near Liverpool, "kicking" took the form of a riot on March 4–5 when soldiers learned that MSA conscripts in 3rd Division units were already headed for Canada while one of their ships had been cancelled as being unfit. Five soldiers died in various affrays. Canadian authorities blamed "Bolshevism" but the British provided more ships. In April and May, there were more riots at Witley and Bramshott, and again more ships were provided. Clashes between the British and their reluctant guests climaxed at Epsom in June with the death of an elderly policeman.

By September, the Overseas Ministry had despatched 267,813 Canadian soldiers and 37,748 wives and children. Despite dire warnings and Kemp's disapproval, 15,182 soldiers took their release in England, though they were outnumbered by 24,753 "Imperials" who went to Canada. Among those left behind were 34 Canadians, including 2 murderers, serving sentences in British prisons. A remnant of Kemp's officials stayed to oversee shipping of weapons and equipment and a British gift of $5 millions' worth of aircraft and spare parts to launch a Canadian air force. The brave promise in 1914 that Canada would bear the full cost of her contingent had degenerated by 1917 into haggling over the cost of the vast quantities of artillery ammunition consumed by the Corps. Arguments about dead horses, barrack damages, and mysterious Serbian soldiers ended in a Canadian agreement in April 1920 to pay $252,567,942.03 for the cost of her overseas army. The Overseas Ministry could at last be dissolved.

The delays in England and Belgium allowed soldiers to complete elaborate documentation and medical examinations before they embarked for Canada. Despite worn-out railways and damage in Halifax, demobilization in Canada proceeded with impressive speed. Men with families disembarked at Saint John, hospital ships docked at Portland, Maine, and most soldiers landed at Halifax's Pier II. A Repatriation Committee, headed by Herbert J. Daly, president of the ill-fated Home Bank, helped organize civic welcomes, reception committees, and volunteers. The Red Cross distributed comforts, boy scouts carried family baggage, and Rotary Clubs organized cars and drivers. CEF battalions formed up, marched through cheering crowds, endured the speeches of municipal dignitaries, and waited for the last command most of them ever wanted to hear from the army: "Dismiss!" Next day, men handed in their rifles and equipment, collected a discharge pin, a transport warrant, $35 for civilian clothing, and a War Service Gratuity that averaged $240. "I was in Civies," Claude Craig recorded in his diary. "It was great."

What happened next? In the 1917 election, soldiers had been promised "full re-establishment", a phrase that left much to the imagination and seemingly a great deal of responsibility to the new Department of Soldiers' Civil Re-establishment, created in February 1918. In practice, it was the old Hospital Commission, with Scammell's doctrine intact. If the disabled could work, so must the able-bodied. Full re-establishment for them meant the right to earn a living, raise a family, and pay taxes — and the sooner the better. Even before the armistice, returning soldiers seemed afflicted by such a lassitude and dependence that some doctors wondered if the Germans had a secret weapon. Perhaps the disease was army life. "Most of the men come back with sluggish mental action," a Hospitals Commission pamphlet explained. "They have been under military discipline so long, clothed, fed and ordered about that they have lost independence." A new Employment Service of Canada, created to help munition workers, was available to help soldiers find a job. To do more was to risk permanent psychological damage.

The one exception to official *laissez-faire* was more apparent than real. Free land for ex-soldiers was an old Canadian tradition. It had also become impossible: the last available public land had been distributed to South African War veterans in 1907. However, both soldiers and the public expected a settlement program, and a series of half-hearted measures culminated in the Soldier Settlement Act of 1918. As presented by Arthur Meighen, it was strictly a business proposition. Soldiers who proved their strength and experience — nurses were excluded — could borrow up to $7,500 at 5 per cent for land, livestock, and buildings. A Soldiers Settlement Board held the title, supervised the settlers, and protected the public's money. When returning soldiers discovered wartime farm prices, whole battalions applied for loans, though only about twenty-five thousand became settlers. Within a few years, when prices had collapsed but the debts remained, the difference between old-fashioned military bounty and the new businesslike soldier settlement became painfully clear.

Apart from soldier settlement and government employment bureaux, most returned men were on their own. Veterans could claim a year's free medical care at military hospitals, and government-sponsored Returned Soldiers Insurance offered them a life policy with no medical examination. Manitoba offered property-tax relief. Ontario, New Brunswick, Saskatchewan, and British Columbia offered otherwise unsaleable land for soldiers' colonies. When universities sought federal help in educating veterans they were rebuffed: it would be "class legislation".

Most veterans accepted their situation, found work, and tried to rebuild their lives. Others carried such crippling burdens of emotional or psychological disability that normal life was impossible. Few ex-soldiers escaped a sense of grievance. It was too easy to see that those who stayed home had done better. Medical officers and lawyers came home to find their practices had been dissolved. So had innumerable businesses. Farmers had lost the profitable wartime years. Even when workers' wages had lagged behind inflation, they had increased but a private's $1.10 a day and $20.00 a month for his family was unchanged from 1914.

The war did not radicalize veterans; it gave them a special stake in the nation they had defended. That underpinned the ethnocentrism of the GWVA and the occasional violence of its members against Greeks in Toronto, Ukrainians in Winnipeg, labour radicals in Vancouver, and the Chinese in a score of small communities. Veterans' conservatism had an egalitarian edge. The GWVA urged members to address each other as "comrade". Preferences for officers rankled. "That an officer with an arm off should get twice as much pension as a private with an arm off," raged Harris Turner, a blinded veteran and Saskatchewan MLA, "is unfair, unjust, unsound, undemocratic, unreasonable, unBritish, unacceptable, outrageous and rotten." (The government got the message.) Naturally, few senior officers felt welcome in veterans' organizations.

In 1917, the GWVA had called itself "the advanced guard" of a returning army, but its priority, like its membership, was the disabled. Grant MacNeil, the GWVA secretary-treasurer after 1918, made himself an expert and a major force in the evolution of veterans' benefits in Canada but he could not speak for the frustrations of the able-bodied veterans. On February 23, 1919, returned men, meeting in a Calgary theatre to escape boredom and the icy cold, persuaded themselves that "full re-establishment" for them was a bonus of $2,000 for each man who had served overseas, to be paid by slackers, profiteers, and, perhaps, by German reparations. Politicians, editors, the Liberal party, found the bonus easy to endorse. GWVA leaders, torn between responsibility and a grass-roots cause, found it a nightmare. The Borden government found the courage to say no: the "Calgary Resolution" would cost a billion dollars, almost half the national debt, and no one could promise that the veterans would not come back for more. With a single dissenting vote — Colonel J.A. Currie — the Unionist caucus stood firm. The Liberals ignored their convention resolution four months earlier. The bonus was dead. During the bonus campaign, GWVA membership soared from twenty thousand to two hundred thousand. It then drained away to rival organizations or, most often, to the more private concern of re-establishment. Grant MacNeil was left with the increasingly lonely fight for pensioners against the Pension Commissioners and their allies in the Senate. In 1925, a fading and penniless GWVA gave way to the generals and the colonels, and the newly formed Canadian Legion took over the veterans' cause.

By 1920, demobilization was over. Canada's wartime army vanished faster than anyone had predicted. Canadians, if they cared, could take pride in generous pensions and innovative programs for the war-disabled. There was no crisis of unemployment in 1919 and four-fifths of the money set aside to help veterans and their families through the winter of 1919–20 went unspent.

RECONSTRUCTION

"Very quickly," Herbert Daly had warned Canadians in 1918, "will the world realize how much easier it was to make the war than to make peace." The Union government had adopted "Reconstruction" as its phrase for planning the post-war world. Like "re-establishment", it was a carefully ambiguous word, at once progressive and conservative. Most Canadians, like their prime minister, yearned for an old, familiar anchorage but knew that it did not exist. Others had dreams of a new society, emerging from the pain of war. Norman James was welcomed home by the mayor of his small Alberta town with the hope that he and other veterans would create a "New Order in Canada". "To be frank with you," James replied, "we were hoping that you would do something about that while we were away."

In fact, governments had been busy. By the end of the war, Ottawa controlled most of the railways, wheat marketing, and coal distribution. In June 1918, it had enforced national registration on women as well as men. The government mildly taxed incomes and profits and, with a war debt approaching $2 billion, it could not stop. The habit of authority grew with feeding. In 1919, Unionist ministers distributed grants to build homes and highways, to control the spread of venereal disease, and to promote technical education — among the first federal-provincial cost-sharing programs. Soldier settlement, at an outlay of $100 million, was the largest land-development operation in Canadian history. Veterans' hospitals, sanatoria, and training schools took Ottawa deep into provincial, private, and charitable domains. So did a Department of Health, created in 1919 because of the influenza epidemic and the fear that returned soldiers would spread a new epidemic of syphilis. By the end of the year, Ottawa controlled the Grand Trunk and its Pacific extension.

By ordinary standards, the government in 1919 had marched at a revolutionary pace but the times were not ordinary. J.W. Dafoe of the *Manitoba Free Press* had warned that anyone in government after the war would face a thankless task: "It is going to be demanded of him that he do things which are mutually contradictory and destructive, and whatever he does will have more critics than friends." Reformers had imagined that the consensus that made a government powerful in wartime would somehow continue into the peace. "During reorganization after the war," Dr. J.L. Todd, the architect of Canada's military pension system, told an American audience, "it will be unbelievably easy to achieve social ideas which, before the war, seemed impracticable and impossible of attainment." Todd was wrong.

Ideas there certainly were. Physicians, anxious to make work for colleagues home from the war, argued for a national health-insurance plan. Thomas Adams, a British urban planner summoned to Ottawa in 1914 to design a national capital, had spent a frustrating war. Now, he announced, was the time for his vision of a city beautiful: veterans would be the major beneficiaries. The Military Hospitals Commission in 1916 proposed a trans-Canada highway as a war memorial, a massive public work for veterans and a recognition of the new automotive age. The West, in particular, seethed with radical ideas. Farm leaders debated the single tax, the benefits of government-managed grain marketing, and the early abolition of political "partyism". Having spawned the veterans' bonus campaign in February, Calgary was the meeting place in March for the Western Labour Conference. Delegates demanded a six-hour day, praised the Bolshevik Revolution, and promised themselves a One Big Union for all workers.

Two months later, thirty thousand Winnipeggers walked out in a six-week general strike, ostensibly to support two local unions, in fact to protest low wages, high prices, and the failure of the post-war world to repay their wartime sacrifices. From Nanaimo to Sydney, workers responded to Winnipeg with sympathetic strikes of their own. By the end of 1919, Canada had lost a greater share of working time to labour disputes than in any year before or since. A Royal Commission on Industrial Relations, headed by Mr. Justice T.G. Mathers, concluded that economic conditions, not foreigners, had caused the unrest and recommended a minimum wage, an eight-hour day, unemployment and health insurance, and the right of free collective-bargaining.

Nothing happened. A National Industrial Conference in September dissolved in wrangling. Doctors forgot about national health insurance until the Depression when, again, they needed patients. The One Big Union came and went, speeded on its way by veterans who attacked organizers and bundled them out of small western towns. The Commission of Conservation, which had employed Adams, was wound up in 1921. The Board of Commerce, created in April 1919 to control cost increases, was gone by the end of the year when its two leading members, Mr. Justice Mathers and W.F. O'Connor, had fought each other to a standstill. The Wheat Board wound up in 1920; the Grain Exchange returned as world prices fell. Prohibition of liquor faltered when the Senate allowed regulations under the War Measures Act to lapse. All provinces but Quebec promptly reinstated it, but "Moderation Leagues", spearheaded by veterans and reinforced by the obvious unenforceability of temperance legislation, gradually won back the bottle if not the bar. Women had won the vote in all provinces but Quebec by 1922 but their feminism was still maternal. The economist Margaret MacMurchy reminded Canadians that "the great employments of women, in comparison with which all other employments appear insignificant, are homemaking and the care of children". Women's share of the Canadian workforce was hardly greater in 1921 than in 1911. Post-war feminist politics focused on motherhood, morality, and the new crypto-science of eugenics.

The real decisions about reconstruction had already been made by banks and businesses and by a government alarmed at its burden of $2 billion in debt. For a moment near the end of the war, business had glimpsed the potential power of government and its frail progressive idealism promptly shrivelled. "Legislation has its function," admitted *Industrial Canada,* the organ of the Canadian Manufacturers' Association, "but legislation which attempts to limit or pervert great natural laws will defeat its own ends...." For industrialists, the tariff was a great natural law and a Canadian Reconstruction Association ensured that governments would hear a firm and persuasive message from free enterprisers. A discreet subsidy to the Trades and Labor Congress added most union leaders to the cause of the tariff and moderate reform, in opposition to the free-trade Progressives. Acting on their own natural laws, the chartered banks celebrated peace by calling in exposed loans, raising interest rates, and curbing inflation with such success that prices, by 1921, had dropped back to 1917 levels. Unfortunately the economy had also collapsed, throwing a quarter of all veterans and most of their disabled comrades out of work. A proper concern for economy prevented the Department of Soldiers' Civil Re-establishment from making a second attempt at training and placement. Other depression victims included thousands of soldier settlers and the humble depositors in Herbert Daly's Home Bank.

In retrospect, Borden and his government should have sought a renewed mandate early in 1919. Instead, the prime minister had crossed the Atlantic and his weary colleagues had soldiered on, encountering all the misery Dafoe had predicted. "I should be happy to return to Canada," Borden wrote from Paris in May, "were it not for politics." That summer, he made an attempt to win over Sir Lomer Gouin. He beat the Quebec premier at golf but he could not bring him to Ottawa. Laurier had died in February and Liberals met in August to choose a new leader. Lady Laurier preferred the elderly and dignified Sir William Fielding. Quebec delegates insisted on William Lyon Mackenzie King because, unlike Fielding, he had been loyal to Sir Wilfrid in 1917. None of them knew how close King had come, in that summer of torn loyalties, to declaring for Unionism.

Doctors persuaded Borden to quit at the end of 1919; desperate Unionists pleaded with him to stay on. Months of recuperation in the southern states and New York left the government without its leader. Finally, on July 1, 1920, Borden resigned. He wanted Sir Thomas White as his successor but the finance minister was as worn out as his leader. Instead, Unionists chose Arthur Meighen, the architect of conscription and of most other policies that demanded a hard-edged mind and debating skill. Meighen knew the odds. Quebec had forgotten nothing and wealthy Montreal would never forgive him for refusing to hand over Canada's railways to the CPR. Agrarian reform and free trade swept rural Canada. The new prime minister returned to the old party, and to the old issue of 1911, the tariff. Mackenzie King refused to be pinned. The sweeping reform policies of the 1919 Liberal convention, he insisted, were "a chart"; the Liberals believed in a tariff that would help farmers, manufacturers, workers — everyone but multi-millionaires. On December 6, 1921, Canadians were too divided to give anyone a majority. A solid Quebec and seats in Ontario and the Maritimes gave King 116 members. Thomas Crerar's new Progressives swept the west and rural Ontario, 65 MPS in all. Meighen salvaged only 50 seats. North Winnipeg remembered the 1919 strike, forgot the war, and elected J.S. Woodsworth, the frail pacifist who had stood by the workers in 1919.

Reconstruction was over. The great conciliator, William Lyon Mackenzie King, could help Canada find peace with her divided selves.

CONCLUSIONS

The Great War of 1914–19 lies like a great angry scar across the history of Western civilization. At least thirteen million people died in the war, most of them young men. So did four old empires. A dozen newly sovereign states emerged, among them Canada. Those who lived through the 1914–19 war recalled it as the great divide in their lives. A golden glow of nostalgia suffused the pre-1914 years, blotting out the reality of poverty, violence, and cruelty. Never again would life be so assured for the middle class or so comfortable for the well born and they, of course, are the people who write history. "Before the war" evoked a romantic magic that somehow died in the mud of Verdun, the Somme, or the Ypres salient. Not for generations and perhaps never again could war be portrayed as romantic or heroic.

Modern historians have sometimes been harsh about this image. If influenza killed fifteen million people in a few months of 1918 was it a greater or a lesser event than the war? Was it European arrogance to claim world status for a conflict that essentially engaged the white nations and their colonies?

Was the Europe of 1914, with its slums and suffering, a haven of civilization or a jewelled corpse? Were the war dead a "lost generation" whose brilliance might have saved the world from future folly or was A.J.P. Taylor correct in his brutal conclusion: "Young males could be more easily spared than at any other time in the world's history"? Why was there no comparable myth after the 1939–45 war, when far more people had perished?

The war transformed much of daily life. Automobiles, cigarette-smoking, and the wristwatch became commonplace. Women abandoned heavy, constricting clothing and, in the 1920s, wore less than at any time in modern history. Would these changes have occurred without war? Wartime saw rapid progress in orthopaedics and rehabilitation medicine. For the first time in any major war, death from disease was far outweighed by death from enemy action, at least on the Western Front, and despite conditions that invited epidemic sickness. Never had the power of immunization and hygienic practices been more clearly demonstrated or in worse conditions.

Probably these changes would have come without a war. Other changes depended on the savage competition of belligerents. The air war forced Germany, France, and Britain to transform aircraft from fragile toys in 1914 to the tough, durable vehicles that, by 1919, were capable of crossing the Atlantic. The United States, birthplace of aeronautical technology in 1903, was left far behind in the war years. Tanks, however, which certainly invited technological innovation, remained vulnerable and undependable until major improvements in suspension and armament in the unmilitary 1920s. Canadians have been acutely conscious of the innovative influence of creating a munitions industry in wartime but, as the historian Michael Bliss has pointed out, most of the IMB's products were technically unsophisticated and its aircraft factory and shipbuilding activities proved utterly uneconomic. Canada's chief wartime success story was the automotive industry but the dramatic growth in car production, a by-product of the sudden wealth of farmers and industrialists, was not widely celebrated. It reflected profiteering.

History would have gone on without a war. Three of the four dead empires were in visible decay before 1914. If Britain was spared a civil war in Ireland in 1914, it resumed in 1916 and again in 1919 and persists, with intermittent savagery, to the present day. Canada would have discovered her sense of nationality without capturing Vimy Ridge and it hardly required a war to reveal the frustrations of "imperial federation".

Yet the war had happened and its consequences remained in broken dreams, broken bodies, and broken families. By 1935, Canada paid its hundred thousand dependent and disabled pensioners $41 million a year, an item second in the national accounts only to servicing a national debt that was $2 billion larger than it might have been without the war. These were the vulgar valuations of loss and suffering that no one could ever measure in a more satisfactory way. For the rest of their lives, the war-disabled would never escape the awkwardness of a missing limb, the shame of disfigurement, or the pain and breathlessness of being gassed. No one could ever count the tens of thousands who bore permanent psychological scars from the war, made all the deeper by public rejection and family friction. Canada's cost in lives and outlay was almost identical to that of the far larger United States, but across Germany, France, Russia, Britain, and the successor states of the Habsburg Empire, the toll could be multiplied a hundredfold.

From mourning, it was easy to move to disillusionment. The pre-war pacifists had denounced the "merchants of death" as manufacturers of war but now their theories explained a terrible reality of profitable devastation. Krupp, Vickers, Schneider, and other vast armament firms had profited from the war. Generals, too, emerged with little credit from a war that they had seemingly prolonged. The same electorates that had accepted their genius in wartime now felt savagely disillusioned at bemedalled commanders who lived in safety while their orders sent hundreds of thousands of uniformed civilians to their deaths. A host of voices insisted that victory could have come swiftly and cheaply if Joffre, von Ludendorff, and, above all, Sir Douglas Haig had not been so blindly stupid. Surely aircraft, more tanks, or a real effort in the Mediterranean would have spared Europe the remorseless savagery of attrition. It would take another war to justify that cruel doctrine. The Second World War would be won only after the Soviet Army, at horrifying cost, had worn down Hitler's *Wehrmacht*. Only then could Stalin's allies win in Italy or Normandy. It took four years of brutal attrition before the Australians and Canadians could win their victories in the autumn of 1918 and, even then, at heavy cost.

Such a horrible calculus had no meaning for the post-war generation. In Canada, autonomy was an argument for turning away from Europe. Having joined the League of Nations, Canada did what she could to undermine its frail provision for collective security. Nor was Ottawa much moved by the shrinking Imperial shadow. In 1922, when British troops faced a resurgent Turkish army at Chanak, the Conservative leader, Arthur Meighen, instinctively repeated Laurier's words of 1914: "Ready, Aye, Ready". A more politically sensitive Mackenzie King understood what had happened to Canadians and said nothing — beyond an assurance that "Parliament would decide."

Veterans of the war showed little enthusiasm for new conflicts. Many CEF officers insisted that their battalions survive in the post-war militia and a

committee headed by the venerable Major-General Sir William Otter surrendered far enough to create a vast paper organization in which new units like
the 3rd Toronto's or the 10th Calgary Highlanders figured with the Royal
Highlanders and the Winnipeg Rifles. It made little difference. Men who had
served in the ranks of the CEF were in no hurry for another dose of drill and
order-taking and their officers, after a first flush of enthusiasm, found themselves too busy trying to earn a living. By 1936, Otter's militia organization
had to be drastically pruned. In Parliament, Canada's first woman MP, Agnes
Macphail, made an annual ritual of her demand that military spending be cut
to a dollar a year and there were sympathetic echoes. In 1922 a Quebec Liberal and CEF veteran, Major C.G. Power, demanded a $300,000 cut in the mili-
tia estimates. By the time his fellow back-benchers had finished, they had
slashed $700,000.

Power's Canadien and Irish constituents found nothing in his isolationism
to criticize. It is easy to exaggerate the depth and durability of the wound conscription left in Quebec. By 1930, Quebec had sufficiently forgiven the Conservatives to give them seats, but the Liberals would do their best to keep evil
memories alive. So would an array of movements and institutions, from Abbé
Groulx's Action Nationale to the new Catholic trade-union organization, created at Hull in 1921. There were no more illusions about a Bonne Entente
between Quebec and Ontario, although, in 1926, an Ontario Conservative
government discreetly buried Regulation 17 and, by retaining a Royal 22e
Régiment in its post-war permanent force, the Militia Department set out to
remedy its pre-1914 neglect of French Canada.

Even Canadians who wanted the 1914–19 war to be the last in human history wanted it commemorated. The reconstruction of the burned-out Parliament Buildings allowed the Borden government to designate its crowning
central structure as a "Peace Tower". For a time, that was all. Dreams of a
National Memorial Gallery, with Lord Beaverbrook's magnificent collection
of war art, withered and the works of Nash, Varley, and Augustus John
remained half-forgotten in storage. The government could alternately plead
cost-cutting and opposition to the glorification of war. Across Canada, communities debated the construction of war memorials and pestered their politicians for German war trophies to decorate their parks and vacant
intersections. An American firm, complained the GWVA, was peddling its
mass-produced sculptures to gullible officials and committees. Winnipeg
launched a war-memorial competition and then made itself ridiculous by
rejecting a series of winning entries because the successful artists had Ger-
man-sounding names.

Canadian veterans had toyed with adopting St. Julien's Day, April 22, as a reminder of sacrificial struggles but the martyred son of St. Symphorosa was easily supplanted by Armistice Day, November 11. A bleak day fostered bleak memories. Poppies, introduced in 1921 as a fund-raising device for the benefit of French and Belgian war orphans, were seized on by the impoverished GWVA to finance its work for pension claimants. In turn, a hostile Senate turned the Poppy Fund into a political scandal that helped discredit the Great War Veterans and bring on the Canadian Legion in 1925. The red paper flowers survived as both a reminder of John McCrae's poem and a source of employment for disabled veterans.

In 1922, France handed over to Canada in perpetuity 250 acres at Hill 145, the crest of Vimy Ridge. Walter Allward designed the memorial: two soaring pillars of marble for the duality of French and English Canada, mounted on a vast concrete plinth. By the 1930s, veterans' organizations everywhere had turned from the barren struggles for compensation and employment to the concern for commemoration. In Canada, the Legion took almost four years to prepare for the unveiling of the Vimy memorial. On July 26, 1936, six thousand ex-soldiers had assembled on the slopes the Canadians had climbed more than nineteen years before. Now, instead of snow and sleet, the sun broke through, uncertainly at first and then with full force. Edward VIII, no longer the boyish prince and not much longer to be king, shared the dais with the French president and lesser Canadian cabinet ministers. Veterans stood, a little self-consciously, enduring the official speeches. Then, swooping low and racing across the memorial and the crowd, came flights of modern fighter planes.

They were unwitting precursors of another war.

A Canadian standing a chilly sentry-go in Vladivostok. Having endorsed the view that an Allied victory could not come before 1920, and that it depended on getting Russia back into Allied ranks, Sir Robert Borden had to back up his words with action. The result was the dispatch of a few thousand MSA men to winter at the eastern tip of Siberia.

Men of a Canadian battalion march past Sir Arthur Currie over the Rhine to Bonn. Canada initially committed two divisions to an Allied occupation force in Germany. The Canadians occupied bridgeheads at Bonn and Cologne.

Technically the Armistice was only an interruption to the fighting, but for Allied soldiers, as well as their enemies, it was time to become civilians again. Men of the 13th Battalion begin their homeward journey from Cologne in a German boxcar.

Canadian soldiers inspect the ruins of Kinmel's "Tin Town" after the March 1919 riots. Shopkeepers who had allegedly profiteered from their soldier-customers were the commonest target of post-Armistice disturbances. The answer was to get homesick soldier-civilians home.

Canadian soldiers board the *Olympic*. The Kinmel riots helped persuade the British authorities that it was better to risk one of their few remaining luxury liners in Halifax's inadequate port facilities than to face further disorder. A "monster ship", the *Olympic* could carry 5,000 troops.

The *Olympic* docks in Halifax. For authorities in Canada, it was better politically to have soldiers waiting in England than stranded in Halifax by the limitations of the worn-out Canadian railways. Put to the test, however, the transportation system strained, creaked, and worked.

A family reunion. For many veterans homecoming proved unexpectedly awkward.
There was an immeasureable gulf in experiences between the men from overseas
and those who had stayed home. Many returned soldiers found that only former
comrades and fellow veterans understood the shared ordeal. For some, the feeling
of alienation never wore off.

A last Victory Loan in 1919 was designed to pay the cost of Soldiers' Civil Re-establishment. Apart from a modest War Service Gratuity, the government reserved almost all its help for the war-disabled. Able-bodied soldiers were expected, for their own good, to help themselves. This poster notwithstanding, it was really "up to him".

Disabled soldiers at work on their handicrafts. Part of their "re-establishment" was a systematic revival of the work ethic and the acquisition of suitable skills. "Ward Occupations" were the first stage in demonstrating that even the most disabled soldiers could become at least partially self-supporting.

A disabled soldier returns to his family. While amputees may be the popular image of war-wounded, fewer than 3,000 of Canada's 80,000 war pensioners had lost limbs. Most were victims of illness, not wounds.

The Soldier Settlement Board, with its expert advice and loans, offered the only
specific assistance to able-bodied veterans — and going on the land after 1919 was
not much of a gift. The frame shack on display in Winnipeg was a sample of what a
soldier-settler could afford with his SSB loan.

Returned men, out of work during the 1921 depression, ask a question many war veterans have asked over the centuries. By pressing for better pensions, unemployment insurance, and special aid for the "burned-out" cases, veterans became an important force in creating Canada's social support system — but veterans of a later war would be the main beneficiaries.

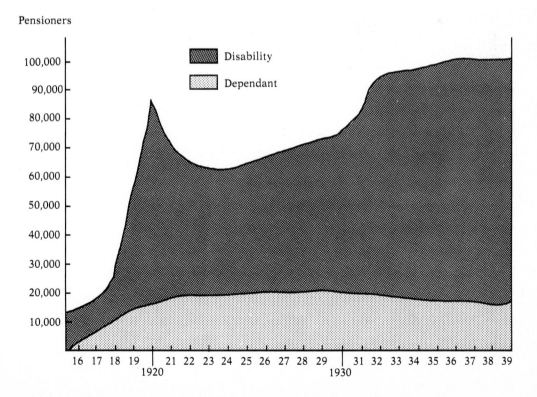

APPENDIX A

ORDER OF BATTLE: THE CANADIAN CORPS AND OTHER CANADIAN FORMATIONS IN THE FIELD, NOVEMBER 1918

1st Canadian Division

Artillery:
    1st Brigade, C.F.A.   2nd Brigade, C.F.A.
      1st Field Battery   5th Field Battery
      3rd Field Battery   6th Field Battery
      4th Field Battery   7th Field Battery
      2nd Howitzer Battery   48th Howitzer Battery
    1st Division Ammunition Column

Engineers:
    1st Brigade, C.E.
      1st Battalion
      2nd Battalion
      3rd Battalion
    1st Division Signal Company

Infantry:
    1st Infantry Brigade
      1st (Western Ontario) Battalion
      2nd (Eastern Ontario) Battalion
      3rd (Toronto Regiment) Battalion
      4th (Central Ontario) Battalion
      1st Trench Mortar Battery

    2nd Infantry Brigade
      5th (Western Cavalry) Battalion
      7th (1st British Columbia Regiment) Battalion
      8th (90th Rifles) Battalion
      10th (Western Canadians) Battalion
      2nd Trench Mortar Battery

    3rd Infantry Brigade
      13th (Royal Highlanders of Canada) Battalion
      14th (Royal Montreal Regiment) Battalion
      15th (48th Highlanders of Canada) Battalion
      16th (The Canadian Scottish) Battalion
      3rd Trench Mortar Battery

Machine Gun Corps: 1st Battalion, C.M.G.C.

Army Service Corps: 1st Divisional Train, C.A.S.C.

Army Medical Corps: 1st, 2nd, 3rd Field Ambulances, C.A.M.C.

2nd Canadian Division

Artillery:
    5th Brigade, C.F.A.   6th Brigade, C.F.A.
      17th Field Battery   15th Field Battery
      18th Field Battery   16th Field Battery
      20th Field Battery   25th Field Battery
      23rd Howitzer Battery   22nd Howitzer Battery

2nd Division Ammunition Column

Engineers: 2nd Brigade, C.E.
    4th Battalion
    5th Battalion
    6th Battalion

2nd Division Signal Company

Infantry: 4th Infantry Brigade
    18th (Western Ontario) Battalion
    19th (Central Ontario) Battalion
    20th (Central Ontario) Battalion
    21st (Eastern Ontario) Battalion
    4th Trench Mortar Battery

    5th Infantry Brigade
    22nd (French Canadian) Battalion
    24th (Victoria Rifles of Canada) Battalion
    25th (Nova Scotia Rifles) Battalion
    26th (New Brunswick) Battalion
    5th Trench Mortar Battery

    6th Infantry Brigade
    27th (City of Winnipeg) Battalion
    28th (Northwest) Battalion
    29th (Vancouver) Battalion
    31st (Alberta) Battalion
    6th Trench Mortar Battery

Machine Gun Corps: 2nd Battalion, C.M.G.C.

Army Service Corps: 2nd Divisional Train, C.A.S.C.

Army Medical Corps: 4th, 5th, 6th Field Ambulances, C.A.M.C.

3rd Canadian Division

Artillery:

9th Brigade, C.F.A.	10th Brigade, C.F.A.
31st Field Battery	38th Field Battery
33rd Field Battery	39th Field Battery
45th Field Battery	40th Field Battery
36th Howitzer Battery	35th Howitzer Battery

3rd Division Ammunition Column

Engineers: 3rd Brigade, C.E.
    7th Battalion
    8th Battalion
    9th Battalion

3rd Division Signal Company

Infantry: 7th Infantry Brigade
    The Royal Canadian Regiment
    Princess Patricia's Canadian Light Infantry
    42nd (Royal Highlanders of Canada) Battalion
    49th (Edmonton Regiment) Battalion
    7th Trench Mortar Battery

8th Infantry Brigade
   1st Canadian Mounted Rifles Battalion
   2nd Canadian Mounted Rifles Battalion
   4th Canadian Mounted Rifles Battalion
   5th Canadian Mounted Rifles Battalion
   8th Trench Mortar Battery

9th Infantry Brigade
   43rd (Cameron Highlanders of Canada) Battalion
   52nd (New Ontario) Battalion
   58th (Central Ontario) Battalion
   60th (Victoria Rifles of Canada) Battalion
      (replaced, April 1917, by 116th [Central Ontario]
      Battalion)
   9th Trench Mortar Battery

Machine Gun Corps: 3rd Battalion, C.M.G.C.

Army Service Corps: 3rd Divisional Train, C.A.S.C.

Army Medical Corps: 8th, 9th, 10th Field Ambulances, C.A.M.C.

4th Canadian Division

Artillery:

3rd Brigade, C.F.A.	4th Brigade, C.F.A.
10th Field Battery	13th Field Battery
11th Field Battery	19th Field Battery
12th Field Battery	27th Field Battery
9th Howitzer Battery	21st Howitzer Battery

4th Division Ammunition Column

Engineers: 4th Brigade, C.E.
   10th Battalion
   11th Battalion
   12th Battalion

4th Division Signal Company

Infantry: 10th Infantry Brigade
   44th (Manitoba) Battalion
      (redesignated "New Brunswick", August 1918)
   46th (South Saskatchewan) Battalion
   47th (British Columbia) Battalion
      (redesignated "Western Ontario", February 1918)
   50th (Calgary) Battalion
   10th Trench Mortar Battery

11th Infantry Brigade
   54th (Kootenay) Battalion
      (redesignated "Central Ontario", August 1917)
   75th (Mississauga) Battalion
   87th (Canadian Grenadier Guards) Battalion
   102nd (North British Columbians) Battalion
      (redesignated "Central Ontario", August 1917)
   11th Trench Mortar Battery

12th Infantry Brigade
  38th (Ottawa) Battalion
  72nd (Seaforth Highlanders of Canada)
    Battalion
  73rd (Royal Highlanders of Canada) Battalion
    (replaced by 85th [Nova Scotia Highlanders]
    Battalion, April 1917)
  78th (Winnipeg Grenadiers) Battalion

Machine Gun Corps: 4th Battalion, C.M.G.C.

Army Service Corps: 4th Divisional Train, C.A.S.C.

Army Medical Corps: 11th, 12th, 13th Field Ambulances, C.A.M.C.

Canadian Corps Troops

Cavalry: Canadian Light Horse

Artillery: Corps Heavy Artillery

1st Brigade, C.G.A.
  1st Siege Battery
  3rd Siege Battery
  7th Siege Battery
  9th Siege Battery

2nd Brigade, C.G.A.
  1st Heavy Battery
  2nd Heavy Battery
  2nd Siege Battery
  4th Siege Battery
  5th Siege Battery
  6th Siege Battery

3rd Brigade, C.G.A.
  8th Siege Battery
  10th Siege Battery
  11th Siege Battery
  12th Siege Battery

5th Divisional Artillery
13th Brigade, C.F.A.
  52nd Field Battery
  53rd Field Battery
  55th Field Battery
  51st Howitzer Battery

14th Brigade, C.F.A.
  60th Field Battery
  61st Field Battery
  66th Field Battery
  58th Howitzer Battery

5th Division Ammunition Column

Engineers: Anti-Aircraft Searchlight Company
3rd Tunnelling Company
Corps Survey Company
1st Tramways Company
2nd Tramways Company

Corps Signal Company

Machine Gun Corps: 1st Motor Machine Gun Brigade, C.M.G.C.
2nd Motor Machine Gun Brigade, C.M.G.C.

Army Service Corps: Corps Troops Motor Transport Company C.A.S.C.
1st, 2nd, 3rd, 4th Division Motor Transport
  Companies, C.A.S.C.

5th Divisional Artillery Motor Transport
   Detachment
Engineers Motor Transport Company, C.A.S.C.
Motor Machine Gun Motor Transport Company,
   C.A.S.C.
5th Divisional Train Detachment, C.A.S.C.

Army Medical Corps: 1st, 2nd, 3rd, 6th, 7th, 8th General
     Hospitals, C.A.M.C.
2nd, 3rd, 7th, 8th, 9th, 10th Stationary
     Hospitals, C.A.M.C.
1st, 2nd, 3rd, 4th, 5th, 6th Forestry Corps Hospitals
1st, 2nd, 3rd, 4th Casualty Clearing
     Stations. C.A.M.C.
14th Field Ambulance, C.A.M.C.

Miscellaneous Units   Canadian Cyclist Battalion
Corps Reinforcement Camp
Corps Schools
Corps Signal Company

Canadian Cavalry Brigade

Cavalry: Royal Canadian Dragoons
Lord Strathcona's Horse (Royal Canadians)
Fort Garry Horse
R.N.W.M.P. Squadron

Artillery: Royal Canadian Horse Artillery Brigade

Army Medical Corps: 7th (Cavalry) Field Ambulance, C.A.M.C.

Army Troops (Attached to the British Expeditionary Force)

Artillery: 8th Army Brigade, C.F.A.
     24th Field Battery
     30th Field Battery
     32nd Field Battery
     43rd Howitzer Battery
     8th Army Brigade Ammunition Column

"E" Anti-Aircraft Battery

Engineers: 1st, 2nd, 3rd, 4th, 5th Army Troops Companies

Railway Troops: Canadian Overseas Railway Construction
     Corps (1st to 13th Battalions)

Forestry Corps: 58 companies, C.F.C.

(No reference is made to formation headquarters or to many small units which performed important services.)

APPENDIX B

CANADIAN EXPEDITIONARY FORCE ENLISTMENTS AND CASUALITIES

	Officers	*Other Ranks*	*Total*
Enlisted as Volunteers	21,616	455,432	477,048
Enlisted under the Military Service Act		142,588	142,588
TOTAL	21,616	598,020	619,636
Killed in action	1,777	33,148	34,925
Missing, presumed dead	157	4,273	4,430
Died of wounds	602	11,658	12,260
Died at sea	28	105	133
Died of disease or injury	425	7,371	7,796
TOTAL DEATHS	2,989	56,555	59,544
Wounded in action	5,496	121,098	126,594
Gassed	361	11,211	11,572
Injuries	1,279	33,505	34,784
TOTAL NON-FATAL CASUALTIES	7,136	165,814	172,950

APPENDIX C

SOCIAL AND ECONOMIC CHANGE IN WARTIME CANADA

A. **Labour:**

Year	*Wage Index (1949 = 100)*	*Union Members (thousands)*	*Time lost in strikes (thousands of days)*
1911	24.0	133	1,821
1914	25.8	166	491
1915	26.0	143	95
1916	27.8	160	237
1917	31.9	205	1,124
1918	37.4	249	648
1919	44.0	378	3,401

APPENDIX C

B. Inflation by Price Indices: (1937 = 100)

Year	Total	Food	Rent	Clothing	Fuel/light
1913	79.5	88	74	88	76
1914	80.0	92	72	89	74
1915	81.4	93	70	97	73
1916	88.1	103	71	110	74
1917	104.3	133	76	130	83
1918	118.1	153	80	152	91
1919	129.8	164	87	175	99
1920	150.4	188	100	213	119
1925	120.8	127	118	141	121

C. Public Finance:

Year	Budgetary Expenditure ($ million)			Total	Budgetary Revenue	National Debt
	Defence	Transportation	Veterans			
1911	10	63	—	136	136	463
1914	72	79	1	246	133	750
1915	173	85	1	338	172	974
1916	311	69	3	497	233	1410
1917	344	94	8	574	261	1871
1918	439	86	30	696	313	2638
1919	347	61	75	740	350	2978
1925	14	74	46	356	383	

ACKNOWLEDGEMENT OF PICTURE SOURCES

The government of Canada holds the copyright for most of the paintings reproduced in this book, and has given permission for their reproduction. Every reasonable effort has been made to trace the ownership of other copyright materials. Information enabling the Publisher to rectify any reference or credit in future printings will be welcomed.

Sources of colour illustrations are acknowledged following the legends on the colour plates in question. Unless otherwise indicated, all are from the National War Museum (NWM), Canadian Museum of Civilization, National Museums of Canada. Photography at the museum was done by William Kent. Sources of black-and-white illustrations are as below. For reasons of space the following abbreviations have been used:

AO: Archives of Ontario, Toronto;
CT/J: City of Toronto Archives, James Collection;
EC: Erindale College;
NAC: National Archives of Canada, Ottawa.

Page *i*: EC; *ii*: AO(11595, 0.1027); *iii*: EC; *vi* (top): NAC(C-68841), (bottom): NAC(PA-1178); *viii*: NAC(PA-1439); 16: CT/J(824); 17 (top): NAC, (bottom): NAC(C-2468); 18 (top): NAC(PA-22739), (bottom): NAC(C-37337); 19: Manitoba Archives (N-2971, Foote Coll. 2309); 20: NAC(C-11264); 21: CT/J; 39: NAC(C-95732); 40 (top): CT/J(728), (bottom): NAC(PA-72600); 41: NAC; 42: NAC; 43 (top): NAC(C-81360), (bottom): Provincial Archives of British Columbia (54987); 44 (top): CT/J(4538), (bottom): CT/J(873); 45: CT/J(981); 46: NAC(C-95733); 47: AO(s4504); 66 (top): after a diagram in *Eye-Deep in Hell*, John Ellis (London: Croom-Helm, 1976), (bottom): EC; 67: NAC(PA-2205); 68: NAC(PA-22708); 69 (top): NAC(PA-66778), (bottom): J.A. Currie collection, EC; 70: CT/J(4538); 71: NAC(PA-1654); 72: NAC(PA-1326); 73 (top): NAC(PA-1416), (bottom): NAC(PA-149311); 74: AO(11595, 0.1464); 75: J.A. Currie collection, EC; 76: J.A. Currie collection, EC; 77: AO(11595, album 2, page 7); 78: EC; 79: EC; 96: NAC(C-97801); 97 (top): CT/J(737), (bottom): AO(s10102); 98: NAC(C-95289); 99: NAC(PA-151); 100: NAC(PA-2572); 101: NAC(PA-72527); 102: NAC(C-27484); 103: NAC(PA-24436); 104: Shortreed collection, EC; 105 (top): NAC(PA-157), (bottom): NAC(PA-742); 125: AO(11595, album 2, page 39); 126 (top): NAC(PA-124), (bottom): NAC(PA-628); 127 (top): NAC(PA-811), (bottom): NAC(PA-868); 128 (top): NAC(PA-786), (bottom): NAC(PA-2326); 129: NAC(PA-832); 130: EC; 131: NAC(PA-717); 132: AO(11595, album 3, page 42); 133: NAC(PA-1356); 151 (top): NAC(C-6859), (bottom): NAC(PA-2045); 152: NAC(PA-2306); 153 (top): NAC(PA-1184), (bottom): EC (by Mrs. G. Anderson); 154: NAC(PA-1994); 155: AO(11595, album 5, page 21); 156 (top): NAC(PA-1020), (bottom): NAC(PA-1931); 157: NAC(PA-1135); 158 (top): NAC(PA-4388), (bottom): NAC(PA-3717); 159: NAC; 179: NAC(C-13224); 180: NAC(PA-1670); 181: NAC(C-80027); 182: NAC(PA-8158); 183: NAC(C-93223); 184: EC; 185 (top): NAC(PA-2162), (bottom): EC; 186: AO(11595, album 2, page 20); 187: AO(11595, album 2, page 19); 188: NAC(PA-115373); 189 (top): NAC(PA-6655), (bottom): NAC(C-241); 208 (top): NAC(C-28029), (bottom): AO(11595, album 2, page 36); 209: EC; 210: NAC(PA-2946); 211 (top): NAC(PA-2955), (bottom): NAC(PA-4107); 212 (top): NAC(C-19953), (bottom): CT/J(sc244-2451); 213: NAC(C-95280); 214: *Saturday Night*; 215: Shortreed collection, EC; 216 (top): NAC(C-102361), (bottom): NAC(PA-2150); 217: Saskatchewan Archives Board CR-B8132(48); 236: NAC(PA-3133); 237: NAC(PA-3198); 238: AO(11595, album 2, page 31); 239: AO(11595, album 2, page 28); 240: AO(11595, album 2, page 35); 241: NAC(PA-3202); 242: NAC(PA-3539); 243: NAC(PA-3270); 244: Provincial Archives of British Columbia (94246/F-5321); 245: AO(11595, 0.3617); 264: EC; 265: NAC(PA-3776); 266 (top): NAC(PA-4013), (bottom): National War Museum; 267: NAC(PA-6049); 268: NAC(PA-2296); 269: NAC; 270: NAC(C-55108); 271 (top): Dept. of Veterans' Affairs, (bottom): NAC; 280: Manitoba Archives (N-2445, Foote Coll. 845); 281 (top): CT/J(903), (bottom): EC.

281

INDEX